COGITATIONS

Wilfred R. Bion

COGITATIONS

New Extended Edition

Wilfred R. Bion

edited by

Francesca Bion

London
KARNAC BOOKS

First published in 1992 by
H. Karnac (Books) Ltd.
58 Gloucester Road
London SW7 4QY

British Library Cataloguing in Publication Data

Bion, Wilfred R. (Wilfred Ruprecht), *1897-1979*
Cogitations.
1. Psychoanalysis
I. Title
150. 195

ISBN 0-946439-98 2

Printed in Great Britain by BPC Wheatons Ltd, Exeter

Thought is only a flash between two long nights,
but this flash is everything.

Henri Poincaré

FOREWORD

'Cogitations' was the name Bion gave to his thoughts transferred to paper. The physical act of writing was, he found, an aid to his thinking—typing would have been too noisy and 'fidgety'. He wrote slowly, neatly, with very few alterations, on loose sheets, most of which he subsequently fastened together in two lots (unfortunately not in chronological order). Many are undated, but I believe that the order in which I have arranged them is not grossly in error. They cover the period from February 1958 to April 1979. In addition to relating the subject matter to his published papers and books, I have applied some Holmesian detective work to variations in the colour of ink and paper, and to the style of handwriting, which he changed from time to time as he tried to improve his hand.

These occasional writings were his attempt to discipline, clarify, and evaluate complex ideas—both his own and those of others—by setting them out visually and by often addressing them to an imaginary audience. He never re-read them, but he must have thought them worth preserving because they escaped consignment to the waste-paper basket during gleeful paper-tearing sessions, especially before leaving Los Angeles in 1979.

They will be of particular interest to those already familiar with Bion's work as an illustration of his doubts, his arguments with himself, and of how his initial ideas developed. They should not be read in isolation by newcomers, but as an adjunct to his published works, especially those of the 1960s.

The compilation of this book affirms my belief that it forms an essential part of Bion's work and that it would be a considerable loss to psycho-analysis if its contents were to remain imprisoned in filing cabinets. It is the last of the posthumous publications, which have given me so much pleasure to prepare.

Francesca Bion
Oxford, 1990

COGITATIONS

Comments in square brackets have been added by the Editor.

Asterisks indicate the passage of time between the writing of one section and the next.

February 1958

Psychotic mechanisms

At last I think I see daylight on a point that has baffled me for a long time: what does the psychotic patient think analysis is? Partly an activity that is followed by consequences such as those that attend on events in the realm of physical fact; partly a mental event in which consequences (as they exist in the world of physical reality) do not exist—there are only sequences. In a dream an act *appears* to have consequences; it has only sequences. What is needed is a spatial model to represent a dream. The verbal description would then be seen as an artefact in which certain elements, in an agglomeration that has no time component and no events that are consequent on other events, are highlighted by the imposition on them of causality and temporality. The capacity to impose on these elements both causality and temporality depends on the existence of a non-psychotic personality. This non-psychotic personality must be capable of (a) frustration, and hence awareness of temporality, (b) guilt and depression, and hence an ability to contemplate causality (since contemplating causes involves the possibility of having to contemplate one's own responsibility for certain events in the chain of causes). The capacity for verbalization is, as I have shown already, itself a function of the depressive position. [*see* 'Notes on the Theory of Schizophrenia', read at the Eighteenth International Psycho-Analytical Congress in London, 1953.]

One result is that verbal reporting of a dream is only possible when enough work has been done for the patient to be able to tolerate temporality and causality, i.e. frustration and guilt-depression, and the patient is therefore able to produce the artefact we call 'a dream' from the 'agglomeration' of mental urine and faeces. [*see* Bion, 'Attacks on Linking', *International Journal of Psycho-Analysis, 40* (1959), Parts 5–6.]

10 January 1959

Scientific method

The patient said he couldn't find a pot to harmonize all the things in his studio. This would be a vagina or womb; an object like that sought by Poincaré [*Science and Method*, p. 30] which

> must unite elements long since known, but till then scattered and seemingly foreign to each other, and suddenly introduce order where the appearance of disorder reigned. Then it enables us to see at a glance each of those elements in the place it occupies in the whole. Not only is the new fact valuable on its own account, but it alone gives a value to the old facts it unites. Our mind is frail as our senses are; it would lose itself in the complexity of the world if that complexity were not harmonious; like the short-sighted, it would only see the details, and would be obliged to forget each of these details before examining the next, because it would be incapable of taking in the whole.

He adds the opinion that 'the only facts worthy of our attention are those that introduce order into this complexity and so make it accessible to us'.

How can something people 'feel' be measured? By postulating temperature after ridding oneself of prejudice of pairs of opposites. Then it is found that things, inanimate objects, are sensitive to temperature though they do not feel 'heat and cold'. What about love and hate? Are they not 'prejudices'? Should it not simply be 'x'—the amount of x, like the amount of temperature? Then one might be able to measure x even if one cannot measure love and hate, or heat and cold.

Braithwaite talks about scientific deductive systems in his *Scientific Explanation*. He says, 'A scientific system consists of a set of hypotheses which form a deductive system; that is, which is arranged in such a way that from some of the hypotheses as premises all the other hypotheses logically follow.' These are arranged in an order of levels such that the hypotheses at the highest level are those that occur *only as premises* in the system. Those at the lowest level occur only as conclusions in the system. Those at intermediate levels occur as conclusions of deductions from higher-level hypotheses, and serve as premises for deductions to lower-level hypotheses [p. 12]. He gives as an example the deductive system associated with the theory of falling bodies. He then says that in most deductive systems each deduction requires more than one premise, but that in his example just given there is only one higher-level hypothesis, used as a premise, from which deductions to lower-level hypotheses are made. But is this really true? Implicit in it are many hypotheses thus: 'Every body near the earth, freely falling towards the earth, falls with an acceleration of thirty-two feet per second per second.' Surely in this is brought together in the one sentence a hypothesis about bodies near the earth, about bodies falling freely, about bodies falling towards the earth (unlike, for example, a rocket going into the sun's orbit), about distance, and about time.

All this is reminiscent of Bradley on causation [*The Principles of Logic,* Vol. I, p. 211]. Is a hypothesis the meeting of mental events, which, in a moment of union, begin a process that issues in the change we call the depressive position? Bradley says,

> We should do better to call the cause the meeting of elements which, in the moment of their union, begin a process which issues in the change we call the effect.

He continues,

> An actual union of actual elements is the cause. Each element by itself and apart from this union is not even a condition. It becomes a condition when you place it ideally in union with others. But in order to do that you must make it an idea. In its character of condition it must so far cease to be fact.

This sounds as if there is a factual situation of multiple causes, a unification in a moment of time, leading to a change that issues in the effect *and* an ideational situation in which the 'elements' need to be made into 'ideas' via symbol formation, so that the ideas can be unified at a moment that then issues in a change we feel as the effect. It is not possible to do this if you cannot tolerate depression, because this ideational counterpart (the same as the 'scientific deductive system'?) is the process Melanie Klein calls the synthesis of the depressive position. And this would mean that the breakdown in symbol formation is the inability to transform an actual union of actual elements into an abstraction, i.e. a scientific deductive system or calculus.

But it is probably necessary to make a distinction between two related processes. Assuming the factual situation of multiple causes (of which Bradley speaks and which I shall later regard as being none other than the elements common to all scientific disciplines, the elements that are also the feature of the paranoid–schizoid position and are synthesized in the depressive position) that have to be transformed into 'ideas' so that they then become part of an ideational system, it is evident that it would be useful to know how this transformation is brought about.

One can regard it psychologically as a process of hypothesis formation; that is to say, elements that appear to be constantly conjoined are implicitly stated to be so by being associated with a word, the word itself then having some of the characteristics of a hypothesis that states that such-and-such experiences and an external event in the world of fact are constantly conjoined.

But for our purposes we need to consider how the ideational system develops into the scientific deductive system. The ideational system I shall regard as relatively primitive and belonging principally to the mental dynamics by which ideas, related to objects, are formed. The scientific deductive system I regard as more sophisticated and related to permanent establishment of knowledge, or to the establishment of knowledge in a form that is permanent and indestructible.

The problem may be most easily broached (though not necessarily most accurately in the sense of being most closely approximated to the facts of development) by considering the groups of senses as the route by which awareness of external fact is acquired. I group them thus: (a) touch and smell, (b) sound, (c) sight.

Group (a) is essentially non-verbal, comprises all elements of what is later called sexual, and is expressed best by sexual acts and various peripheral manifestations of sexual acts. These peripheral acts often have the characteristics of (b) and (c) but are in essence sexual acts, and only (b) and (c) in outward appearance. Thus words are employed in love-making but are then actions and not conveyors of ideas except incidentally. This is made obvious in certain analytic situations, particularly in the analysis of the psychoses, where the patient clearly reacts to words as if he had experienced a sexual approach by the analyst. Group (b) is verbal and musical, but the verbal characteristics that are relevant are not those of content so much as those that are related to the establishment of patterns of sound. Group (c) is essentially verbal and pictorial, or ideogrammatic.

What does the psycho-analyst do? He observes a mass of 'elements long since known but'—till he gives his interpretation—'scattered and seemingly foreign to each other'. If he can tolerate the depressive position, he can give this interpretation; the interpretation itself is one of those 'only facts worthy of our attention' which, according to Poincaré, 'introduce order into this complexity and so make it accessible to us'. The patient is in this way helped to find, through the analyst's ability to select, one of these unifying facts.

The fact that I here equate with what Bradley calls 'the actual element' is in a sense in no way different from the facts or actual elements that are the objects of curiosity, elucidation, and study in any science whatever, although this fact may be obscured because it is a 'fact' or 'actual element' of the kind that the analyst is inviting the patient to study—namely, the patient's own.

It will be observed that in the theory I am putting forward I am postulating a phenomenon with three facets:

(1) what Bradley would call 'actual elements in an actual union', which is identical with what the scientist would call 'observable data' in a relationship with each other that is equally observable,

(2) an ideational counterpart of the above, which is dependent upon the individual's ability to translate an 'actual element'

into an idea. (The psychotic fails to do this, and even when he verbalizes still thinks that words are things.) This operation depends on the individual's capacity to tolerate the depression of the depressive position and therefore to achieve symbol formation. This phase is identical with the scientist's ability to produce a scientific deductive system and the representation of this, which is called calculus [Braithwaite, p. 23],

(3) a mental development that is associated with an ability 'to see facts as they really are' [Samuel Johnson to Bennet Langton, *see* p. 114 of text for details] and internally with a sense of well-being that has an instantaneous ephemeral effect and a lasting sense of permanently increased mental stability.

The peculiarity that distinguishes the psycho-analyst from his analysand is that the analyst is able to select the worthwhile fact, produce the deductive system and its associated calculus, experience the moment of union when the elements meet to give rise to a feeling that the cause has been found, and begin a process that issues in a change that produces a feeling that an effect and its cause have been linked [Poincaré, on defect of logic, p. 126; Braithwaite, p. 24].

The analysand, on the other hand, is made aware of an hypothesis in a deductive system which he may or may not be able to use as a premise for further deductions. The deductive system thus formed may enable him in his turn to select one of these unifying facts of which Poincaré speaks.

At this point it is necessary to review what I have already said from a somewhat different angle: if we are to assume, with Bradley, that there are elements in actuality that come together at an actual moment to initiate the process of change that leads to what we call the effect, those elements and that moment must be determined ideationally by the selective process through which, according to Poincaré, the individual picks on 'worthwhile facts'. I would therefore suggest that in the description of elements in actuality of which Bradley speaks, he is not really accurate in supposing that they unite at an actual moment to produce an actual process of change that issues in an actual event. Rather, it is true to say that in actuality a stream of elements exists, some of which are *seen* to unite at a moment that, like the elements themselves, is selected *by the predisposition of the observer* and are seen to issue in a process of change and its attendant effect—events that are a peculiarity of the observer's outlook. I suggest then that the stream of elements remains constant in actuality, but the union of those elements and the choice of the elements that are supposed to unite, together with the choice of the moment at which the union is supposed to be effected, depends upon the observer and in particular on what we should call the observer's disposition (if we are analysts) or scientific discipline. If a steel ball drops on a marble floor, the elements that are seen to unite at a particular moment to initiate the process of change will differ if the observers are, say, a physicist, an astronomer, or a philosopher addicted to Berkeley's new theory of vision.

The question that arises now is this: how far is the scientific outlook, the attempt to understand, a compromise between the necessity, imposed by the compulsion to survive the 'reality principle', of knowing the facts of external reality, and the necessity, imposed by the psyche's intolerance of the paranoid–schizoid position or the depressive position, to move freely from one position to the other and back without depressively coloured persecutory feelings on the one hand, and depressive feelings untinged with feelings of persecution on the other?

The quotations on scientific method which I have cited from Poincaré and on causation from Bradley are open to the objection that they are expressions of the inner tensions of the personalities of their authors, and in view of the subject matter of this paper cannot be taken as valid descriptions of scientific method. Since it is my object to show that scientific method itself lacks the 'objectivity' that is widely attributed to it, and may indeed spring from very deep-seated elements in the personality which seek fulfilment, it is obvious that the very thesis of this paper may be taken as a refutation of its premises.

To this I can only reply that I am aware of the objection and have therefore devoted considerable thought to using only such descriptions of scientific method as appear to me to be unsurpassed for clarity of expression and the authority that their writers may be held to have as exponents of scientific thought. I have carefully excluded quotations that display illogicalities or evidence of any weakness that would invite criticism on scientific grounds by those accustomed to scientific method.

It is commonly held that the function of a science is to establish general laws covering the behaviour of empirical events or objects in such a way that it becomes possible to make reliable predictions of events as yet unknown [Braithwaite, *Scientific Explanation,* p. 1]. Braithwaite points out that once a generalization is formulated that all whales are mammals, it enables us to predict that the next whale we meet will be a mammal. He goes on to hint, however, that many questions that science is expected to make answerable are historical, and in particular such questions as are directed to the elucidation of causation. Leaving aside for the time being the impingement of this aspect of the problem on the discussions by physicists and philosophers, I wish to emphasize the fact that the historical question may be regarded as the reciprocal of prediction in that the function of the scientific generalization is to make it possible to summarize past experience in such a way that when, as it were, a whale turns out *not* to be a mammal, it will at once become clear either that an error has been made in the original formulation of the hypothesis, or is about to be made. It follows that the scientific law is closely related to, and an epitome of, experience; that it has relationships with memory, and that a capacity for the formulation of scientific generalization must be an essential function of any personality if it is to be capable of learning by experience (i.e. storing experience in an epitome and comparing a fact with the expectation engendered by the 'law'). In essence those postulates remain true even when we deal, as analysts, with primitive and rudimentary manifestations of this capacity far removed from the sophisticated demonstrations of the capacity evident in the best work, say, of modern physicists.

Most of Braithwaite's introductory discussion of what can be considered as legitimate material for scientific study—as data on which scientific law can properly be formulated—shows that what is at issue is really a matter of choice. He himself makes the choice when he says that he concerns himself with 'the relationship of public scientific laws to public facts of observations'

[*Scientific Explanation*, p. 6] and eschews consideration of the problems involved in the transition from private knowledge, as the phenomenalist would regard it, 'to public knowledge of the material objects of common sense'. Whatever choice is made, it is to be expected that it brings its own problems with it, and this point is well understood by the student of scientific method. What is not so easily appreciated is the immediacy of the impingement of the problems with which the philosopher of science is familiar on the mental phenomena that modern psycho-analytic methods make overt. Braithwaite's decision so to limit his field as to exclude the problems that confront the philosopher of perception [p. 6] involves using 'the observations which form the basis of scientific laws as being observations (as common sense understands the word) of material objects and their properties' [p. 7]. This at once raises the question, what is common sense?—a problem that has received inadequate attention because without modern psycho-analytic technique and theory it is not possible to make any useful approach to the question, or perhaps even to realize that a most significant phenomenon lies embedded in the term, which is itself a striking emanation of common sense.

Let us approach it clinically: a patient enters the consulting room, notices that the couch is in some disorder but, making only a minor adjustment, lies on it and proceeds with his associations. In due course evidence from his associations indicates that at this particular juncture, and taken with sundry other facts not germane to this discussion, he is experiencing an increase in anxiety and, furthermore, that the anxiety has as its ideational content the disordered couch as part of the furniture of a scene of parental intercourse. This conclusion, and the interpretation that is the psycho-analytic act by which it is expressed, is arrived at on the basis of observed facts seen in the light of a psycho-analytic hypothesis. But common sense tells this patient that he is lying on an ordinary couch and that ordinary people, as he himself might say, would know that that is what it is and that its disorder was due to the movements of the previous patient upon it.

To prevent too minute a discussion, I propose that we may now say that common sense is a term commonly employed to cover experiences in which the speaker feels that his contemporaries, individuals whom he knows, would without hesitation hold the view he has put forward in common with each other. Common sense, the highest common factor of sense, so to speak, would support his view of what the senses convey. Furthermore, he has a feeling of certitude, of confidence, associated with a belief that all his senses are in harmony and support each on the evidence of the rest. In this sense also, private to the individual himself, the term, 'common sense', is felt to be an adequate description covering an experience felt to be supported by all the senses without disharmony. As contrast, I may cite the experience in which a tactile impression of, say, fur—sudden and unpredicted—gives rise to the idea of an animal, which then has to be confirmed or refuted visually; and so, it is hoped, the common-sense view is achieved.

But there is a difficulty. So far one might say that the patient's view is essentially at one with the strictly scientific view that Braithwaite investigates after limiting the scope of his survey in the way I have shown above. The analyst, however, is also able to claim that his interpretation is based on common sense; but it is common only to some psycho-analysts who may be presumed to witness the same events and make the same deductions.

The analyst's problem is not associated with the objection that the phenomenologist might raise, although it can be argued that an awareness of the phenomenological philosopher's criticism of scientific theory is implicitly supported by the analyst's view that all analysts should be psycho-analysed. The phenomenological philosopher's objection is obviously not met by the psycho-analyst's procedure, and for the time being we shall discuss this problem by relegating it to the sphere concerned with the transformation of private knowledge to public knowledge.

The serious problem can be emphasized if I maintain that the hypothesis on which I base my interpretation is itself an embodiment of common sense in the sense in which I have already described the term. The hypothesis purports to be a generalization from 'common sensations' applicable on an occasion when there arise again 'common sensations' that appear to lend themselves to generalization in the same hypothesis.

It may be argued, and in fact is argued, that these are not common sensations and that the generalizations from them cannot be attributed to the dictates of common sense. As Hanson has pointed out, such an argument levelled at a physicist who says he is measuring a wave length justifies the demand that the questioner should be acquainted with the discipline of electricity and magnetism as it is investigated by the techniques of modern physics. These techniques may be said to have two components. The first is dependent on mechanical aids that multiply the number of sensory perceptions. (I exclude considerations of what appear to be transformations but are not, such as when an impression of weight is conferred not by direct imposition on the hand but by the visual image presented by the pointer of a scale.) This multiplication of sensory experiences provides a field in which common sense can operate to determine what is the 'common sense' of the available sensory experiences now they have been augmented. Clearly I am attributing a very important position to whatever it is in the psyche that is ordinarily called common sense whose function it is to determine the 'common sense' of the sensory experiences. Furthermore, it may seem that a certain minimum of sense experiences is necessary before it can be reasonably said that common sense can determine what is the sense that is common to all of them. This is a folklore version of the sophisticated scientist's need to establish adequate correlations (cf. A. D. Ritchie on the inadequacy of 'the far-off stars are redder' as a basis for the red shift and the expanding universe). [*Studies in the History and Methods of the Sciences,* p. 215.]

The second component is dependent on the mental equipment of the observer. The philosopher of science concerns himself, as is already apparent from the brief survey I have made of Braithwaite's demarcation of the area that he wishes to discuss, with a limited aspect of the observer's mental equipment. Even the phenomenological philosopher of scientific method intends to restrict his field, though it is doubtful whether he means to restrict it so severely as in fact it is—thanks to the lack of the psycho-analytic discoveries that could have given greater freedom. The psycho-analyst, as is to be expected, excludes no part of the mental equipment from his survey except in so far as his knowledge and capacity by their own limitations forbid automatically the fullness of inquiry he would desire. His investigation of scientific technique has been imposed on him first by Freud's impulsion to investigate the human mind scientifically, and second by Freud's realization that his discoveries compelled suspicions of the mental equipment of the investigator—Freud himself in the first instance.

The exigencies of psycho-analytic history have forced this investigation into a somewhat limited channel: the scientists investigated are predominantly psycho-analysts, which means that their grasp of methodology may be rudimentary in the extreme and lacking in even the elementary sophistication that could be expected, say, of a physicist who came for analysis. The weight of the investigation has perforce been directed to elucidation of what we now regard as the psycho-pathology of the psycho-neuroses. These limitations are, however, not as great as might be supposed, and are certainly not in my opinion as great as my own description makes them appear to be. For this reason I am persuaded that much psycho-analytic work done has been an investigation of the scientific technique or mental component, but not under that name. One has only to consider Freud's Theory of the Reality Principle and its dominance to appreciate that he is describing a development that must include in its more sophisticated manifestations the elaboration of what we now call scientific techniques of—or techniques known to science as—deduction, induction, hypothesis, etc.

Although I expressly disclaim anything new in what I have to say here—precisely because in my view psycho-analysis has all along concerned itself with and elucidated these problems—yet I believe that there may be something novel in the juxtaposition of the facts which will serve to focus psycho-analytic attention more directly and purposively on elements that have still not been sufficiently regarded.

This brings me to the difficulty that I have had to approach through this long digression. The individual whose development has allowed the establishment of the reality principle to take place has established—with varying degrees of sophistication—a vast mass of hypotheses in the course of his life. Most of these have some degree of justification both in the external circumstances of the period in which the formulation occurred, and in the quality and degree of mental equipment available to the individual at the time. In other words, we do not need to assume that they were unjustified, although, as with the case I have mentioned, the patient is not slow to say that the *analyst's* reconstruction of what he believes to be the patient's original but still current hypothetical formulation is unjustified. So it is—on the level of mind on which the patient is at his most adult, most sophisticated, most scientific.

I shall return later to further discussion of common sense, but for the present I propose to leave this subject to carry further our investigation of the scientific hypothesis.

Braithwaite favours the view that the scientific hypothesis consists of a generalization and nothing else. He admits that Hume's formulation of the theory of constant conjunction is open to grave criticism and that it has done much to obscure the value of the view that he (Braithwaite) puts forward, though with important modifications. In particular he stresses the close connection that exists between Hume's view of constant conjunction, and Hume's view that there is no element beyond a generalization in a scientific hypothesis except a psychological fact about the association of ideas or beliefs in the mind of the person believing the law. It is evident to Braithwaite that there is a desire to find something in a hypothesis which goes beyond a generalization abstracted from facts observed by common sense, whether aided by mechanical apparatus or not. As an instance he cites the desire to believe that a scientific law asserts, in addition to the generalization, that there exists some kind of relationship between the facts about which the generalization is made which is analogous to the logical relation holding between premise and conclusion in a deductive inference. Further instances of this tendency, cited by him, are the desire to believe in the existence of a relation of activity analogous to that occurring in volition or, finally, a quite specific relation not analogous to anything else.

To a psycho-analyst it is clear that the demands that could be made on any scientific law are endless and need by no means be restricted to the few Braithwaite mentions [in *Scientific Explanation,* p. 10]. The point to which I would draw attention is the scientist's view that the scientific hypothesis is a generalization abstracted from the fact that certain facts have been found to be constantly conjoined—the constant conjunction theory. The complication is that clinical experience shows how strong is the desire to formulate a hypothesis that will state that certain events are constantly conjoined and that therefore we must regard the relationship to the facts from which it is supposed to be educed as a generalization, as being two-way; that is to say that the hypothesis may be regarded as (a) educed from constantly conjoined facts, and (b) designed, however it may be derived, to affirm that certain facts are constantly conjoined. It will be observed that the latter view is quite compatible with the former—incompatibility of the two views is not the point. But, assuming both views are correct, we may say that the scientific hypothesis fulfils the following three functions:

First, a private experience is transmuted into a public communication (whether it is in fact made public or not).

Second, the types of certain experiences, facts, or events are stated to be agglomerated, articulated, or integrated in time (past, present or future), the hypothesis being thus associated with memory and prediction. This function is intrinsically related to reality and cannot without deliberation be divorced from reality testing, that is, experiment and practical application; e.g. 'red sky at night, shepherd's delight' has to be tested out if it is to retain its vitality, even if the testing jeopardizes its existence.

Third, the mental bringing together of mental elements corresponding to Bradley's 'meeting of elements which, in the moment of union, begin a process that issues in the change we call the effect' (I refer, of course, not to any supposed meeting of elements in external reality, but to the ideational counterpart of such an event; my comparison is between this ideational counterpart and the hypothesis as the ideational counterpart of the particular events to which the deductive system may be applied), and the selection of certain mental elements analogous to those mathematician's facts that, in Poincaré's words, 'unite elements long since known but till then scattered and seemingly foreign to each other', so that we can see each element in the place it occupies in the whole.

It will be appreciated that in the whole of this discussion of the nature of the scientific deductive system, the hypothesis embedded in its framework, and the calculus which is its representational counterpart, I have accepted as scientifically sound the idea that common sense may be, and should be, accepted as the arbiter that decides what are the facts in external reality to which these mental activities relate. The philosopher of science has always been brought to a standstill at this point, caught between the logic of the idealist philosopher on the one hand, and the feeling of unreality to which an acceptance of such logic would expose him on the other. There is essentially no difference between the reactions of Braithwaite and Doctor Johnson to the demands of the idealist.

It is possible that the scientist's dilemma, and therefore our own, may be seen differently if we now return to clinical psycho-analysis for the light it may throw on common sense and on that particular instance of scientific hypothesis and deduction known to us as a psycho-analytic interpretation.

Description 1 (D.1). Let us consider the following episode taken from the analysis of a psychotic patient. The patient, who is used to lying on the couch, looks apprehensively and cautiously about him, finally seating himself precariously on the very edge of the couch. His survey is perfunctory, as if confirming some preconception; his expression changes to one of dejection. After some minutes he has become established in his posture; he does not move, he does not talk, he is no longer apparently even anxious—just dejected. I draw his attention to his behaviour and to my presence, of which he seems to be only vaguely aware, by saying, "You are not lying down today". He replies, looking at the couch, "There is blood everywhere". His tone implies distaste, and his reply carries the suggestion that it is the presence of blood everywhere that makes him unwilling to lie down.

I maintain that the description I have given is a common-sense one; I am not in two minds about any of the statements I have made, and I believe that any ordinary human being of my acquaintance would agree that the account is an accurate description, even when I employ terms such as, 'as if confirming some preconception'. Such a phrase is sanctioned by usage and may be expected to convey an impression with which the reader could match his own. Unfortunately, in this instance the reader can have no impression of the episode of which I speak other than that conveyed by me. But he can have impressions of what he may regard as similar experiences of his own. It therefore seems fair to say that I have given him an opportunity for the exercise of his common sense so that he can decide for himself whether or not his common sense tells him that an event such as I describe actually took place or not. In short, I am saying that it is common sense to say and believe that the facts were what I said they were.

To begin with I propose to maintain, with Braithwaite, that it is legitimate for my present purposes to ignore the problems that are associated with the phenomenological scientific philosopher's outlook, and to consider as facts those events that my common sense tells me are facts. The justification for this lies in the experience of scientists that it is conducive to a growth of knowledge to behave as if events that common sense says are facts provide adequate material for the formation of contingent propositions on the one hand, and objective tests of a hypothesis on the other. There is also a historical justification in such a procedure, for common-sense synthesis has always been the precursor of a scientific ordering in a scientific system. I repeat, therefore, that common sense declares that the facts are as I have stated them and thereby provide a basis for scientific work.

From this premise I select the possible trains of thought that I might pursue: one touches the nature of the common sense to which I appeal and to which, in conformity with the views of a powerful school of philosophers to which I adhere, I accord an extremely important role. For the time being I shall leave this thought in abeyance, merely contenting myself with a partial limitation of the term to cover that aspect of the personality which is a compact of a component of the senses, common to two or more of the senses, and which in my belief has a social component analogous to that which Freud supposed might be the case with the sexual impulses, and which appears to me to be true of all emotional drives [Freud, 'Instincts and their Vicissitudes', 1915c, *SE 14*]. This train of thought I leave for discussion later.

The second train of thought following my premise that I have made a common-sense observation leads me to put two questions. Where is the patient's common sense? What has happened to it? I shall later consider the reciprocal of these questions starting from the point of view that the patient's description of the facts is the common-sense view, but for the present I consider only these two questions.

Description 2 (D.2). Is there any reason to doubt that the patient's judgement that there is blood everywhere is in his opinion a common-sense view? There are the following reasons for doubting it: he has shown in previous similar situations that he does not believe I share his view; the readiness with which he volunteered his explanation for not lying on the couch is an expression of confidence that I shall tolerate his opinion, not that I shall share it. He is even, at this advanced stage of the analysis, quite capable of making no response, because he knows that *his* view is not the 'common' sense one, and he prefers that the difference in outlook should not become public. He may be supposed, therefore, to feel that his sense of 'blood everywhere' is not common sense, is not in accord with the 'common' view demanded of him as a price of his membership of the group.

One answer to the question, 'Where is his common sense?' is therefore that it is where it always has been; it is still a part of that non-psychotic part of the personality which I believe, together with Mauritz Katan and other observers, always to remain in existence. None the less, the question still stands because from one point of view the patient does not behave as if he has any common sense or, if he has any, that it could be of any use to him. I am not, of course, suggesting that this is deducible from the one instance I have attempted to describe; it is a deduction from many similar episodes. Indeed, it is arguable that the patient has no conceivable interest in common sense, still less the question that I have put to myself about it. And yet the patient appears to feel that he has some identity of interest with me as the analyst, or he would not keep coming for analysis.

But now I think I see the answers to my two questions. Where is the patient's common sense? Obviously, it is 'everywhere'. What has happened to it? Equally obviously, it has been turned into blood—'blood everywhere'. If I am correct, then the patient and I are well on the way to establishing a 'common-sense' view, that is to say a view common to him and to me. But it is equally clear that my interpretation of the facts I mentioned in *D.1* involves me in having produced a new description, *D.2*. The description, *D.2*, of the facts owes its difference from *D.1* to the new hypothesis in the light of which I now regard the episode. I argued that I am entitled to regard *D.1* as common sense: I am prepared to argue that *D.2* has a sense common to me and my patient. But can I now maintain that *D.2* is a common-sense description in a wider, extra-analytic context, and if so, in what way?

Let us first turn to discuss the idea that *D.2* is a common-sense description in the limited field of that which is common to the patient and me. It is evident that even in this limited respect the interpretation of the patient's behaviour that I have proposed cannot, on the facts I have given so far, be regarded as a 'sense' common to the patient and myself. It is an idea selected or accepted in a penumbra of circumstances which suggest a resemblance to the new fact for which Poincaré says the mathematician seeks—'the link that unites facts which have a deep but hidden analogy' [*Science and Method,* p. 27]. For if it is indeed a fact that the blood which the patient describes as being everywhere is the transmuted common sense for which I am looking, then this fact does link a number of other facts in a way that demonstrates a deep but hidden analogy. Thus the patient, as I know, believes he is mad and has always felt himself to be unlike others, to have a feeling compatible with that of having no 'sense' felt in common with others, and no senses that appear to have a factor common to each other. This he often expresses (as do two other patients) in a reiterated plaint about almost any feeling he has—"I don't know why". I know that if he saw blood everywhere, and then also felt the blood everywhere, and furthermore thought he smelt it everywhere, then he would think he knew why—it would just be common sense to see blood everywhere because his common sense told him it was everywhere. Since, however, his common sense does not tell him so, it may be a matter of some interest and significance to consider *what* sense has told him so. *D.2* has thus served to point one possible direction for further inquiry, and at the same time to link the present fact, his statement about the blood, with previously observed facts touching his profound sense of isolation and uniqueness. I know, furthermore, that this patient considers the sight of blood to be significant; it is felt to be something that has been lost, and the loss is felt to be associated with disaster for the object that has lost it. In the episode I have recounted, its presence was associated with feelings of depression and persecution (these last being observations of my common sense). I know the patient's hatred of reality is strongly coloured by the feeling that a sense of reality carries with it a stimulation of the socially polarized aspect of his emotional drives, and that this stimulation is felt to menace the ego-centric aspect of his emotional drives and therefore his narcissism, thus increasing his fear of annihilation. I know, therefore, that a belief that his common sense has been lost, destroyed or alienated is quite compatible with and illuminant of his previously expressed hatred of reality or the mental apparatus that might link him with it.

It may be supposed that I am arguing that my interpretation is based on previous observations, that it is a scientific hypothesis in the sense that that term is used by those who consider a hypothesis to be a generalization from a number of particular observations of fact. But I no longer feel that this view is adequate, although it still seems to me to have substance. I do not wish to exclude from debate the influence exerted by numerous stimuli, subliminal or overt, which are received over a period of psycho-analytic experience. I think it would be misleading to suggest that the interpretation, *D.2*, owes nothing to the stream of stimuli which I, as analyst, have received. But I consider it to be equally misleading to say that *D.2* is 'based on experience'. Such a description should be reserved for beliefs, interpretations, hypotheses, which have demonstrably undergone what common sense would recognize as reality-testing. (Once more I appeal to common sense, that is to say a group or socially orientated sense whose 'purposes' go beyond the individual. I, as individual, need to consider what the 'group' will accept as reality-testing before I can feel that my view has the sanction of 'my' common sense.) I shall therefore suggest that *D.2* has, as one of the components to which it owes its emergence, the influence of external events on the analyst's psyche both in shaping the form the interpretation takes as a crystallization of experience, the memory component, and as a compendium facilitating prediction, and by virtue of that, reality-testing.

There remains the element whose existence was suspected by Hume and classified by him as 'psychological'. This element is most obtrusive before the point at which the common-sense synthesis of experience becomes a scientific ordering in a scientific system. It is worth remarking at this point Braithwaite's comment:

> There is no hard and fast line at the point at which the common-sense synthesis of experience becomes a scientific ordering in a scientific system. Just as, in tracing back commonsense thought either in the individual or in the race, there is no point at which there were no generalizations believed, so in the history of a science there is rarely any one historical date at which it is possible to say that the first hypothesis was adumbrated. [*Scientific Explanation,* p. 28]

To this I would add that the same holds true of the history of an analysis—there is rarely a precise moment at which it can be said that a particular interpretation was first enunciated. Nevertheless, even though it is in fact difficult to say that a given moment is *the* moment, we may yet suppose such a moment to exist, and it is before this point is reached that the so-called psychological factors are suspected of playing a dominant role in the scientific activity. In other words, there is reason to look to the mentality of the analyst himself for the major contribution of elements in the totality of elements which issues in the interpretation *D.2*, namely that the patient feels his common sense not as an integral part of his personality but as blood, dangerous and persecuting, lying about him everywhere. Before Hume's insistence that there is nothing in a scientific hypothesis but a generalization and that any added element does not belong to the scientific generalization properly speaking, but is only the psychological factor in the observer which he recognized as a tendency in the human mind for certain ideas to be associated together, philosophers of science were not prepared to admit either that this something extra to the generalization did not exist, or that its existence lay in the personality of the human being. It was supposed that this something was analogous to the logic of the human mind. My view diverges from the view that the scientific hypothesis or law includes more than a generalization and that that something is a function of external reality. It approximates to the views of those epistemologists—Kant, Whewell, Mill, Peirce, Poincaré, Russell and Popper—who tend to the beliefs compatible with the idea that scientific knowledge is the result of the growth of common-sense knowledge. My agreements—and disagreements—with these epistemologists are a direct consequence of a psycho-analytic investigation of the phenomena known to all of them under various synonyms for scientific common sense. It is my view that the impasse in which the scientists and philosophers of science find themselves is not capable of further adumbration, let alone resolution, without the employment of psycho-analytic research, and more precisely research into the phenomena collectively called common sense which are the main theme of this inquiry. I say the main theme, but in fact I propose to make it so only because its data, elusive though they are, are none the less more accessible to preliminary investigation than phenomena associated with intuition, the first hypothesis, the inspiration (Karl Popper, *The Logic of Scientific Discovery*, pp. 31, 32). If I do not elucidate this last, it will be because I cannot. In fact I do not consider that the elaboration of a deductive system from facts declared by common sense to be so can be separated from the earlier phenomenon which is a precondition for the elaboration of a deductive system, namely the inspiration. I propose, therefore, to make no strenuous effort to separate the phenomena from each other.

I shall first consider the opposite of the hunch. "I don't know why", says the patient. "I don't understand", replies the patient to a particularly clear interpretation I have just given him. By 'particularly clear' I mean one that has, in my opinion, drawn together a number of apparently unrelated facts in a way that demonstrates their relationship, and does so in terms so precise that the expression of the interpretation does not vitiate the deduction that is intrinsically dependent on its mode of expression. These two statements, 'I don't know why', and, 'I don't understand', are as active, as affirmative as 'I know', or, 'I understand'. In effect my interpretation has said, 'This is why . . .', and, 'Listen to what I am telling you, and you will find I have made you understand . . .'. Both statements are implicit declarations by me that the relationship between the patient and myself is an analogue of the relationship that might exist between his capacity for inspiration, whatever that is, and the ideational counterpart of apparently unrelated elements scattered and apparently foreign to one another. I have in effect said, 'I know why . . .', i.e. I unite elements. The patient has in effect said, 'I, unlike you, do *not* know why . . .'. My point is that this statement is a declaration of equality with me; not simply rivalry, but equality of status. 'I unite . . .' is one statement. 'I disunite . . .' is the antiphonal reply. I propose to clarify my point in a series of formulas thus:

(1) I unite ⟷ I disunite;

(2) I synthesize ⟷ I analyse;

(3) I metabolize ⟷ I katabolize;

(4) I analyse violently ⟷ I split;

(5) I synthesize violently ⟷ I fuse.

Analysis and synthesis are both involved in understanding. If the act is carried out lovingly it leads to understanding; if carried out violently, i.e. violently with hate, then it leads to splitting and cruel juxtaposition or fusion.

16 May 1959

Common sense

On Friday X's anxiety was far more marked: he hated me, or felt I was not what he thought me; he was disillusioned; my practice had gone; I was ill or dying. But these disjointed scraps were at least *possible* interpretations about a real man; I could see that he *could* hold such a view about facts that *might* be observed by him. Why was this?

It was a kind of disjointed rage, a fragmented hatred, but said with fear. This is the importance of the father, and this is the importance of the mother. He can get inside her as a tank from which the father can be attacked. The patient retreats into a state of mind, e.g. insanity, from which he can launch his attacks.

Where then is his common sense? Why blood? Blood is not faeces. It is essential to his life—like common sense. It has become bad *outside* him; not turned to faeces inside him, but bad and dangerous outside.

The blood—common sense—the semen in which he sits, is dangerous and bad. It is laughter, sexual laughter; noise, horns, drills, banging. It is all the bizarre objects. It is a kind of orgasm that cannot be contained within a disciplined framework. The disciplined framework is reason, mathematics, logic. The analyst becomes a very frightening, aggressive object who takes control of the genitalia so as to give effect to, to fulfil a violent oedipal assault of a murderous kind on the father *and* mother. "I am going to make you shoot your mother. Look what I've got! The penis and balls with which I shall make you shoot your mother!"

The violence seems to be related to a kind of greed in which no choice can be made because nothing can be discarded. This operates against any advance in analysis; no cure can take place because no infantile mechanism is to be given up. And nothing can be taken in because of the conflicting aim to take something else in. Cigars *and* breast milk, pap *and* caviare. Projective identification of food: asceticism and gormandizing.

Megalomania. A matter of having to *be* as well as *have* everything. Common sense produces, from this point of view, a restrictive state of mind; it conflicts with megalomanic narcissism. Without common sense, phantasy can be felt as fact.

Indolence can be the need to remain free to indulge phantasy: again, common sense is the obstructing force.

Public-ation is an essential of scientific method, and this means that common sense plays a vital part. If it is inoperative for any reason, the individual in whom it is inoperative cannot publish, and unpublished work is unscientific work.

* * *

The individual analyst has two main contacts: his patients and society. In the first certainly, and in the second probably, he will have it brought home to him how little he knows and how poor his work is. In this respect his position is not unlike that of the soldier in war who is aware of his own troubles but not of his enemy's. It must therefore be borne in mind that the fundamental importance of our work demands that kind of fortitude and high morale which places the welfare of the analytic group and its work before the welfare of the individual analyst, and sometimes before the welfare even of a particular patient. This, taken in conjunction with the isolation in which analyst and patient work, means that the analyst must, in addition to the commonly recognized equipment, possess a social consciousness of a very high degree—common sense must never be allowed to become dimmed, even when work is concentrated on the more arcane and narcissistic attributes of the analyst's patients. In other words, when concentration is focused predominantly on psychotic mechanisms, the non-psychotic aspects of the work must be as present to the analyst's mind as his awareness of the non-psychotic aspects of the psychotic patient's personality are in the analysis he is conducting. Or, to put it another way, the analyst must never cease, even in the midst of his analytic work, to be a member of one or more social groups.

12 July 1959

I am nonplussed yet excited, as if on some important trail I cannot get hold of. X is not random reconstruction: then what does he do? Could it be logically or mathematically described? If he is saying something apparently insignificant, he can produce coherent, recognizably coherent, speech. Then he may become vehement and speak emphatically. "Then we went down the road. It was" (persuasive and confidential) "just a quite ordinary road. And I said to him, 'This won't do' (quietly emphatic and faintly reminiscent of the 'I said it very loud and clear' verses of Lewis Carroll). I just made it obvious to him that it just *would not do*", the last three words spoken quietly but each one separately emphasized. Has it any meaning for me? And if it has, what is that meaning? And is the meaning it has of any importance except as an indication of my personality and how it reacts to a particular form of stimulus? Yes, obviously it has, because I have just spoken of a 'particular form of stimulus' and this at once suggests (a) it *is* a stimulus, and (b) it has a particular form.

14 July 1959

It is clear that if the search is for the harmonizing fact that marks the transition from the paranoid–schizoid to the depressive position (Poincaré, *Science and Method,* p. 30, and Braithwaite on causation), then much depends on the nature of the elements that are seen to be harmoniously coherent on the discovery of the harmonizing fact, and on the mental make-up of the investigator who discovers, or (according to Poincaré) selects the harmonizing fact. To a religious such a fact might well be quite different from that selected by a physicist. The fact or formula discovered by a mathematician would differ again. The reader of the works written by such pioneer discoverers would have an experience similar to the emotional experience of the discoverer; he would discover the discovery, or the book, or the sentence, or the phrase in which the selected fact was embodied. But—and here lies the central fact—in all these instances, as I have already shown, a series of facts out of an infinitely larger totality of facts is given coherence by the selected fact, and that is all; not only is *the fact* selected, but all the cohering facts also are a selection. Thus one fact is observed to 'explain' a great number of other facts, which facts may be considered to belong to the domain of Physics. But this is no more than saying that all the facts that are not given coherence by the selected or discovered fact are either unknown, ignored, or regarded as belonging to some other discipline or system. A result of this is that some kind of objective reality is attributed to the coherent system of facts, whereas there is no evidence to suppose that such a system, say physics, is anything more than an appearance artificially produced by the limitations of the human mind unable to do more than see a tiny fraction of the totality of facts, and prone to attribute to that fraction of facts a relationship intrinsic to itself, while the supposed relationship between the facts is only a relationship that each fact has to the capacities of the human observer.

This argument can be extended further by considering not physics but the whole of what we call a scientific outlook, the outlook and methods common to all the sciences, as being a peculiarity of the human mind analogous to that peculiarity of human visual capacity which makes it sensitive to a comparatively small range of wavelengths.

The supposition that man's mathematical ability receives (from the apparently endless series of discoveries that have in the past two thousand years been associated with the application of mathematical techniques to physical and astronomical phenomena) some kind of title to be considered as itself an intrinsic objective quality in the universe it has helped to illuminate, can now be seen as open to question. It is arguable that it is simply a peculiarity of the human mind which tends to illuminate just those phenomena that lie within its powers of illumination, and so does not prove that the universe has mathematical qualities, any more than the eye's sensitivity to certain wavelengths proves that there is in the universe an objective essential quality which can be called 'visibility'.

* * *

The reason why a mathematical statement is given such importance by the scientist is that the deductions made from it appear to correspond with the parallel developments in the scientific deductive system which it represents, and in the corresponding world of empirical data. But this may merely mean that mathematical logic is the expression of the ultimate limits of human mental capacity—that an appearance of finality is observed in a mathematical statement of natural phenomena which in reality belongs to the inability of the human mind to go further, and not to the exhaustion of the natural phenomena under observation.

This is the reciprocal of my reply to Prichard (*Knowledge and Perception*). That is to say that just as it is idle to deny the title of 'knowledge' to what a human being knows because it is possible to imagine that another being might know more, so is it idle to suppose that because some mathematically precise behaviour appears to be observed, say in astronomical phenomena, this mathematically precise behaviour is any more than that aspect of the behaviour which we as human beings are capable of observing.

15 July 1959
(4.30 a.m. Blast it!)

X said . . . well, what? He used words in such a way that they seemed to indicate that his mother or relatives had cut off supplies; that he could sell out £500 of shares and go to the cottage, in which case there would only be £50 and that just could not buy food. "That's all there is to it." I attempted to draw attention to the fact that even while there was an opportunity for analysis, he could make no use of it. He defends by taking this as an accusation in which he is to blame and thus denies the existence of a very bad obstructive object. The rational comes in, therefore, not as the product of an elucidation, but as a defence against the elucidation. If I put to him that his mother is a very dangerous object denying him food, then I am giving him material to defend himself against the common-sense view, and am myself felt to be disturbed to an extent which makes me unable to see the common-sense view.

There is something curious about this kind of defence which is analogous to an interpretation in which the elements are so ordered that the narcissism of the patient is spared. But I have already said that narcissism, apparently primary narcissism [Freud, 'Instincts and their Vicissitudes', 1915c, *SE 14*], is related to the fact that common sense is a function of the patient's relationship to his group, and in his relationship with the group the individual's welfare is secondary to the survival of the group. Darwin's theory of the survival of the fittest needs to be replaced by a theory of the survival of the fittest to survive in a group—as far as the survival of the individual is concerned. That is, he must be possessed with a high degree of common sense: (1) an ability to see what everyone else sees when subjected to the same stimulus, (2) an ability to believe in survival of the dead after death in a sort of Heaven or Valhalla or what-not, (3) an ability to hallucinate or manipulate facts so as to produce material for a delusion that there exists an inexhaustible fund of love in the group for himself. If for some reason the patient lacks these, or some similar series of capacities for attaining subordination to the group, he has to defend himself against his fear of the group—which is known to be indifferent to his fate as an *individual*—by destroying his common sense or sense of group pressures on himself as an individual, as the only method by which he can preserve his narcissism. In the extreme form of defence in the psychotic the result of these destructive attacks appears as a superabundance of primary narcissism. But this is an *appearance*—the supposedly primary narcissism must be recognized as secondary to a fear of 'social-ism'.

This digression brings me back to the psychotic defence against interpretation which I said was analogous to the analyst's attempt to evade any conveyance by the interpretation of an element which constitutes, or is felt to constitute, an attack on the patient's narcissism. In practice this means evading the elucidation of illusory, delusory, or hallucinatory mechanisms for making the patient feel loved, lest such elucidation should show him that such love as he wishes to feel that he receives does not in fact exist. This in turn means that the analyst has to convey by various means that he loves the patient, and that in this respect he is a representative of the common sense of the patient's social group which loves the patient more than it loves itself. This latter belief can of course be supported by the patient by his believing that analysis itself is an expression of such group love for him. Or, in early infant terms, that the breast is a gift to him from the family group.

In so far as the patient is successful in evading the attacks on his narcissism, he experiences a hallucinatory gratification of his craving for love. This, like all hallucinatory gratification, leaves the patient unsatisfied. He therefore greedily resorts to a strengthening of his capacity for hallucination, but there is naturally no corresponding increase in satisfaction.

18 July 1959

(An inability to dream and hatred of common sense)
implies
(destructive attacks on all linking and anti-social acting out)
[*see* p. 58, discussion of symbol for 'implies', –)–].

The anti-social acting out is an attempt to destroy the common sense which the patient cannot get rid of. In analysis it contributes to the danger of murderous attacks on the analyst. The analyst's common-sense interpretations are attacked by being seen and felt as sexual assaults. But does the patient really feel them as sexual assaults, or is this an instance of anti-social, i.e. anti-common-sense, attacks on common sense, a sort of 'You're another' retort to someone who is felt to frustrate?

Social-ism versus Narcissism = Frustration of all instincts.

The aimless wandering is described in terms such as, 'down the road' and, 'I don't know why'. But these terms also give a lively impression of the protesting and bewildered parent who is suspicious but can get no relief for anxiety either through confirmation of anxiety, or final or even temporary dismissal of doubts. Is this his conscience playing up both him and me by being delinquent, by being a delinquent super-ego which knows just how to produce the maximum anxiety?

How does this link up with the common sense? The most obvious would be Freud's early super-ego which he equated or associated with social guilt. If this is so, Freud's denial of guilt before the Oedipal situation, except for social guilt, is a more fruitful theory than Melanie Klein's [*Developments in Psycho-Analysis,* p. 272 et seq.]. But splitting attacks on the super-ego, common sense, would lead to a mass of super-egos—the bizarre objects I spoke of in 'Differentiation of the Psychotic from the

Non-psychotic Part of the Personality'. It is a murderous super-ego. He rebels against it but it is itself delinquent.

What is the relationship between common sense, super-ego, narcissism?

The super-ego is certainly opposed to his existence: it is opposed, *a fortiori,* to his living. It is opposed to morals, e.g. his dream: his father makes a sexual approach to his wife while he (the patient) looks out of the window helplessly.

* * *

The idea (Prichard, *Knowledge and Perception*) that we come to wonder if we can learn anything at all if we start inquiring how we come to know anything is fallacious in that it depends on the supposition that someone exists who knows more than we know, that what we know is not knowledge because in the eyes of this other person's supposedly superior knowledge what we know is inaccurate. But even when in fact someone else exists who knows more, or even when we know better ourselves—as for example when we say we know the sun rises when in fact the earth rotates—that does not invalidate our claim to have a particular piece of knowledge. There is a sense in which it is true knowledge that the sun rises and not accurate that the earth rotates, depending on the context of the phrase.

24 July 1959

The suspicion that the actual events of the session are being turned into a dream came back to me today with X when at one point I suspected that my interpretation was being made into a dream. Thus, he sees a tunnel with a train in it. The train stops. "Won't be able to get cured. Too early and since I just missed it there will not be another for a long time. Minute fragments like faeces . . . two chairs and the three-piece suite; stool–chair. I can't talk properly." Then he started on the 'dream'. It was clear to me that a distinction was being made between talking 'properly' and some kind of talking in visual images.

In an attempt to see how these elements were put together, the first difficulty was that the terrifying super-ego would be put together. When it came to synthesis, after this interpretation, the problem was to see how elements were combined. I suspect that Freud's displacement etc. is relevant; he took up only the negative attitude, dreams as 'concealing' something, not the way in which the *necessary* dream is *constructed*.

[Undated]

The tropisms

The tropisms may be communicated. In certain circumstances they are too powerful for the modes of communication available to the personality. This, presumably, may be because the personality is too weak or ill-developed if the traumatic situation arrives prematurely. But when this situation does arise, all the future development of the personality depends on whether an object, the breast, exists into which the tropisms can be projected. If it does not, the result is disaster which ultimately takes the form of loss of contact with reality, apathy, or mania. And in this context I include in mania feelings of depression that must be distinguished from the depression of the neuroses. In extreme cases it is an agitated melancholia, but it need not be extreme; the maniacal quality may be so slight as to be recognizable as an obsessive depression, but its essential quality is aggressiveness and hate.

If such an object exists, a breast capable of tolerating projective identifications that are thrust into it (for it is to projective identification in relation to the breast that I have now returned), then the outcome may be supposed to be more favourable, or at least in suspense.

Associated with the strength of the tropisms, but probably secondary to it, is an intolerance of frustration. Psychopathologically this has not the fundamental importance of the tropisms; clinically it presents a grave problem as it jeopardizes the analytic approach since frustration is essential to it—not extrinsic.

The action appropriate to the tropisms is seeking. I have so far considered this activity as it might be thought to relate to murder, parasitism, and creation—the three tropisms. Thus, considered individually, the tropisms are seen to issue in seeking (1) an object to murder or be murdered by, (2) a parasite or a host, (3) an object to create or by which to be created. But taken as a whole, and not individually, the action appropriate to the tropisms in the patient who comes for treatment is a seeking for an object with which projective identification is possible. This is due to the fact that in such a patient the tropism of creation is stronger than the tropism of murder.

Suppose that the search ends in the discovery of the object, but the object, the primitive breast, is found to be intolerant of projective identification. For the sake of simplicity in exposition I shall suppose that this intolerance shows itself in two main forms: anxiety (persecution) and hate, or apathy. It is these two classes of response that contribute the environmental component in the development of the psychotic part of the personality. Ultimately both lead to the rejection of the tropism which, it must always be remembered, is a part of the projecting personality. But there are important differences in the rejection: the persecuted object causes the personality partly to reintroject the tropism, now exacerbated, and wholly to introject a peculiar form of primitive super-ego hostile to projective identification even as a method of communication, and so, by extension, to all forms of communication. But, as I have said, the tropism has only been partly reintrojected. For the most part it is felt to exist, not in the primitive breast which has refused it admission, not in the immature psyche which dare not take it back, but enclosed within the vehicle of communication itself, be that sound, sight, or touch. Thus enclosed, the tropism and its envelope become persecuted and persecuting.

The tropisms are the matrix from which all mental life springs. For maturation to be possible they need to be won from the void and communicated. Just as a breast, or its equivalent, is necessary for the infant life to be sustained, so it is necessary that a mental counterpart, the primitive breast, should exist for mental life to be sustained. The vehicle of communication—the infant's cry, tactile and visual senses—is engaged in order not only to communicate but also to control the tropism. If all goes well the communication, by projective identification, leads (as Melanie Klein has described) to the deposition in the breast of the tropisms that the infant can neither control, modify, nor develop, but which can be so controlled and developed after they have been modified by the object.

If this breaks down, then the vehicle of communication, the contact with reality, the links of every kind of which I have spoken, suffer a significant fate. This applies particularly to the communicating particles that are felt to lie with their enclosed tropisms, rejected by psyche and object alike.

25 July 1959

I shall assume that the patient's fear of the murderous super-ego prevents his approaching the Positions [paranoid–schizoid and depressive positions]. This in turn means that he is unable to dream, for it is in dream that the Positions are negotiated. He therefore postpones this experience till the analytic session in which he hopes he will have support, or perhaps, feeling he has support, dares to have the dream he cannot have without the consciousness of support.

He has to dream—the important thing here is not the content of the dream, but his having to 'dream', a positive transitive act for which a transitive verb is necessary. Not only the creative person needs to dream to accomplish the act of creation involving experience of the Positions, but also the lesser mortal who needs to do it to 'understand' the interpretation, each good interpretation being, as I have said before, an event that is, or should be, significant as one of thc selected facts to which Poincaré draws attention. The patient who consistently 'cannot understand' may not simply be resisting, but resisting in a particular way. Indeed it may be that here lies the essential difference between the resistance as something peculiar to the neurotic and relegation to the unconscious, and psychotic destruction of the means for understanding which is associated with an apparently full consciousness of what is ordinarily the furniture of the unconscious. "I do not understand", or, "do not know why", or "do not know how", etc. may be taken either as a *positive* statement of *inability* to dream, or a defiant assertion of a capacity for *not* dreaming.

If this is so, psycho-analytic use of the dream as a method by which the unconscious is made conscious is an employment in reverse of what is in nature the machinery that is employed in the transformation of the conscious into material suitable for storage in the unconscious. In other words, the dream-work we know is only a small aspect of dreaming proper—dreaming proper being a continuous process belonging to the *waking* life and in action all through the waking hours, but not usually observable then except with the psychotic patient. The possibility of observing it in the psychotic depends on some peculiarity which makes his unconscious observable. Is this peculiarity the dispersal of the ego, 'common sense', the links with reality, leaving the id exposed? At any rate the hypothesis that in an analytic session I can see the patient dream has proved to be very valuable especially with its counterpart of seeing the contrasting activity of hallucination.

To return to the patient's fear of the Positions and the potential emergence at that stage of a murderous super-ego: the patient tries to cope with this by dreaming with the analyst—or does he just continue what he does all the time? He may then be so afraid that he produces an artefact that is not a dream but a hallucination, and then can make no use of it because he can get no more from a hallucination than he could get milk from an imaginary breast.

Or he may 'dream' (a) introjectively, (b) projectively.

[Undated]

The Dream is an emotional event of which we usually only hear a report or have a memory, although as we shall see it is a matter of some doubt what we mean when we think, or say, we remember a dream. I wish now to extend the term, 'dream', to cover the kind of events that take place in an analysis of a schizophrenic—events that appear to me to merit the description, 'dreams'.

One of the points I wish to discuss is related to the fact that the actual events of the session, as they are apparent to the analyst, are being 'dreamed' by the patient *not* in the sense that he believes that the events observed by him are the same as the events observed by the analyst (except for the fact that he believes them to be a part of a dream, and the analyst believes them to be a part of reality), but in the sense that these same events that are being *perceived* by the analyst are being perceived by the patient and treated to a process of being dreamed by him. That is, these events are having something done to them mentally, and that which is being done to them is what I call being dreamed—subjected to a process which I hope to describe in more detail.

[Undated]

Schematic presentation of dreaming

Murderous super-ego: therefore avoidance of the depressive positions is achieved by not dreaming, or by dreaming with precautions, e.g. of being with the analyst or, like Y, only allowing the dream to develop when he knows someone is there; instead of quietening down when his mother arrives, his dream appears to become *more* vivid and *worse*. It also explains why X seems to cling so tenaciously to my badness in the session.

First Stage

a. No dreams (in the ordinary sense of night-time phenomena).

b. Dreams suppressed and has hallucinations as a substitute. These hallucinations are excretory, projective.

Second Stage

a. No dreams.

b. Dreams suppressed but has hallucinations as a substitute. These are *intended* to be introjectory, but because of fear of the super-ego and, paradoxically, creating the super-ego by synthesis, it is not rewarding as the true dream would be, and in any case the hallucination cannot yield the free associations etc. which are what make a true dream yield its meaning. So: no free associations and no development of personality is possible. The patient cannot get sustenance from a hallucination.

Third Stage

a. Dreams reported. No free associations and not easily distinguishable from hallucinations—"I was standing at the window as usual." Dream seems to be excretory in function.

b. Confusion. Projective identification—splitting almost exclusively with 'dreaming the session'. That is to say, the session is dreamed; my interpretations and all other events of which he is aware, are not seen, listened to, heard in the ordinary way but are subjected to 'inaccessible-ization'. Thus: train stuck in tunnel—two chairs and a three-piece suite—a stool–chair. Mostly excretory to deal with the ego qualities of the interpretations by dispersal.

Fourth Stage

a. Dreams, more frequent but lacking associations and mostly excretory—arm drops off when he gives a traffic signal, thus indicating uselessness of attempting to warn because parts of the body persist in wanting to be

b. Introjective and projective. The dream-work intended to convert material into a form where it is compact and can be stored—an important function because of memory. His mind being a kind of 'gut', mental storage seems to

destructive. It lies on the grass—in a tantrum?—but there are no associations. Does the analyst know the meaning, or is it obvious?

mean that the dream is a mental digestive process. The nature of the dream and its function vary according to stimuli. The week-end break seems always to lead to sessional dreaming—I think of the excretory kind, but in later stage perhaps more introjective and retentive.

27 July 1959

I think the fear of dreams must contribute to making the patient anxious to avoid the dream-work of the conscious state. Should it simply be introjection that is avoided? No: because according to me the process of introjection is carried out by the patient's 'dreaming' the current events. Introjection –)– Dreaming, would be the formula [*see* p. 58].

Anxiety in the analyst is a sign that the analyst is refusing to 'dream' the patient's material: not (dream) = resist = not (introject). It may be worth considering, when a patient is resisting, whether the resistance bears characteristics relating it to phenomena Freud described as 'dream-work'. But *Freud* meant by dream-work that unconscious material, which would otherwise be perfectly comprehensible, was transformed into a dream, and that the dream-work needed to be undone to make the now incomprehensible dream comprehensible [*New Introductory Lectures,* 1933a, *SE 22*, p. 25]. *I* mean that the conscious material has to be subjected to dream-work to render it fit for storing, selection, and suitable for transformation from paranoid–schizoid position to depressive position, and that unconscious pre-verbal material has to be subjected to reciprocal dream-work for the same purpose. *Freud* says Aristotle states that a dream is the way the mind works in sleep: *I* say it is the way it works when awake (*New Introductory Lectures* [1933a, *SE 22*], pp. 26–27). Freud says the state of sleep represents a turning away from the world, the real external world, and 'thus provides a necessary condition for the development of a psychosis'. Is this why X talks of losing consciousness? It follows on dream-work which is intended to be destroyed, or has been destroyed, as part of an attack on linking.

28 July 1959

The dream

The dream is the mechanism by which

(1) the ego links the sense data of external experience with the associated conscious awareness of the sense impression;

(2) the stream of unconnected impressions and events are made suitable for storing in memory;

(3) these stored events are reviewed and one is chosen which enables facts already 'known', i.e. stored, to be harmonized so that the relationship between them is established and the place of each element seen in its relationship to the whole;

(4) the interplay between paranoid–schizoid and depressive positions is made possible by a selected fact which is known as the 'harmonizing or unifying fact' spatially, and the 'cause' temporally, or when time is an essential element in the relationship between the elements.

The dream, therefore, is the mechanism by which there comes into operation,

(a) the social conscience, associated with splitting of the super-ego and retreat from the depressive position to the paranoid–schizoid position. This seems identical with the social guilt and true super-ego which can only come into being with the Oedipus complex, but which I think is a highly persecutory super-ego which becomes more persecutory since it is split up. Each split itself becomes a complete super-ego and this leads to further splitting, the fragmentation becoming progressively more minute. This contributes to the state where dreams are 'invisible', wet, and being awake is 'dry';

(b) the individual super-ego, a murderous object, which becomes manifest if synthesis of the fragments of the paranoid-schizoid position is effected by dream-work bringing the depressive position into being.

Social and individual super-ego both contribute by their fearfulness to patients' need to make destructive attacks in dream mechanism. When this happens in the session, the patient will show fear that he is dead or has lost consciousness, because the dream is that which makes available, as part of the personality, both the events of external emotional reality and the events of internal pre-verbal psychic reality. If the dream-work capacity is destroyed, the patient feels dread which is peculiarly terrifying because it is nameless, and because the namelessness itself springs from the destruction of the patient's capacity for dream-work which is the mechanism responsible for naming.

The domain of the dream

Into the domain of the dream flow the sense impressions associated with the coming into being of the reality principle and the pre-verbal impressions associated with the pleasure–pain principle. None of these can be associated with consciousness, memory, recall, unconsciousness, repression, or suppression unless transformed by dream-work. The domain of the dream is the storehouse in which the transformed impressions are stored after they have been transformed. Dream-work is responsible for rendering pre-communicable material 'storable' and communicable; the same for stimuli and impressions derived from the contact of the personality with the external world. Contact with reality is *not* dependent on dream-work; accessibility to the personality of the material derived from this contact *is* dependent on dream-work. The failure of dream-work and the consequent lack of availability of experience of external or internal psychic reality gives rise to the peculiar state of the psychotic who seems to have a contact with reality but is able to make singularly little use of it either for learning by experience or for immediate consumption.

In this respect the dream seems to play a part in the mental life of the individual which is analogous to the digestive processes in the alimentary life of the individual. Why?

The domain of the dream must be seen as containing an amorphous mass of unconnected and undifferentiated elements. These will be felt by the patient to be dangerous and bad, or potentially good, according to factors in his personality with which I cannot at present be engaged. In so far as this is clinically recognizable, the form in which it manifests itself is a nameless feeling of dread, but there may be others. In so far as dream-work is operative, the course of events in the vicissitudes of these elements can be seen to take different forms: visual, auditory, haptic, olfactory. . . .

* * *

An example of what I mean by 'dreaming' the environment in which the individual finds himself may be found in the group in the elaboration of a myth such as the story that Newton, seeing an apple fall, discovered the Laws of Gravitation. The statement is the outcome of the dream-work, and its object is the embodiment, in a pictorial symbol, of facts which the individuals in a group need to transform so that they can be stored and recalled at will. The pictorial symbol, once formed and stored, can then be recovered and interpreted by the individual to yield the contents that he has felt he needed to store. A peculiarity of psychoanalysis is that the scientific deductive system is a series of hypotheses about hypotheses about hypotheses . . . (e.g. Freud, *Interpretation of Dreams* [1900a, *SE 4*], p. 16), a neurological hypothesis about the individual's hypothesis about himself. Also X's alimentary hypothesis about his hypothesis about his persecuting authority. Also my Kleinian hypothesis about X's hypothesis about his hypothesis about his persecuting authority.

This deserves comparison with the physicist's quantum mechanics hypothesis about basic data which in fact are statistical hypotheses [Northrop, 'Introduction to Heisenberg', *Physics and Philosophy*].

1 August 1959

Freud says,

> It is easy to see how the remarkable preference shown by the memory in dreams for indifferent, and consequently unnoticed, elements in waking experience is bound to lead people to overlook in general the dependence of dreams upon waking life and all events to make it difficult in any particular instance to prove that dependence. [*Interpretation of Dreams,* 1900a, *SE 4*, p. 19]

My belief is that the dependence of waking life on dreams has been overlooked and is even more important. Waking life = ego activity, and in particular the play of logical thought on the synthesis of elements, i.e. particles characteristic of the paranoid–schizoid position. The function of the dream is to render these elements suitable for storage, and so to constitute the contents of what we call memory. Waking life = ego activity = logical operation. This in turn is essential for synthesis and communicability or publication.

'The way in which memory behaves in dreams is undoubtedly of the greatest importance for any theory of memory in general' [*Interpretation of Dreams,* 1900a, *SE 4,* p. 20]. In my idea above, the dream symbolization and dream-work is what makes memory possible.

2 August 1959

Vomiting and greed as most recalcitrant symptoms: the intense desire to chew and then to feel it going down; the movement of the jaws, the biting is very satisfactory. Some feeling of rebellion likewise—a kind of "Why-should-I-be-denied-the-good-things-of-life?" attitude. The good things are denied because the desire is to chew, and the object is only within visual grasp. But then the destructiveness is transferred to, and is consequently felt to impregnate, looking itself.

Much the same is true of smell as of sight, in that with neither sense must the object be in the physical contact necessary for biting and chewing. Good smells are felt to be turned into bad by the destructiveness with which they are savoured.

This frustration carries over into a relationship with the man's anus because he is predominantly representing the cruelly destroyed breast. Or, rather, the masculine anus represents it, and is itself a cruelly destructive mouth 'producing' bad smells and bad food.

Stammering is also most recalcitrant. Intolerance of frustration leads to intolerance of stimulation.

* * *

Dreams

> We close our most important sensory channels, our eyes, and try to protect the other senses from all stimuli or from any modification of the stimuli acting on them.
>
> The sensory stimuli that reach us during sleep may very well become sources of dreams. [Freud, *Interpretation of Dreams*, 1900a, *SE 4*, p. 23]

Then why is it that dreams we report, or have reported to us, are so often in terms of visual images?

Is it not a 'modification of the stimuli' reaching us? And could this be something to do with the dream-work as an attempt to achieve 'common sense' as part of the synthesizing function of the dream? It may be an aspect of 'linking' one sense to another; the transformation of tactile stimuli into visual excretions as in hallucination. If this is so, it would fit in with Freud's idea that sleep is to be preserved. [*Interpretation of Dreams,* 1900a, *SE 5,* p. 573 et seq.]. The hallucinated patient then *would* be doing what I said he was doing when I described him as taking in the interpretation and evacuating it as far as possible away from himself by 'seeing' it, i.e. visually evacuating it as a hallucination. If this is so, the dream proper may be an attempt at visual and flatus-like evacuation.

Calculus formation notes

There is a need for a sign for 'contributes to' = 'adds to' = 'augments'.

Thus: greed, frustration 'augments' envy.

Also a sign for 'initiates' = 'generates'.

Thus: greed, frustration 'generates' hallucination. Or, frustration, intolerance 'generates' hallucination.

Also a symbol or sign for 'of', meaning 'associated with', so as to express frustration 'of' sexual desire in the sense of the frustration being particularized as to the stimulus involved.

3 August 1959

A dream can be concerned with evacuation of an undesired thought, feeling, image, or with its storage. In either instance it must convert either an empirical external fact or an internal psychic reality into a form that renders it suitable for storage or evacuation. In this respect, too, it seems analogous to a digestive process. But is it? Or is it not that the 'name' of the process is similar to the 'name' of the digestive process? From where does this seeming similarity arise?

4 August 1959

One way of dealing with the problem of scientific evidence for dream theories would be to restrict the search for data to experience shared by analyst and patient, or at which analyst and patient are both present. Such occasions might be all those on which the patient said he had had a dream, or all those on which there appear to be events taking place, e.g. the patient sits up and looks around in a dazed way; the analyst, identifying himself with the patient, feels that the experience the patient is having would be more understandable if the patient were asleep and dreaming.

'More understandable.' Why? Because it is more appropriate to the facts as the analyst sees them. But this means that if the analyst were feeling what the patient seems to be feeling, then he, the analyst, would be disposed to say, "I must have been dreaming".

Just then I found I had been asleep; just before I woke I seemed to be saying to F that I was feeling I was going mad because I could not sort out the feeling I was having in the dream about having a dream and who I was. The dream seemed to be that I was trying to solve the problem I am in fact trying to solve, but with the addition of the fear of going mad—a sort of mental disintegration.

Last night, as I was trying to understand a passage in Quine's *Mathematical Logic* [p. 31] in which 'negative' occurred, I had a dream—having fallen into a sleep or doze—in which a negro appeared. The dream, I thought as I wakened, was associated with 'neg' being both negro and negative. But why did I not write it down then? And now I think of negative and native: 'natives' is associated with memories of India, my mother, and natives as being coloured people like Indians who were 'inferior'.

Also 'dative' as being a present, and dates which I liked. 'Ablative', to lift off or take away. Negro, as he appeared in the dream, now seems to me to be not a real person but an ideogram. My theory is that this ideogram has enabled me to store all these ideas which I am now producing—maybe because I am a dreamer. Perhaps there is a class of persons, or a class of dreamers, to which it might be useful to say some people belong. If so, and if it is true that schizophrenics cannot dream, it would need to be stated that they were not members of that class. (A point to remember in the elaboration of a theoretical deductive system for the schizophrenic patient.)

What do I mean by saying that the negro in the dream was not a real person? Of course he was not. But I suppose that while I was asleep and in that part of mind, if any, in which I am still asleep, he must have been thought of as just a real person, a fact, what I have called an 'undigested' fact. But now I regard him as an ideogram, and this means that some fact has been 'digested' and that the visual image of the negro, which I am now recalling, is a significant element in the process of (the mental counterpart of) digestion. Are 'undigested facts' then used in the process of 'digesting' other facts? Is their 'indigestibility' a quality that renders them useful for this function, as if it were some kind of container for an eroding liquid which must be able itself to resist the erosion by its contents?

On this basis there is always some 'undigested part' of a dream-product ('dream-product' is usually called the dream itself), although my point is that if the person can dream, then he can 'digest' facts and so learn from experience. Obviously what is needed is to consider what 'digesting' facts consists of in detail.

5 August 1959

α

Frustration, according to Freud, enforces the installation of the reality principle ('Formulations on the Two Principles of Mental Functioning' [1911b, *SE 12*], pp. 218–226). But the psychotic with his hatred of reality evades the installation of the reality principle. His intolerance of frustration makes for intolerance of reality and contributes to his hatred of reality. This leads to reinforcement of projective identification as a method of evacuation. This in turn leads to dreams that are evacuations, not introjectory operations—hence 'dreams' of the psychotic, which are really evacuations of such α as he has been unable to prevent. The dream-elements in the psychotic dream are really the discarded residue of α-elements that have survived mutilations of α.

Thus, in the psychotic we find no capacity for reverie, no α, or a very deficient α, and so none of the capacities—or extremely macilent capacities—which depend on α, namely attention, passing of judgement, memory, and dream-pictures, or pictorial imagery that is capable of yielding associations.

But this in turn means that he destroys the capacity for thought which is essential to action in reality and which makes bearable the frustration—an essential concomitant of the interval between a wish and its fulfilment. So the psychotic's attempt to evade frustration ends in producing a personality more than ever subject to frustration without the softening or moderating mechanism that would have been available through α and thought. In consequence he is more than ever intolerant of a frustration that is more than ever intolerable. And thus a self-perpetuating situation is created in which more and more frustration is produced by more and more effort devoted to its evasion by the destruction of the capacity for dreaming which, had he retained it, might have enabled him to moderate frustration.

* * *

How does a dream evade frustration? By distortion of facts of reality, and by displacement of facts of reality. In short, by dream-work on the perception of facts—not, in this context, dream-work on the dream-thoughts except in so far as the dream-thoughts are thoughts portraying the facts. Freud attributes to dream-work the function of concealing the facts of internal mental life only—the dream-thoughts only. I attribute to it the function of evading the frustration to which the dream-thoughts, and therefore the interpretation of dream-thoughts, would give rise if allowed to function properly—that is, as mechanisms associated with the legitimate tasks involved in real modification of frustration. Consequently, since such legitimate tasks always carry an element of frustration, excessive intolerance of frustration short-sightedly leads to the attempt at evasion of the frustration intrinsic to the task of modification of the frustration.

α is concerned with, and is identical with, unconscious waking thinking designed, as a part of the reality principle, to aid in the task of real, as opposed to pathological, modification of frustration.

* * *

Freud, approaching the problem as one of interpreting the dream [*Interpretation of Dreams,* 1900a, *SE 4,* p. 136], regards the dream-work as 'distorting' the wish-fulfilment. The α approach regards the wish-fulfilment ≡ frustration-avoidance, and the distortion as being of the *facts*—notably a distortion of the fact of frustration. [≡, the sign for 'equivalent to'.]

But it must be noted that I make a distinction between α which is essential to attention, storage of memory, thinking, the positions, consciousness attached to sense organs, notation, passing of judgement, motor discharge (what about sleep-walking?), and the use to which this developing form of thinking ('originally unconscious', as Freud says, and according to me still unconscious) is put—particularly in its use 'to support increased tensions' or, as I would say, in frustration-avoidance or frustration-evasion.

6 August 1959

α

The waking unconscious thinking. Does this have the function I attribute to α, or does α carry out the transformation of sense impressions which makes these storable in such a form that they are available for waking unconscious thinking? When Y winces at each word said, it seems clear that the words are not, outwardly at least, being transformed by α into a form, 'notation', that makes the experience of the analysis available to him.

But the transformation by α is not all by symbol formation. For example, it is clearly of consequence to know from a particular transaction in which the individual possessor of two apples, when given two more, ends up having four apples, that this peculiarity applies always, namely that if two things of any kind whatever are added to two others of the same kind, the result will be a total of four such objects.

That 2 + 2 = 4 is sometimes said to be self-evident, an axiom. But it is by no means clear that this is or always has been so, any more than it has always been obvious that if I want something in my room which is out of reach I shall have to leave my chair, walk over to it and fetch it. At some point even the process of walking required thought, probably conscious thought. My suggestion is that it still requires thought, but that it is now waking unconscious thought which has been made possible by α. And it is similarly thanks to the operation of α that it seems obvious that 2 + 2 = 4. If α has not operated, it is probable that it would not be 'obvious' at all.

At first sight it seems that the mathematical capacities of the individual must depend on an α-operation which effects abstraction or generalization, but as usual these convenient simplifications, by their nature, are only approximations, and in some instances the approximation is found not to be sufficiently close. It is probably more true to say that concretization, pictorial or otherwise, may be inseparable from the faculty of abstraction or generalization. Let us then consider this from a new angle.

Let us first suppose that 2 + 2 is established in the individual's mind as = 4. Let us then remember that it is notorious that the mathematicians have never been able to advance their science with sufficient rapidity to be of service to the biological scientist (Braithwaite, *Scientific Explanation,* p. 49) and still less to the psycho-analyst. (It is usually put the other way round—the psycho-analyst is censured for being unscientific because he cannot produce a calculus which is the counterpart of the scientist's deductive systems, e.g. Eysenck.) Let us then transfer the statement, 1 + 1 = 2, to the field of biological science by considering what happens if 1 rabbit (male) is added to 1 rabbit (female), all enclosed in a suitable hutch. In this instance 1 + 1 may easily be found to make quite a considerably larger number than 2 rabbits. Such a fact, thanks to α, may not present any great difficulty. But there are situations in which waking unconscious thought is not enough, and these situations demand a change in mathematical outlook which may be as revolutionary and arduous as the elaboration of a positional geometry from a foundation of Euclidean geometry.

* * *

Interpretation of Dreams

([1900a], *SE 4,* p. 54)

Most of the criticisms cited are hostile and indicate the need in a waking state to disparage the dream. This is compatible with the α-theory that there is a failure of 'digestion mentally'. It would explain partly why the 'facts' and their ideational counterpart had not been digested if the rational conscious attitude was so hostile to the ideational counterpart of the stimulus, wherever in reality it originated. For such hostility would be likely to inhibit dream-work-α, and in so far as the inhibition failed—for after all the patient has dreamed—the hostility now extends to the product of the dream-work.

* * *

Logic and dreams

Logic is possibly that element by which it is hoped to establish coherence between elements that otherwise remain separate and persecutory, as in the paranoid–schizoid position.

8 August 1959

In what way does logic show itself? What signs betray its presence or absence? How can it be seen that the signs employed in logic, whether peculiar to logic or not, are being logically employed? In view of Quine's criticisms (*Mathematical Logic,* pp. 31, 32, 33) of Russell and Whitehead, it seems evident that even the best logicians have great difficulty in being logical.

Is it possible that there is no necessary, inescapable deduction from any premise that is not merely a repetition of a definitory formula? For example, if 'two' means two, and 'and' means and, and 'two' means two, and 'equals' means equals, and 'four' means four, then two and two equals four.

In the instances quoted by Quine it seems as if the symbol or sign, $-\supset-$, has been so abstracted that it has lost precision necessary for the purpose for which Quine wishes to use it. What is the relationship between 'implies', $-\supset-$, used by Russell and Whitehead, and '$-\supset-$' used by Quine? By what process is 'implies' denuded of its ordinary speech meanings so that it becomes precise? How is it determined when the sign has been suffiently abstracted from its ordinary speech meanings to give it the required precision, yet not so much that it has become too generalized and so open to Quine's kind of criticism when scientifically employed? It looks as if the ordinary meanings of 'implies' have crept back into Russell and Whitehead's use of the sign, $-\supset-$. If this is so, then the fault does not lie in the sign but in the fact that the sign has to be employed by human beings who are governed, obviously, by the limitations of their mental equipment. This is similar to the situation with other tools. The tool can be made, be it bomb or $-\supset-$, but there still remains the problem of the use to which it is to be put and the motives impelling the person who employs it.

Why have ordinary meanings (if ___ is true then ___ is true; ___ is false or ___ is true; ___ implies ___; if ___ then ___) crept back into the symbol, –)–, employed by Russell and Whitehead? Or, alternatively, by what process has Quine stripped off all meanings from '–)–' other than some counterpart of 'if ___ then ___'? Consciously one might say that he is in process of stripping it off in the discussion in *Mathematical Logic* (pp. 31–33) and that there it is done by showing that the use of '–)–', as Russell and Whitehead use it, can give rise to different trains of deduction all in themselves correct, but leading to deductions that are either contradictory or absurd. (Northrup, Introduction to Heisenberg, *Physics and Philosophy*, pp. 26, 27 on complementarity and contradiction and Freud.) Could this be related to juxtapositions in α of contradictions and absurdities? But the contradictions or absurdities of dreams are different. And the concretization that is involved in verbal images or ideograms may be very important for preserving precision. How do you abstract the generalized idea of 'table'? How do you concretize and keep precise 'implies'? Is it achieved by dream-work similar to the process of abstraction in *Euclid* I.1, or I.5, or I.47?

* * *

X

His statements that he feels anxious—"I don't know why"—may, in addition to being denials, support very strongly, in view of their constant reiteration, my idea that there is a breakdown of dream-work-α, which makes it impossible for the feelings to be ideogrammaticized and so verbalized. This breakdown is due to the need to prevent the synthesis, in the depressive position, of a frightening super-ego.

9 August 1959

Heisenberg: *Physics and Philosophy*

P. 32 'Influence of physics on the general situation.'
No: the influence of physics has simply been to modify the potency of the man with power to use the atomic bomb. It has no political aspect, but advances in physics have had political *consequences*. But Heisenberg shows that his meaning is not properly expressed by his first paragraph when he goes on in the second to show 'that every tool carries with it the spirit by which it has been created'. And here I think of the theory I put forward that man's tool-making capacity is hypertrophying as the defensive armour of stegosaurus hypertrophied and led to its extinction.

p. 32 'What will be the outcome of this impact of a special branch of modern science on different powerful old traditions?'

I prefer, 'What will be the impact of powerful old traditions on this special branch of modern science?' as alternative reading.

p. 36 'Light could either be interpreted as consisting of electromagnetic waves . . . or as consisting of light quanta, energy packets travelling through space with high velocity. . . . Einstein . . . was not able to dispute the complete contradiction between this wave picture and the idea of the light quanta.'

Is it possible that the explanation fundamentally has to be in terms of primitive phantasies?—e.g. elementary particles (paranoid–schizoid), or wave theory (depressive)—because these are limitations in the human mind which cannot be transcended?

p. 37 'No planetary system following the laws of Newton's

> mechanics would ever go back to its original configuration after a collision with another such system.'

The collision and return to normal fit in also with the primitive primal scene.

p. 43 'Instead of asking: How can one in the known mathematical scheme express a given experimental situation? the other question was put: Is it true, perhaps, that only such experimental situations can arise in nature as can be expressed in the mathematical formalism?'

Or can only those phenomena be seen which lie within the scope of man's mathematical capacity? Or can maths and fact come together only if dream-work is available to make abstraction and concretization possible?

10 August 1959

Dream-work-α

Under the title dream-work-α I propose to bring together a number of mental activities all of which are familiar to practising psycho-analysts, although they may not have previously associated them together in this way and may not indeed feel the need or value of associating them in the way I propose after they have familiarized themselves with what I am about to say.

The title, 'dream-work', has already a meaning of great value. I wish to extend some of the ideas already associated with it and to limit others. It has seemed to me least likely to cause confusion if I group my ideas under a new title which indicates the affiliations of my ideas and yet makes clear that a distinction is being proposed from the theories already grouped under the term, 'dream-work'.

The main sources, other than the stimulations of psycho-analytical practice and historical affiliations of these grouped ideas, are three-fold.

(1) Freud's *Interpretation of Dreams* [1900a, *SE 4, 5*] and especially the elaboration of his theories of dream-work.

(2) Freud's paper, 'Two Principles of Mental Functioning' [1911b, *SE 12*] and his *New Introductory Lectures on Psycho-Analysis* [1933a, *SE 22*]. Essential to this orientation are the views he expresses on narcissism and the future development of that concept in his paper, 'Instincts and their Vicissitudes' [1915c, *SE 14*].

(3) Melanie Klein's theories of splitting, projective identification, and the paranoid–schizoid and depressive positions. In one very important respect I have made extensive use of her description of the difference of her views on guilt and

super-ego formation [*Developments in Psycho-Analysis,* p. 273 et seq. and p. 281 et seq.] from those of Freud in what I want to say about the nature of social guilt, acting out, and delinquency in the psychotic patient.

I shall now set out the characteristics of dream-work-α, or, for the sake of brevity, α.

Dream-work-α is continuous night and day. It operates on the receipt of stimuli arising within and without the psyche. It operates on the mental counterpart of events of external reality, or on what Bradley calls the ideational counterpart of external fact. This ideational counterpart on which α operates appears to be the consciousness associated with certain sense impressions, that which Freud calls the consciousness attached to the sense organs [1900a, *SE 5*, p. 615]. What this is I am not able to suggest. I have no clinical experience that I feel would be valuable to differentiate from other clinical experiences and label as a part of that which constitutes the consciousness attached to the sense organs. There have been occasions when a patient has spoken of a sensation in a way that made me think it might be an example of a mental phenomenon before it had been transformed by α. There have been instances, as I shall show, where the patient speaks of, say, a table in a way that makes it clear that he is not meaning or expressing what is ordinarily meant or expressed when the word is used. The difference usually lies in the fact that for different people the same words have, in addition to their common meaning, a different penumbra of associations. But in the instances that I have in mind the difference lies in what seems to be a *lack* of associations. It is as if the word were a counterpart of the pure note in music, devoid of undertones or overtones; as if, meaning nothing but 'table', it came near to meaning nothing at all.

There are other experiences that appear to be those of emotion, fear, anxiety, dread, to which the patient seems unable to attach either a name or an image, or to recognize them as corresponding to any verbal expression he has ever heard or uttered. In so far as he realizes that the experience is one that he wishes to associate with a cause, he can only say that he has such-and-such a feeling but does not know why. These experiences also appear to be untransformed by α. The table is not a memory; it is an indigested fact; it has not been 'dreamed'; it has not been transformed by α. The same is true of the emotional experience.

Is it possible to get nearer to describing what α does? It pays attention to the sense impression. But in order to do this the impression must be made durable. It must be transformed so that it is suitable for storage and recall. In short, it has to be submitted to α-activity, and that is impossible unless durability is conferred on the impression and is itself a part of the process by which durability is conferred. The impression must be ideogrammaticized. That is to say, if the experience is a pain, the psyche must have a visual image of rubbing an elbow, or a tearful face, or some such. But now there enters a new feature depending on whether the pleasure–pain or the reality principle is dominant. If the reality principle is dominant, then the object of the ideogram will be to make the experience suitable for storage and recall; if the pleasure–pain principle is dominant, the tendency will be to have as the object of the ideogram its value as an excretable object.

Freud has pointed out that under the dominance of the pleasure principle the object of action is excretion of accumulations of affect (changes of mien etc.), in contrast with action under dominance of the reality principle when its object is to effect changes in environment. In accordance with this, the nature of the visual image will be different if the pleasure principle is dominant from what it would be under the dominance of the reality principle. The grimace of pain or the elbow-rubbing, under pleasure–pain, will be the end-product of a mechanism designed to relieve the psyche of an emotional experience in such a way that the emotional experience can be felt to have been not only excreted but evacuated into a container. In practice, such an omnipotent phantasy can most easily be given the appearance of reality if its expression is not limited to the formation of an ideogram within the psyche, but is expressed through the musculature in an actual grimace of pain or an actual rubbing of the elbow. Muscular action of this kind in the consulting room may sometimes be distinguished from the action designed to change the environment by the peculiarity of the emotional reaction engendered in the beholder. If it is an evacuatory muscular expression of an ideogram, the analyst is aware of having feelings aroused in him which have no component appropriate to action to satisfy those feelings—the evacuating patient's aim is to ensure that the unwanted feelings are inescapably contained in their new receptacle. If the act is carried out under dominance of the reality principle, then the ideogram—whether retained within the psyche or externalized by the musculature—has as its aim a subsequent alteration of the environment. This means that the ideogram expressed by the musculature is felt by the analyst to be by way of a communication and an invitation to do something—not, as is the case in the contrasting state of expression of an evacuatory ideogram, to be an intrusion into him to which he feels he is passively to submit.

In addition to the effect which depends on the dominance of the pleasure–pain or of the reality principle, there is the effect produced by the degree to which the personality is characterized by an excessive tendency to splitting and projective identification. If the tendency is excessive, then the value of dream-work-α is at once altered, for clearly its operation will not aid in the storage of experience if the psyche makes use of experiences that might otherwise be stored in a fund we usually know as memory. But the part played by projective identification is of such wide significance that we shall have to refer to it frequently in other contexts, and I therefore do not propose to elaborate points here which will become clear later.

So far I have had to confess that I cannot really do more than indicate the kind of material that is worked on by α. Perhaps the fact that, according to the theory I am attempting to adumbrate, the expression of these very views depends on the operation of α and that these views cannot be expressed (according to the same theory) until they have been operated on by α, means that there is no way of making a more precise approach verbally. Various kinds of tic, including a stammer, reports of supposed dreams in which there is apparently no content but a powerful emotional experience, reports of dreams in which visual images are devoid of associations of emotion—these for the present appear to be as near as we are likely to get to an understanding of the mental material on which α works. To some extent it will be possible to supplement this if we can get to know what the reality is of which the material on which α works is the counterpart. The experience that offers most hope of this is the situation in analysis in which it is possible for the analyst to see for himself the current facts on which α is operating then and there as the facts unfold.

For the present I must turn to consider further the relationship of α to the mechanisms of projective identification and splitting. I shall have more to say later about its relationship to the pleasure principle and the consequences for the wish-fulfilment aspect of dreams. The immediate point is the adverse effect on the personality when the dream-work-α is associated with the pleasure principle and excessive projective identification. X's dream of 'looking out of the window as usual' while his father interferes with his wife becomes an evacuatory process, an attempt to get rid of 'those feelings' by projection of them into me. But do not visual images symbolize or represent in some way? And if so, has no dream-work-α taken place? Probably it has; it seems likely that certain feelings have been ideogrammaticized, but *not* for purposes of digestion mentally—only as receptacles to contain, to imprison the idea or feeling and then to eject it. In that case the visual image itself is used as the target for projective identification and then is used as a missile container for further projective identification. If so, perhaps the visual element in dreams is significant because it is felt that the feeling can be excreted further and more effectively if it is put into an object *seen,* perhaps in a hallucinatory manner, because such an object does not need, as with other senses, to be at close quarters for contact. Therefore, in a projectively identified dream, the dream itself is felt to be analogous to a hallucinated object, not for hallucinatory gratification of ingestion, but for hallucinatory excretion. Then the next step—the ejection by the eyes of the hallucination containing the undesired emotional experience.

These feelings preclude the possiblity of regarding the dream as a real 'object'—as indeed is the intention—and so preclude the possibility of feeling the dream experience to be potentially effective in its proper function. It is suspect as being only the *appearance* of a life-promoting phenomenon, and so the patient's sense of being unable to dream is unaffected. For the true dream *is* felt as life-promoting, whereas the dream employed as a container for projective identification is felt to be an artefact, as deficient in life-promoting qualities as a hallucinated breast is felt to be deficient in food. But its very function as a container for the unwanted would make it suspect in any case.

The fact that the dream is being employed in an excretory function contributes to the patient's feeling that he is unable to dream or, rather, his thought is far less exact than the phrase, 'unable to dream', would suggest, and does nothing to decrease his feeling that he is lacking in an essential mental capacity.

So far this discussion suggests that a dream exists and that it is characterized by visual images; further, that the dream-work and its production can be employed for two dissimilar purposes. One is concerned with the transformation of stimuli received from the world of external reality and internal psychic reality so that they can be stored (memory) in a form making them accessible to recall (attention) and synthesis with each other.

The other purpose, with which I am here predominantly concerned, is the use of the visual images of the dream for purposes of control and ejection of unwanted (pleasure–pain-determined want) emotional experience. The visual image of the dream is then felt as a hallucinated—that is to say artificially produced—container intended to hold in, imprison, inoculate the emotional experience the personality feels too feeble to contain without danger of rupture, and so to serve as a vehicle for the evacuatory process. The dream itself is then felt to be an act of evacuation in much the same way as the visual hallucination is felt to be a positive act of expulsion through the eyes [*see* 'On Hallucination', *Second Thoughts*, p. 67].

If one kind of patient feels he cannot dream, what does the other kind of patient feel—the kind that feels he *can* dream? I propose to limit the term, 'dream', to the phenomenon as it appears in the light of the common-sense view that we all have dreams, know they occur when we are asleep, and know what they are when we have them. This dream is popularly believed to be due to indigestion: I suggest that the belief expressed in the aphorism, 'in vino veritas', should be extended to expressions of popular common sense, at least in this instance. In short, I suggest that what is ordinarily reported as a dream should be regarded by us as a sign of indigestion, but not simply physical indigestion. Rather, it should be taken as a symptom of mental indigestion. Or, to phrase it more exactly, as a sign—when a patient reports a dream to us and we are satisfied that he means by this what we all ordinarily understand by a dream—that there has been a failure of dream-work-α. The failure may of course be due to precisely such causes as the use of visual imagery in the service of projective identification which I have just been describing, but there are other more common causes of failure of dream-work-α, and there are also degrees of frequency with which the patient resorts to the use of dream imagery in the service of projective identification. Investigation of the dream as a symptom of a failure of dream-work-α means that we have to reconsider the series of hypotheses that I have grouped together under the heading of dream-work-α.

The first cause of breakdown in capacity to dream is associated with the synthesizing function of α in relation to the super-ego.

11 August 1959

One of the dangers of the failure to dream α in the session is that the patient then splits the murderous super-ego and evacuates it. He is now surrounded by murderous fragments of super-ego, each of which immediately develops into a super-ego. These, being externalized, are not seen in the real-life objects with which he is surrounded, and a situation is produced similar to that described by Freud as typical of 'social guilt'. Since the patient not only fears but wishes to be re-united with his murderous super-ego fragments, the danger is that he now acts out. And he does this in a way calculated to make the social forces of reality harbour murderous wishes against him. Hence the danger that he will force this by actually committing a murder.

21 August 1959

α

There is a great difficulty in making the step between the scientific deductive system and the low-level hypothesis that is susceptible of clinical verification. The gap between the actual clinical (experimental) data and the theory that is being tested and is to contribute to the formation of an interpretation, seems to me to be very big; it is not only the 'size' of the gap, but the actual dimension in which it exists, which is so difficult to determine. Once the two have been brought together, it becomes simpler.

It is very important that the analyst knows not what *is* happening, but that he *thinks* it is happening. That is the only certitude to which he lays claim. If he does not know that he thinks such-and-such is happening, he has no grounds for making the interpretation. This may help to bridge the gap. The theory that is being subjected to empirical test must be related to its power to enable the analyst to feel certain that he *thinks* that x is the case—not to its power to make it certain that x *is* the case. The fact susceptible of empirical test is the certainty, or the degree of certainty, that the analyst can achieve about what he thinks is going on. He could say, "I quite realize that my view may be entirely wrong, but I do know that I am certain at any rate that *this* is my view".

8 September 1959

α

The inability of the psychotic to 'digest' his experience mentally because of his lack of capacity for α contributes to the situation with which most observers are familiar, namely the easy accessibility to the *observer* of what should be the psychotic's unconscious. These elements remain detectable because the patient cannot make them unconscious. They are therefore also, as I have shown, not available to *him* because there has been no dream-work-α done to make them unconscious and therefore available to him. He is a man both unable to make these elements unconscious and unable to profit by experience, for profiting by experience means being able to make the material consciously perceived into material that can be mentally stored in such a way that it is susceptible of both concretization and abstraction.

A child learning to walk is engaged in attempting to make conscious material unconscious; only when this is done can it walk. The same is true of every piece of learning ever done—its success depends on the central operations by which dream-work-α is able to transform conscious material into unconscious material suitable for unconscious waking thinking.

The non-psychotic, and the non-psychotic part of the personality, is afraid of making something conscious—the typical neurotic fear in psycho-analysis—because making it conscious is feared as being the same as 'bringing it out into the open'; this in turn is felt to be the same as evacuating it and making it conscious in such a way that it can never be made unconscious again, and therefore unavailable ever again for unconscious waking thinking. And this in turn is felt to be indistinguishable from being psychotic. This is one of the reasons for the neurotic's fear that successful analysis will make him mad.

The psychotic fears α partly because its operation is felt to bring in the super-ego, and partly because making something unconscious is felt to be equivalent to losing it and consciousness for ever, i.e. death.

The neurotic fears interpretation partly because making something conscious is the same as making it unavailable for unconscious waking thought (equivalent to insane state). Unconscious waking thought is occupied with transitions from paranoid–schizoid position to depressive position (Poincaré, *Science and Method*, p. 30).

12 September 1959

In 'Two Principles of Mental Functioning' [1911b, *SE 12*] Freud speaks of a capacity for *attention* as associated with the development of the reality principle; he did not follow up this theme. The name seems peculiarly appropriate to a phenomenon I wish to discuss, but I am loath to take over and possibly distort any scientific term already serving a useful function. For this reason I have discarded the term, 'dream-work', which in some respects covered a number of phenomena bearing an apparent similarity to those I wished to discuss. I considered employing some term such as 'dream-work-α', or simply 'α', but the first only obviated some of the objections implicit in the use of 'dream-work', and the second, though avoiding too strong a penumbra of already-existing associations, erred on the side of being too abstract. The term, 'reverie', had many virtues but carried an implication of divorce from practicality or action, which was alien to my purpose. I hope to avoid a greater number of the possible objections than is possible in the use of any other terms I have considered by using the term, 'attention'. The word does not seem to have been used sufficiently by Freud to make my use of it liable to debase a meaning it already has and so to destroy precision. At the same time it is possible that my use of it may be a legitimate extension of an opening for investigation which Freud made but did not follow up.

13 September 1959

The contact with a psychotic patient is an emotional experience, presenting some precise features that differentiate it from the experience of contact of a more usual kind; the analyst does not meet a personality, but a hastily organized improvisation of a personality, or perhaps of a mood. It is an improvisation of fragments; if the impression is predominantly of friendliness, there will nevertheless be easily discernible fragments of hostility embedded in the conglomerate that has been assembled to do service, for the occasion, as a personality. If the impression is predominantly of depression, the mosaic of fragments will reveal incongruous bits of a smile without context other than a kind of contiguity with surrounding fragments; tears without depth, jocosity without friendliness, bits of hate—all these and many more fragmentary emotions or ideas jostle each other to present a labile façade.

But at once the question arises: is it a façade? If so, what lies behind it? Or, if it means that this improvised personality is all, or nearly all, there is, who or what is responsible for the improvisation? If it is a façade, what does it conceal, and to what end?

The encounter is not unlike the more everyday event of a face-to-face conversation with someone who has a marked squint: at which eye does one look? For the analyst the problem is central, not peripheral. He must decide whether he is speaking to the apparently improvised personality, to the improviser who has had the improvisation forced upon him so as to effect a meeting with the analyst, or to an improviser whose improvisation is one behind which he wishes to remain concealed.

Suppose the patient to be, or to have been, capable of normality: the conglomerate of fragments of personality which serves the patient for a personality can only be regarded as evidence of a disaster. The discussion of such a case is difficult because we are concerned not with the ordinary structures of the human personality for which terms such as ego, id, super-ego have been made available by Freud, but with the shattered fragments of these which have now been reassembled but not rearticulated.

19 September 1959

Scientific method

Heisenberg shows (*Physics and Philosophy*, p. 89) that a set of concepts has a limitation that is not obvious from the set of concepts itself. The 'set' of relativity and the 'set' of Newtonian mechanics approached each other within the limit where velocities in the system are very small compared with the speed of light.

Similarly it may be true that a scientific deductive system is valid in a certain limited system that is not deductive from the scientific deductive system itself; moreover, that two separate scientific deductive systems approximate to each other in a certain limited system whose limits are not deducible from the concepts of either of the two scientific deductive systems.

In Freud's work the social field in which the individual works is taken as 'given', but now it is essential that the environment must become the object of further theoretical studies. Only in this way can narcissism and the narcissistic psychoses be understood.

* * *

Cogito ergo sum

I am, therefore I think: I think, therefore I am. If α is destroyed, thought becomes impossible and the personality ceases to exist. The schizophrenic's fear of annihilation may be associated with an experiencing of his non-existence as a personality. It raises the question: what is the personality? What is the limiting field for the concept of personality? There can be no personality if there is no thinking, no self consciousness. There may be persons, but not personality unless there is a function of self consciousness. Self consciousness, the function, is the *sine qua non* of personality. To say someone has personality is to mean that he is aware of himself, not sporadically but permanently as a continuous phenomenon.

The stammer is a repudiation of awareness, an evacuation of awareness of what is currently taking place; it is the antithesis of α. It is therefore incompatible with a state of self consciousness. And therefore, and to that extent, the stammerer has no personality?

This is not true; any stammerer would I think be said to have a marked personality, often irascible.

26 September 1959

The patient's relationship is, tenuously, with the analyst as analyst; it is predominantly with the couple in the room—any couple, but most obviously the couple formed by the analyst and himself; it is with himself only in a somewhat peculiar manner in that he is either identified with himself or with the couple.

The relationship is not so much with the couple as with the couple as two objects linked together. The predominant element in the relationship between the patient and the couple is that aspect of the relationship which is formed with the link between the two objects. The most obvious link is that provided by his free associations and the analyst's interpretations.

The link changes in character. For my immediate purpose we may suppose that the analyst feels called upon to give a sexual interpretation. He may say, in response to previous material and in accordance with psycho-analytical principles, "You are showing that you feel I am a man doing something sexual to a woman". This statement turns the relationship between analyst and patient into a sexual relationship, and the verbal exchange has become a sexual link.

The patient does not subject this interpretation to α except tenuously and in non-psychotic aspects (parts) of his personality, but of that I do not wish just now to speak. Instead he subjects it to splitting attacks that are destructive in intent; it is taken in only to be subjected to splitting and ejection.

For this purpose mechanisms exist to carry out the double function. The splitting is carried out by some part of the psyche which is symbolically or pictorially represented by teeth, typewriter (working in reverse as it were—the words are taken in aurally, broken up into letters of the alphabet, and thus not only fragmented but transformed from sound into visual objects and ejected through the eyes to become further mutilated, so that they are now minute, unrecognizable shapes at a distance), gramophone (also working in reverse), and so on. The sensory apparatus employed for ejection is related to the distance to which the fragmented objects are propelled. Visual apparatus is used for distant ejection; tactile sense carries no further than the skin in one direction, and to various organs of the body in the other.

Owing to the conflicting reparative and creative drives, this evacuatory process may not reach the extremes that are represented by invisible visual hallucinations that are the outcome of transformation into pictorial images, extremely minute fragmentation, and ejection by the eyes to a great distance. Some degree of pictorialization and other transformations take place to form the (from the analyst's point of view) bizarre, hallucinatory objects.

This situation which has now developed in the consulting room must be distinguished from that of which I shall treat in the scientific deductive system entitled Hallucination and Dream, dealing with the problem of transition from one position to another when the depressive position is indissolubly linked with the materialization (realization) of a murderous super-ego. For the present I want to consider the fate of the content, the characteristics, of the link between the analyst and patient which has been thus subjected to splitting and evacuation.

"Well then, if you want to know", he said, becoming confidential, "last night I had a most enjoyable evening. People smoking: intelligent, friendly atmosphere, and *then* . . .", becoming indignant, in a noisy voice, "the waitress brought me only half a cup of coffee, and that ab-so-lutely finished it". Dropping his voice, "I couldn't do a thing after that. Not a thing." Almost whispering, "That finished it".

* * *

The schizophrenic's relationship is not with the analyst predominantly but with the analyst + himself. That is to say, it is predominantly a social transference—dualism to narcissism.

The persecutors are products of the *immediate* destruction of the conversation. That is to say, if $a + p$ are talking sexually, then p evacuates as he destroys as he hears the sexual pair. At the same time he reconstructs; his verbal meaning etc. is the reconstruction, and that is audible in the form of his description of the persecutors.

27 September 1959

X has feelings of persecution about various sensory impressions he receives. Are all these sense impressions indications of a process of mental digestion? When he hears banging, is it because he has to get into a state of mind appropriate to being in a mother's inside to spy on her digestive processes—a kind of sexual intercourse in which she (I, in the analysis) is digesting him by banging him to bits, clicking (his frequent complaint) him to bits, just turning him not into a person but a conglomeration of bits of faeces, a stool? In this case his attempt to get into the analyst is identical emotionally with getting 'deeply' into parental sexual intercourse—digestion of one parent by the other. ('Deeply' here means multi-dimensionally extreme—in space, in time, in 'thoroughness', in emotional involvement. A mathematical symbol is required for this concept, or something similarly exact yet abstract.) He has to see the supposed parental intercourse in minute detail and to the bitter end. But as he proceeds, he loses touch with his 'base'.

29 September 1959

Today X was anxious to insist that my voice was stronger and better—that I had got it back again. And as a corollary, that it had been very weak. Obviously the idea was that *he* had put me right—not that he had damaged me. Only if he is allowed to be the analyst can the analysis proceed. But all this is an acting out of phantasy. It differs from normal analysis in which the phantasy has to be interpreted; here it is acted, and the analyst has to agree that the phantasy is a fact.

Drowsiness is coming to me; it is part of the relaxation I have to achieve if my ideas are to be accessible. I must *dream* along, but then I risk going fast asleep. I have had to shut my eyes because they sting. Then I nearly went to sleep. "Watch the wall my darling, while the Gentlemen go by." [Rudyard Kipling, 'A Smuggler's Song'.] A smuggling process I must not know anything about. A wrapping up and packing of the goods I wish to remove from the environment. Does this mean that α is to *hide* things from the conscious? If so, it is nearer to Freud's view of dream-work. The conscious is the servant of the unconscious. It is the conscious whose job it is to lie and deceive and protect the unconscious in its activities.

2 October 1959

X

When I begin to think of an unusually full session, I can remember nothing. This makes me wonder if my wish for his co-operation leads me to exaggerate what he did.

He came into the room handing me his cheque. He lay down from the end of the couch. He speaks. "I wondered whether to write it standing up. I couldn't find a lavatory or a train in which to do it. If I did it downstairs it would keep you standing." Now I am not sure that he did not say, "If I wrote it in the waiting room it would keep you standing", or if it was that if he wrote it downstairs it would keep me waiting. The point is that I suspect that from time to time he speaks with, from his point of view, great precision, and that if I treat it conversationally I am guilty of splashing the good food about, as it were.

Perhaps I should consider schizophrenic precision—a meticulous accuracy—and schizophrenic destructiveness.

4 October 1959

In spite of the advances of science in recent years, the methods employed in scientific work are under critical scrutiny. The moral questioning amongst scientists themselves of the use to which scientific knowledge is being put is scarcely relevant to discussion of the methods themselves, yet it has contributed to that discussion.

In philosophy the question is not new though it is unnecessary to go back earlier than Hume to find the origins of the present controversies. The problem as it appears to the philosopher has been stated by Prichard (*Knowledge and Perception,* p. 69). He says,

> Though we are aware that any knowledge at which we arrive is the result of a process on our part, we do not reflect on the nature of the process—at any rate in any systematic way—and make it the object of a special study. But sooner or later knowledge of our mistakes and the desire to be sure that we are getting the genuine article, i.e. something which is really knowledge, lead us to reflect on the process . . . in the end we find ourselves having to ask whether we are capable of knowing at all and are not merely under the illusion of thinking that we can know.

In the natural sciences the quantum mechanical theories have disturbed the classical concept of an objective world of facts which is studied objectively. And the work of Freud has at the same time excited criticism that it is unscientific because it does not conform to the standards associated with classical physics and chemistry; it constitutes an attack on the pretensions of the human being to possess a capacity for objective observation and judgement by showing how often the manifestations of human beliefs and attitudes are remarkable for their efficacy as a disguise for unconscious impulses rather than for their contribution to knowledge of the subjects they purport to discuss.

But, it may be argued, do not the facts discovered as a result of the application of scientific methods constitute a proof that the methods employed—for example mathematical formulas in the prediction of astronomical phenomena—have a validity independent of the observer who elaborates and employs them, that the methods belong to ontology, not epistemology, and are 'objective', not 'subjective'? Unfortunately not, for as Heisenberg has shown through the interpretation of quantum mechanical theory made by himself, Nils Bohr, and others of the Copenhagen School, no single fact is unrelated to and uninfluenced by the totality of facts, and that totality must remain unknown. Even the concept of space may have only a very limited application because there need be no reality corresponding to the concept. As Poincaré has pointed out, our methods of mensuration, which have played and still play a considerable part in the concept of space, are clearly related to man's awareness of his own body (*Science and Method,* p. 100), and can in fact be ignored as they are ignored in the positional geometry of Riemann. No psycho-analyst would be surprised at the attribution of the origins of mensuration to the experiences of infancy and childhood.

Since the philosophy of modern physics—the most successful and most rigorous of scientific disciplines—can be seen here to be quite compatible with a philosophical view of unco-ordinated and incoherent elements similar to the mental domain of isolated elements from which Poincaré describes the mathematician as attempting to escape by his discovery of the selected 'fact', and since moreover the mental state described by Poincaré is quite compatible or even identical with that described by Melanie Klein in her discussion of the paranoid–schizoid and depressive positions, it is reasonable to suppose that the investigation and explanation of these unco-ordinated elements will be dictated by the impulse described by Poincaré and investigated in detail psycho-analytically by Melanie Klein and her co-workers, and limited by the mental capacity which in the final analysis is the tool by which the investigation is carried out. This in turn means that of the totality of facts, only those will be investigated which are illuminated and rendered comprehensible by existing mathematical calculi. If they lie beyond the scope of such methods, they will not be discovered; if they are discovered, then obviously they will be such facts as conform to, and so appear to confirm, the mathematical calculi that have been employed. There is no reason to suppose that the totality of facts, or even any considerable proportion of them, support the view that there is a realization (Semple and Kneebone, *Algebraic Projective Geometry,* p. 4) which corresponds to the mathematical calculi and the scientific deductive systems they represent. For the psycho-analyst there is every reason to regard mathematical phenomena as belonging to the domain of epistemology, and therefore as a matter for psycho-analytical investigation, and in particular that mathematics should be regarded as having, as Heisenberg says of 'every word or concept', 'only a limited range of applicability' (*Physics and Philosophy,* p. 111). As he says,

> When we represent a group of connections by a closed and coherent set of concepts, axioms, definitions and laws which in turn is represented by a mathematical scheme, we have in fact isolated and idealized this group of connections with the purpose of clarification. But even if complete clarity has been achieved in this way, it is not known how accurately the set of concepts describes reality. [p. 96]

In short, mathematics must be regarded by the psycho-analyst as one of the limiting classes that belong to psycho-analysis in so far as it attempts to be a coherent system of concepts, and in particular as one of the methods by which the paranoid–schizoid and depressive systems are brought into a dynamic relationship with each other, and therefore as an aspect of those mental phenomena that are concerned in the achievement of mental development by facilitating that dynamic relationship. It will therefore be seen that from a psycho-analytical point of view mathematics does not belong to the realm of ontology nor yet even of epistemology, but rather to that class of mental functioning which, since transition from paranoid–schizoid to depressive positions and back is essential to mental development, is essential to sanity itself.

This is not to belittle mathematics but to show how fallacious is the view that pre-eminent importance in any one sphere, however important, confers some universally equal significance in all—a fallacy that has tended to make some observers suppose that failure to produce calculi representing the deductive system of biology, and in particular of psycho-analysis, is necessarily a condemnation of the subject for which no calculi exist. Mathematics may have a very important role as an object of study psycho-analytically, and at the same time and for the same reason be an important element in the mental processes of the individual which makes it possible for him to be a psycho-analyst.

6 October 1959

X

"Have got paint onto my sleeve." He went on and on about this; he couldn't get it off; it might injure my "new couch"; complaints of noises.

Some of the session was explicable in terms of being right inside the mother and witnessing sexual intercourse from there; some in terms of a sexual relationship with me which was achieved by sexualizing a miserable relationship. He spoke of smoke coming from top-storey rooms—two rooms; a fire-engine going to a house where only a week before there had been a fire. These I interpreted as primal scene. But I felt it was more free association on my part to stimuli produced by him. The session had a certain coherence—as interpreted by me. It is extraordinary how little I can have any confidence in the work done; so much seems to be done by myself that any 'result' in the session is open to the objection that it is achieved by the analyst out of his own mind without any element of real contribution by the patient. Yet he criticizes as if any departure from an exactly correct interpretation is an inexcusable imprecision. It is far easier for me to recall an interpretation of mine than the material on which it was based. But nevertheless there were interpretations today which felt right. One touched on the fact that he behaved and felt like a baby—either D or the unborn one—so that the baby would not envy him as the parent. In this way the parent was not allowed to have anything the baby could not have.

The relationship with me is governed by the same watchfulness towards a murderously envious force which appears to be somewhere about. It is often as if material produced for inspection and interpretation is removed in the very act of interpretation. I showed him that a miserable relationship with me was made tolerable by being sexualized.

7 October 1959

X

The pullover which is beautifully knitted by his wife but not suited for the baby's cold. Trains that did not behave as they should (not as frustration-evading dreams). "Had a dream; remembered it as I got off the couch last time. I had painted a picture; stuck on to one corner of it was the payment for it. I don't know how it got there." (Frustration evasion.) He had been talking of his wish to earn a living by painting.

How much should I interpret on classical lines? He showed he did not think it a dream by the way he said, "I don't know how it (the payment) got there". It was therefore quite likely to be more of a hallucination than a dream. And I had been able to show him, with the dream and the two trains, how he expected the trains to act as frustration-evasion items, and not as frustration-modifying 'facts'—real trains, which took you somewhere at the cost of tolerating frustration.

This session seems to me so exciting in bearing out, together with previous sessions, the theory of α and the theories about frustration evasion and frustration modification that I can hardly trust myself to bring any kind of reasoned criticism to bear on the matter. Further, there is no doubt of the very great improvement that is taking place.

11 October 1959

Resistance

What is being resisted? The investigation? The interpretation? The emotional experience of investigation? The possibility of the discovery of something? The arousal of emotions? The elements of the paranoid–schizoid position? The junction of paranoid–schizoid with depressive? The onset of the depressive position?

While I write this, considering it is probably all of them, I find myself thinking with hate and fear of Z: a pictorial image of myself standing up at a meeting and attacking him for being a disaster to his profession. And it occurs to me that it is this visual image of which I am frightened. I do not want the experience of the visual image. A fear of this kind, carried far enough, would inhibit or destroy α—the process by which immediate fact is transformed into 'storable' material and not just introjected as undigested fact. Visual image of my self being expelled from the meeting and making a noble, impassioned plea.

The elements are then fragments of the destroyed 'couple', and this fits in with observation of X.

But what of mathematics and music? Geometry is a kind of visual image; music can evoke visual images.

* * *

This question was followed by a long digression of thought and physical activity. Why? Partly because I could not see any further, but partly because I felt I was confronted with unknown elements that do not fit into my scheme or any scheme. Any synthesis always involves more unknowns appearing—that is to say, the appearance of a whole mass of more 'elements'. These presumably require a new deductive system, a new theory, or a part of a new but unknown deductive system. At this point it is clear that the objection to the depressive position is not only the emergence of the object synthesized, but of a whole mass of more unsynthesized objects. Thus one reason for the fear of the synthesized punitive super-ego is that its emergence is inseparable from the emergence of more 'elements' which are seen, partly in the light of the recreated punitive super-ego, as being fresh evidence of the destructiveness of the personality. It is a revelation not only of past destructiveness but of new destructiveness freshly wrought. A creative act is felt to be the signal for the discovery of a revelation of further and greater tasks of reparation. This contributes to the sense of overwhelming fatigue that some patients experience.

What then leads to resistance in music or maths? To my mind it is the sphinx, the plague (of 'elements'?), the dread of the experience of the paranoid–schizoid/depressive position interplay. Why are the 'elements' so deadly? The animal that goes on four legs, two legs, three legs seems related to the three-kneed thing with equal legs [*see* pp. 201–202].

* * *

The task confronting the analyst is to bring intuition and reason to bear on an emotional experience between two people (of whom he is one) in such a way that not only he but also the analysand gains an understanding of the analysand's response to that emotional situation, and does so through an appreciation of the evidence to which the analyst is drawing attention in the course of his interpretations. It is not enough for the analyst to be convinced that there is evidence for the truth of his interpretations; he must have enough evidence available to afford the analysand the opportunity of being persuaded, by his reason, of the cogency of the intepretation.

Such is the ideal; in fact the analyst's environment, in which I include his state of mind whatever the elements are that contribute to it, and the disturbed mental state of the analysand introduce hazards that make an analysis relate to this ideal with varying degrees of approximation.

The analytic experience is a complex of many experiences, which individually are familiar both to analyst and analysand and therefore tend to give a deceptively simple appearance to a situation that has, by bringing these familiar experiences together, become unique. Everything that happens in a consulting room has happened quite commonly to both participants before, but never in quite the same way. The behaviour that is under observation is in detail the behaviour of ordinary human beings, and even the interpretations given are no different in essence from the kind of interpretations that in ordinary life we have been used to give and receive throughout our lives, even though we have not so much as heard of psycho-analysis. Nevertheless, the interpretations appear to a layman to be far-fetched and bizarre, a quality they owe to the extension that ordinary interpretative capacity receives through development of the analyst's intuition and the aid he obtains from the body of psycho-analytic theory with which he is familiar.

These theories are always a matter for some degree of controversy even among psycho-analysts, partly because development of the subject means that there are always some theories that are under trial, partly because there are some theories that, though long accepted, seem to require revision, and partly because the application of a theory, perhaps sound in itself, has been defective and so has led to suspicion of the theory.

The theories of psycho-analysis are peculiar in that their use in the consulting room emphasizes, in a manner rare in other sciences, their function as actual tools which the analyst has to use in his practice. In other sciences the theories inform the use to which various tools and appliances are put: in psycho-analysis the theory is the tool itself.

16 October 1959

Various forms of dream manifestation

1. Organic

(a) The patient may be concussed—an unlikely contingency but one to be borne in mind in view of the patient's disturbed condition, and therefore the possibility that he has been in an accident.

(b) He may be drunk.

(c) He may have taken some other drug—cocaine, barbiturates, etc.

2. Psychological

(a) α is in progress. That is to say, he is attempting to transform immediately current events in the room into assimilable form. This pre-supposes that his α capacity is rudimentary and is being expressed aloud presumably to get the analyst's help. But it may slide off into

(b) dreaming. This is the emergence of an activity which the patient dare not allow himself out of the analyst's presence through dread of the dream's *manifest* content, and in particular destroyed objects, un-α'd objects *and* super-ego.

(c) An artificially contrived dream or a hallucinated dream—the latter must be distinguished from the hallucination. Without this distinction the inability to produce associations cannot be properly understood and there is blurring of the distinction between the process intended to evacuate (hallucination) and a process concerned with a need to introject. The artificially contrived dream *sounds* what it is; it is consciously fabricated, and that, I think, must be taken as the distinction from the hallucinated dream. The hallucinated dream is one produced under duress; the patient *must* dream, and it is this compulsion which leads to an uncontrolled hallucinated dream.

(d) Hallucination: olfactory, auditory, visual. The function is evacuatory, and it is stimulated by immediate events. If the analyst knows the content of the hallucination, then he must see it as an immediate situation not transformed (digested) at all. Thus the patient starts up, pointing and saying, "My wife, it's my wife! She's coming for me! Stop her!" This is a visual image—he is evacuating it through his eyes. It might be argued that this is how he sees me and that I must therefore be transformed mentally into a visual image of his dead wife. In fact it is a view that is plausible but untenable for reasons I shall give later. He does not in any true sense see me or have any other sensory perception of me. I remain an undigested fact because his very partial sensory awareness of my presence has acted as a stimulus to his projective mechanisms and he has ejected an old, undigested fact. I shall not for the moment consider the nature and origin of the visual image of his dead wife, which is here a fact undigested in the past, except to say that it is probably a past dream fragment which he did not originally digest, that it dates from a time when he could dream and that it therefore has great prognostic significance. Indeed it could be taken as a sign suggesting the possibility of psychoanalytic repair and cure because it indicates that there is something to repair. For the moment I want to consider only that, excluding any effect interpretation may have, the original undigested fact, the image of the dead wife, remains undigested; in addition there is a new undigested fact, namely my presence and intervention as the analyst. There is every reason to suppose—again excluding the effect any interpretation may have—that the new undigested fact, in addition to the old one, will at some future date reappear.

17 October 1959

The Dream

The term, 'dream', I shall always use for the phenomena described by Freud under that term. The dream is an emotional experience that is developmentally unsuccessful in that it is an attempt to fulfil the functions which are incompatible; it is in the domain of the reality principle and the pleasure principle, and represents an attempt to satisfy both. That is to say, it is an attempt to achieve frustration evasion and frustration modification and fails in both. In so far as it is an attempt at modification of frustration, it requires an interpretation; as an attempt at frustration evasion, it has failed to satisfy because the wish-fulfilment element in it leaves the personality aware that the wish has not been fulfilled in reality. The dream thus occupies a conspicuous role in treatment; it contains, and is itself a manifestation of, painful stresses. But for this same reason its importance is less central amongst the processes involved in the maintenance of smooth development; the crucial mechanisms are those associated with rendering the perceptions of experience fit for storage in the psyche, namely α, and for making these stored transformations of experience available again when the psyche needs them. The problem is, what are these crucial mechanisms? It may be that we can never know, that we can only postulate their existence in order to explain hypotheses that are capable of translation into empirically verifiable data, and that we shall have to work with these postulates without assuming that corresponding realities will at some time be discovered. I regard α as a postulate of this nature.

* * *

α-destruction

One consequence is starvation of the psyche in its supply of reality. There is therefore nothing that can be opposed to phantasy. This is an additional reason for failure to wake up; there is not enough 'up' to wake up to.

Two conditions need differentiation:

(1) a feeling that he cannot dream; this is so strong that it inhibits realization that he is dreaming;

(2) an actual inability to dream.

The appearance of dreaming that the patient then presents can be due to phenomena that look alike but are actually different, according to whether they are associated with (1) or (2). If (1), then the disjointed elements are α-elements that the patient cannot synthesize, e.g. through fear of super-ego, or hatred of reality, or dread of depression. If (2), then the disjointed elements are β-elements.

* * *

The aftermath of the destruction of α

The patient is now enclosed in a state of mind that is no longer adequate for his needs. He is mentally and psychically starved of matter necessary for his development. In short, his attempt to evade frustration has, by cutting him off from reality, produced a frustration more intense than any he has tried to avoid. He is 'imprisoned in psycho-analysis'.

The attempt to escape involves the restoration of α which has been destroyed by splitting and projective identification; the fragments have to be recovered and reunited. In addition to the difficulties incidental to this, especially great when the fragmentation has been into extremely minute pieces, is the danger I have indicated which is anticipated from the restoration of an extremely destructive super-ego, which restoration is unavoidable if any restoration at all is attempted. Therefore the process of repair is constantly hampered by a coincidental destructive procedure.

The result is a complex and confusing clinical picture in which the analyst must attempt to demonstrate the fragments that the patient attempts to juxtapose. During this process the destructive super-ego emerges, and contemporaneous destructive attempts are made, at the instigation of the super-ego, to undo the attempts at juxtaposition and repair.

Thus the patient will produce a fragment of a visual image. Another fragment will be produced, perhaps many sessions later. If all goes well, more fragments are produced, perhaps with decreasing intervals of time, until at last it becomes possible to indicate the relationship of some of these fragments of visual images to each other. The reaction will show that the dreaded super-ego is discerned by the patient in the shadowy lineaments of the juxtaposed fragments. This is the signal for splitting attacks on the super-ego and further dispersal of the fragments. But the fragmented super-ego engages in destruction on its own account and splits itself in the process of splitting the ego. The mutual destruction conflicts with the still proceeding reparative efforts.

But we must now consider another consequence of the destruction of α. Since its destruction makes it impossible to store experience, retaining only undigested 'facts', the patient feels he contains not visual images of things but things themselves. Reciprocally, things themselves are regarded by him in the same way as non-psychotics and the non-psychotic part of his personality regard 'thoughts' and 'ideas'; they are expected by him to behave as if they were visual images in his mind. I have described some of the consequences of this elsewhere; the result I want to consider here is the patient's inability to dream and its exacerbation of the frustration, and its contribution to the frustration that the destruction of α was intended to evade but which has been intensified instead. The starvation of the psyche of all elements needed for growth and development gives extreme urgency to the patient's inability to dream. But this activity is extra-sessional and impregnated with the dangers incidental to a restored super-ego. The fear of this conflicts with the necessity to restore the capacity to dream, for the fear is of nothing less than annihilation. Consequently the patient, as we have already seen, needs to restrict these attempts to sessions. Then, and only then, is he sure of the external aid that the presence of the analyst affords. It is this that leads to the events I have already described in which the patient strives to dream in the session. But, in the instance I am giving, the patient cannot dream. The combination of incapacity to dream with the urgency imposed by psychic starvation gives rise to the phenomenon I have described as the hallucinated dream which affords no associations—associations being equated with sustenance.

25 October 1959

Truth—need for, and need to keep maladjustment in repair

Psycho-analytic procedure pre-supposes that the welfare of the patient demands a constant supply of truth as inevitably as his physical survival demands food. It further presupposes that discovery of the truth about himself is a precondition of an ability to learn the truth, or at least to seek it in his relationship with himself and others. It is supposed at first that he cannot discover the truth about himself without assistance from the analyst and others.

It is likely that this belief has an empirical foundation in that all are familiar with the fact, probably learned very early in life, that a mistaken idea leads to mistaken action, which leads to frustration and other forms of suffering. But a true view can do the same, and on the choice that is made depends the nature of the suffering experienced. The choice is really a choice of method; the essential difference for our purposes in the nature of the choice made is that one is in favour of the method of frustration evasion, and the other in favour of the method of frustration modification. Freud's pleasure principle would seem to tend in the direction of frustration evasion, his reality principle in the direction (in his view) of frustration modification. But in fact, as Freud saw, the impulse to pleasure is not absent under the domination of the reality principle, nor is the reality principle absent under the dominance of the pleasure principle. Much depends on the fact that the choice is influenced by what is, and what is conceived to be, the reality when the choice is made. But the decision is seriously affected by the individual ability or inability to tolerate enduring frustration. If the patient is unable to endure frustration—that is, frustration over a period of time—he will lean towards the methods of frustration evasion.

Whichever choice is made, work has to be done—a point that may escape the attention of the patient, and of those on whom he depends in the most severe cases of all, namely psychotic patients. For the apparatus of denial, endopsychic and social, is formidable indeed if it is to be as effective as it in fact is. The scientifically minded individual has to be what is ordinarily called well-adjusted, but it is equally true that the individual who is dominated by the goal of frustration evasion has to be what is ordinarily called maladjusted and is under compulsion to keep his maladjustment in constant repair—a point that becomes increasingly clear in the psycho-analysis of the psychotic patient. Nor can his labours cease at the borders of his own personality; as the scientist has to seek the aid of groups, institutions, elaborate apparatus, and social support as well as maintain his mental acumen, so the individual oriented to frustration evasion has to enlist the aid of, or actually initiate, social institutions to help in the task of denial of reality. The actual social institutions need not differ: those used by the scientifically oriented and by frustration-evaders can be the same but used differently. It is obvious that a psychotic will use the institution of marriage, the family and the state differently from the frustration-modifier. What is not sufficiently appreciated is that it is purposive; this becomes clear to the analyst who has to deal with a psychotic patient and his various groups, such as his family. The analyst who is oblivious of this fact and imagines that he can enlist the aid of the family to produce the conditions in which treatment is possible, is ignoring the patient's belief that *he* can enlist the aid of the family and his other groups to produce the conditions in which evasion of frustration is possible. In extreme cases, where murderous destructiveness is directed against the sexual parents and their offspring, the original frustration is of the impulse to murder the parents and commit suicide. This impulse is frustrated by the helplessness of the patient as an infant. With growth this helplessness is removed, but psychological development introduces new barriers to the satisfaction of murderous envy and destructiveness. This struggle between life and death instincts informs the operation of all the complex mechanisms that are demonstrated in the course of an analysis of a psychotic patient. It also contributes powerfully to the patient's need to preserve his psychosis as a complex of methods of frustration evasion, which in turn is felt to be a method by which his murderous impulses are satisfied, and by which he can also satisfy his need to preserve his objects. Both impulses are frustrated, but he strives to evade awareness of either frustration—a goal that cannot be achieved by frustration modification.

30 October 1959

X

He looked clean and cool, rather than sweaty and scruffy as he usually does, then began with the usual evocative associations—evocative *and* provocative, so as to ensure either reassurance of love or reassurance of hate. He was more coherent. *Yet it is hard to recall anything he said.* This is typical even though something is said. I was able to show him that by taking a minutely fragmented view he could avoid feeling the seriousness of the situation, which was revealed if all the minor statements of dissatisfaction were added up. This I think suggests splitting attacks on the depressive position. Thus the depressive stupor becomes a mass of tiny persecutory depressions: the door slams; singing in his head; a pain in his ankle; "I don't know why; I'm sorry; the waitress brought some coffee; only half a cup"; and—despairingly, "*I could not go on*".

This can be regarded as a splitting attack on depression, or an attempt to bring the fragments of persecuting depression together in a creative way, i.e. to form a whole; or a series of pictorial images, ideograms, which will not coalesce; or 'undigested' fragments, i.e. not proper pictorial images but facts sensually perceived yet remaining as bits of sensory awareness that have not been rendered fit for storage and are therefore not memories proper.

This explains my being the person who is dead, who, as he said, has "had it". In other words, if the pieces are brought together and *do* coalesce, it is seen that the fragments are really me, only in pieces. And since I cannot exist like that, I must be dead.

[Undated]

I am reminded of the Millais Culpin case: the patient committed suicide after an interview when Culpin told him that analysis was not suitable for him. Culpin was blamed by the coroner and attacked in *The Times,* which suggested that an end should be put to psycho-analysis.

With this patient it is essential never to forget that one is dealing with a schizophrenic. That is to say that one should never forget that the patient is both murderous and irresponsible, and that 'common sense', i.e. the common sense of the society, dictates a particular diagnosis and a particular attitude of individual members of the society to the patient. Resistance to this dictation carries the penalties which the group always threatens to exact from those who resist its dictates. The 'common sense' of the patient, however invisible and undetectable it may seem to be, tells him this, for he *has* common sense though he makes uncommon use of it.

Although the analyst must never cease to be a member of his group, and must be correspondingly sensitive to its dictates and the risks his ignoring of these dictates carries, neither must he ever permit the 'socialism' of his orientation to obscure the immediate vivid reality that confronts him in the consulting room. The patient knows this too; he is prepared to play his part in exacting a heavy penalty if the analyst does not behave with the perspicacity that is not only demanded by the work, but also by the patient's determination that the analyst should support, by his conduct in devoting his exclusive attention to the patient—no matter at what cost to himself—the patient's narcissism against his 'socialism'. (And also be as socially ostracized.)

The analyst is thus forced to experience the split which the patient himself suffers between his narcissism and his socialism. That this split exists is made apparent by the patient's reaction to the analyst's ministrations to his narcissism. We have seen that the patient resents the analyst's awareness of social pressures and obligations, but he equally resents the pressures that originate in the exactions of his narcissism and does so by exploiting the interest the analyst shows in his welfare as a failure on the part of the analyst to show the common sense which everyone, except the analyst, might be supposed to possess.

* * *

The super-ego

The mirror image in time and space, as it appears in *Alice Through the Looking-Glass,* is a version of a psychotic state that bears much the same relation to the psychotic state as do the events in a dream to the anxieties the dream expresses. That is to say, it is a version that makes the intolerable tolerable. The patient who looked at the blood mounting up his sleeve was experiencing murder, or rather being murdered, in reverse. At the point when his blood will be fully restored to his circulatory system he will experience being murdered. And then he will be all right.

Yet this is not quite right. It is far more than a mirror image—perhaps an inverted mirror image, such as might be obtained through a focal point of a lens.

I am not able to co-ordinate what I said about the bizarre objects as being pieces of super-ego or containing pieces of super-ego, with common sense as being the sense of the group and therefore its moral sense. Yet there is some point of intersection. (Certainly: because the group and its common sense is felt to be indistinguishable from particles of his destroyed common sense.)

It may be that the point of entry is the Ps $\rightarrow$ D, the search for the significant unifying fact which is called 'the cause' when time is a component. It is the synthesis of the murderous super-ego (which takes place at the moment when all other syntheses take place) that makes Ps → D so hazardous.

But in postulating socialism as the other pole of narcissism, I had in mind the idea that the patient's socialism menaces his primacy as an individual, and the group demands of him subordination to aims lying outside his personality. This is especially true with regard to aggression. Is it also true of morality? Is there a moral instinct which is also bi-polar, one in which the patient is impelled in conflicting directions because his individual moral view conflicts with the moral view he holds as a member of the group?

The conflict in the individual between socialism and narcissism

In his paper, 'Instincts and their Vicissitudes' [1915c, *SE 14*], Freud makes the suggestion that the relation between the ego and sexuality may be regarded in two apparently equally well justified ways. In the one, the individual is regarded as of prime importance; in the other, as a transitory appendage to the germ plasm bequeathed to him by the race. He postulates, expressly disavowing any greater authority for his statement than that appertaining to a postulate, that the conflict is between sexuality and the ego instincts. He suggests that study, particularly of the schizophrenias, might require modification of the theory.

I agree that one side of the conflict is associated with the ego, but it seems to me that difficulties are caused by making a division between ego instincts on the one hand and the sexual instincts on the other. A more fruitful division is one between narcissism on the one hand, and what I shall call socialism on the other. By these two terms I wish to indicate the two poles of all instincts. This bi-polarity of the instincts refers to their operation as elements in the fulfilment of the individual's life as an individual, and as elements in his life as a social or, as Aristotle would describe it, as a 'political' animal. The exclusive mention of sexuality ignores the striking fact that the individual has an even more dangerous problem to solve in the operation of his aggressive impulses, which, thanks to this bi-polarity, may impose on him the need to fight for his group with the essential possibility of his death, while it also imposes on him the need for action in the interests of his survival. There need be no conflict, but experience shows that in fact there is such a conflict—not between sexuality and ego instincts, but rather between his narcissism and his socialism, and this conflict may manifest itself no matter what the instincts are that are dominant at the time.

The ego is involved, for the ego is that which establishes a connection with internal and external realities. It is therefore within the ego that the conflict between narcissism and socialism has to be fought out. This struggle contributes to the forces that lead, in certain circumstances, to the splitting—and in extreme cases the weakening and finally the destruction—of the ego. But the ego is also under attack because it is the part of the personality that leads to the awareness of the conflicting demands of the group and the individual and is therefore felt to be the cause of the pain the individual experiences on account of the ego's contact with both external or group realities, and internal or ego-centric realities—i.e. because of its contact with the demands of narcissism and socialism. There is, therefore, in extreme cases, a weakening or even destruction of the ego through splitting attacks that derive from the primitive instinctual drives which seek satisfaction for both poles of their nature and turn against the psychic organ that appears to frustrate both alike. Hence the appearance, noted by Freud, of hatred of reality—now hatred of the ego which links with reality—characteristic of the severely disturbed patient seen in the psychoses.

It will be remarked that this view demands a revision of our ideas of the narcissistic neuroses and psychoses: they must be considered as cases in which primary narcissism is matched by an equally strong 'socialism' or group membership.

[Undated]

No free associations

When the patient talks about blood, I know what it means and I can produce plenty of associations, but the patient produces none. So I can either let an association of his pass without proper interpretation, and so feel an opportunity is lost, or I can use my own associations and give an interpretation that, in my giving of it, makes me abandon my position as an analyst and become a participant in *his* game—a game played according to rules of which I am not aware. But I do this if I do *not* give an interpretation.

From this point of view it might be put thus:

P. Blood. Now it's your turn to play.

A. (silent)

P. (to himself) What! Doesn't know what blood is? He must be mad.

A. Blood is your common sense which you feel is seeping away.

P. Yes. (And then follow more remarks which are in fact not comprehensible to me, but are to him because they are part of a game which only he understands. This game is a sexual one—sexual, that is, in the eyes of someone.)

[Undated]

The super-ego

The patient is gay, debonair. What has he to be so cheerful about? He is happily married, has a little son to whom he is devoted; his wife, like himself, is wealthy and devoted to him; his home is charming and—what makes it better—he has done much of the carpentry himself; they have both decorated the rooms. Their friends are many and influential, also interesting and creative; a few are artists whose names are known. All is for the best in the best of all possible worlds—the quotation would be known to him. God, likewise, is in His Heaven, all's right with the world. What then is the matter?

But who said there is anything the matter? The patient certainly has not said so—quite the contrary. The summary of his circumstances that I have given is not only obtained from him but is, as I know, the theme on which he is about to embroider as he comes into the room, the theme and its variations to which I have listened for three years in every session he has attended. His analyst and his response to his analyst's treatment both fit in with the rest of his good fortune; it is a pleasure for him to be treated by so brilliant an analyst as myself, and naturally a pleasure for me to have such an agreeable and rewarding patient.

Occasionally there seems to be some discordant note, an interpretation that, after I have given it, seems not to have been quite happy. The patient is, however, able to pass it off with the kind of easy tact with which an accomplished host or hostess—perhaps the latter conveys the more accurate impression—might pass off the solecism of one of the less sophisticated guests. The surface of urbanity, temporarily almost ruffled, is restored, and we return to 'the analysis'.

I said the patient has not mentioned that anything is the matter, but this is only partly true. At times he reports, somewhat whimsically, experiences, say at a party, which are less than agreeable. A woman, ill-tempered and known to be unpopular, has spoken to him impatiently, harshly almost. I am reminded of the lines,

> The good are so harsh to the clever,
> The clever so rude to the good.
>
> [Elizabeth Wordsworth, 'St. Christopher and Other Poems: Good and Clever'.]

Sometimes he has spoken as if the other guests too were hostile. None of the episodes he reports appears by itself to be of any consequence, but the effect of these scattered reports could be cumulative. I assume, of course, that as analyst I am able to be sufficiently sensitive for such impacts to influence me. The wide dispersal of such reports itself plays a part in producing the cumulative effect on me. I am given the impression that the actual events are of infrequent occurrence. But suppose they are not: is it possible that in fact this man is really hated?

The facts, as I know them, are that he reports such trivial episodes about once a fortnight. They are minor elements in the analytic material of the sessions in which they appear—minor, that is, if one accepts the balance of significance that the patient by intonation and emphasis imposes on his material.

Let us suppose that the reports correspond to the actual events the patient experiences both as to character and frequency. In that case, I wonder whether he is not perhaps somewhat naive and over-sensitive, perhaps even persecuted. He may simply be conceited, as I know he is, and incapable of judging his importance, or lack of importance. Certainly this view would be quite compatible with his capacity for exploiting the indulgence that is extended to him to produce a conviction of his own worth as the central factor in the agreeable episodes of his life.

My description makes it appear that there are two alternatives: either that the patient is hated, or that he is over-indulged, naive, and persecuted. But in fact there is no reason why these views should be regarded as alternatives.

[Undated]

α

The elements to which the student at the Pons Asinorum says goodbye [Euclid I.5] have their counterpart in other mathematical situations. Thus there are the elements that are combined in a particular way to form the notation employed in determinants. But even when the mathematician does not employ the term, there are situations in which it is possible to see that what in fact could with justification be called 'elements' are being combined according to certain rules to produce formulas. These elements seem to vary considerably; it may be interesting to collect them together for investigation.

There are numbers; there are letters of the alphabet; there are points, lines, circles, angles; there are signs such as <, +, −; there are letters of the Greek alphabet, capital and lower case. All without exception are written, and though the marks that the writer makes have names—such as 'greater than', 'plus', 'minus', 'alpha', 'beta'—in fact mathematicians do not appear to use these signs for talking in the way that words are used in conversation. It must be supposed, therefore, that the object in synthesizing these elements is different from the object in verbalization, though the synthesizing process seems similar.

Why do not mathematicians speak mathematics? Is it that a string of mathematical formulas cannot be made to say, "It's a nice day"? Is the vocabulary not big enough? No: it must obviously be that its primary purpose is not conversational, although it is clear that one of the functions of mathematics is public-ation.

We shall have to consider three points: (1) the nature of the elements, (2) the nature of the methods employed to bring them together, and (3) the nature of the objects that are created by the syntheses of the elements (Poincaré, *Science and Method,* p. 30; *The Thirteen Books of Euclid's Elements,* I.1, I.5, I.47).

It may appear that I am suggesting that synthesis must be associated simply with a bringing together of the elements according to some known rule to form, say, a polynomial or a determinant. But we cannot assume such a restriction and exclude the bringing together of these elements in a quite different manner; for example, in such a way that would issue in a dream, or in some structure such as that suggested by Stendhal's description of a painting as, '*de la morale construite*'.

Certainly with the psychotic personality there is a failure to dream, which seems to be parallel with an inability to achieve fully the depressive position. It may therefore be said that the capacity to synthesize issues in two main events: (1) the logical construct, a mathematical formula, sentence, etc. and (2) a dream.

The inability to dream: I leave aside for the present the minute fragmentation etc. that may be associated with an inability to dream or, as I think, with dreams that are devoid of sense impressions, i.e. visual impression, auditory, olfactory, maybe tactile and taste impressions that are felt to be a kind of urination. I concentrate on the situation itself in which the patient has dreams devoid of sensory impressions, or all sense impressions and no dreams. If such a patient reports a dream, I suggest he is really reporting a hallucination and that he always feels it to be a 'queer dream'. I suggest that an inability to dream is itself so serious that the patient is compelled to have a dream, a 'queer dream' that is a counterpart, on the level of dream thinking, of the hallucinatory gratification experienced in waking life when true gratification is impossible.

Seen in this light, X's objection to noise may be his objection to a sense impression as well as to the thing his sense impression conveys to him. The deprivation of sense impression must then lead to an inability to dream and a need to hallucinate sense impressions as a substitute for the dream.

But (and it is striking that I am having great difficulty in remembering or seeing the relationship of each bit of this with the bit that has preceded it or that is coming next) this lack of sensory experience must be related to my theory about 'common sense'. And equally, my theory that his dream is a hallucination will explain adequately (?) why he has no associations. A hallucination of a dream can no more yield associations than a hallucinated breast can yield milk.

This failure to dream is felt as such a grave disaster that the patient continues to hallucinate during the day, to hallucinate a dream, or so to manipulate facts that he is able to feel he is having a dream—which is the daylight counterpart of the night-time hallucination of a dream. But it is also the attempt to suck a dream out of an experience of reality or actuality. And in this respect the dream that yields no associations and the reality that yields no dreams are alike; they are similar to hallucinatory gratification.

Apparently X can get nothing from analysis. In feeling it is a hallucination in which he cannot have either love or hate, I am an object manipulated—like a masturbatory object—to obtain gratification but which yields none. Why is this? Does it mean that envy is primary and precludes the possibility of any gratification, even hallucinatory gratification?

I cannot be satisfied that this is so. I suspect any 'explanation' of which a 'cause' is an essential part; it seems open to the criticism I have made of the theories of causation, namely that there is no actual cause and that the appearance of one is due to the 'realization' of a scientific deductive system, perhaps a premature or hallucinatory 'realization'.

* * *

[Later addition to this page]
24 February 1960

It may be worth considering the attempted transfer of the dreaming function to conscious rational levels of mind instead of the levels, now out of action, on which they usually occur.

January 1960

α and objects

In today's session there were clearly brought together two sets of objects:

1. One set is similar to, if not identical with, the bizarre objects: the woman with freckles and red hair was felt by him to be part of his personality, a 'thing', an undigested object. This and similar objects, or fragments of objects, can be brought together, but cruelly to each other; or in combination, dangerously to him. They are also useless for dream thoughts, for storage as memory, or, as Freud said, for notation, and therefore no good for unconscious waking thinking. Furthermore, they are feared as evidence of the disintegration, under destructive attack, of his personality. They are feared as hostile to him because they have been destroyed so that they now exist only as fragments and not as wholes. They are felt as an internal or external *social* conscience of a hostile and murderous kind because of what he has done to them.

2. The second set, the α-objects, the red-haired, freckled woman, are felt to be visual images and to be capable of association. But it is felt that these visual images, by virtue of their suitability for dream-thought, make imminent the depressive position. This carries with it the danger, the certain danger, of the emergence of a murderous super-ego ('brutal'); and also the problem of the onset of the depressive position, namely depression, a synthesis that reveals the enormity of the destruction already done, and the illimitable vista of the yet unintegrated elements that have *not* been synthesized.

[Undated]

> Let us endeavour to see things as they are, and then enquire whether we ought to complain. Whether to see life as it is will give us much consolation, I know not; but the consolation that is drawn from truth, if any there be, is solid and durable; that which may be derived from error must be, like its original, fallacious and fugitive.
>
> Samuel Johnson, in a letter to Bennet Langton, 21 September 1758, *Boswell's Life of Johnson*, vol. 1, p.339

I assume that the permanently therapeutic effect of a psycho-analysis, if any, depends on the extent to which the analysand has been able to use the experience to see one aspect of his life, namely himself as he is. It is the function of the psycho-analyst to use the experience of such facilities for contact as the patient is able to extend to him, to elucidate the truth about the patient's personality and mental characteristics, and to exhibit them to the patient in a way that makes it possible for him to entertain a reasonable conviction that the statements (propositions) made about himself represent facts.

It follows that a psycho-analysis is a joint activity of analysand and analyst to determine the truth; that being so, the two are engaged—no matter how imperfectly—on what is in intention a scientific activity.

But not at all, it might be objected by a painter; why should the two not be engaged in an artistic activity? An analysand who is a painter or a musician may indeed be hostile to the dominant role played by speech in analysis, and the hostility may include amongst its complexity of component strands some that could be related to a belief in the intrinsic superiority of art to science.

I shall exclude this problem because I wish to limit this to that aspect of the psycho-analysis which can be made explicit verbally—although I may on some other occasion investigate the implications for psycho-analysis of the artist's claim to be concerned with truth, including the claim of the artist in words. I content myself with the observation that the analyst is only concerned with the truth of a particularly limited area of knowledge.

If a psycho-analysis is indeed a scientific activity, it should, in proportion as it is properly conducted, display logical features common to all the sciences, and in so far as its conduct is imperfect will display phenomena of illogicality, irrationality, unscientific conduct, some of which are already well known to psycho-analysts, and all of which must be present in every attempt to establish facts scientifically—no matter in what field of human knowledge, and no matter how great a degree of success is obtained in achieving a properly scientific conduct of the investigation. The awareness of the pressure of these illogical elements has led those whose work forces upon them the recognition of the need for the establishment of the truth to define rules of such a kind that obedience to them might lead to the exclusion of these irrational elements. The wish to establish effective rules of this kind has contributed much to the adumbration of a scientific method and to its continuing discussion and formulation.

The discussion may for convenience be regarded as centring on what is, or should be, the scientific method, and on what are, or should be, the aims of those who employ such methods. One attitude expresses itself in a need to declare what the rules or laws are that have to be obeyed if a scientific investigation is to be carried out. Indeed, if there is to be a scientific method, it is the rules of the method which constitute the qualities that make it appropriate to call it a method. But why should there be a scientific method at all? Why not call it 'science'? The answer is twofold:

(1) In the pursuit of a science, thought has to be translated into action; something has to be done. And it is this fact, often unrecognized, that limits the freedom of thought and imposes the need for rules to give effect to the limitation. This same feature, the need for action as an essential characteristic of scien-

tific activity, constitutes the main source of all the differences that have been noticed to exist between science and mathematics. Science is about something, purely by virtue of the fact that something has to be done, that thought has to be translated into action, and it is the action into which it has to be translated that the scientific thoughts are about. But mathematics do not have to be translated into action; the mathematician can elaborate his system of logically necessary propositions, but it is not about anything unless someone chooses to use it as a subsidiary to his scientific system—and even so it cannot with reason be said even then to be 'about', say, chemistry or physics or a bank balance, any more than a gearbox can be said to be 'about' a motor car. But though the very nature of scientific method (as intrinsically bound up with the translation of thought into action) exacts the promulgation of rules, this is not the only element from which the pressure to regularize springs.

(2) I have already spoken of the phenomena of illogicality, irrationality, and unscientific conduct that obtrude in human activity—as anyone, even without psycho-analytic experience, knows. These elements, whether they are discerned in the observer or in the environment, arouse pain usually of the mental variety known as anxiety, and in certain people impel them to embrace a scientific outlook and to give effect to their cravings in the production of a scientific method with the characteristics I have adumbrated, and designed to produce results of a kind that seem to earn for themselves the title, 'laws of nature'. The use of the term, 'law', like many others employed, is intended to satisfy two classes of conditions. First, the emotional state of the individual who wishes to foster, against his sense of internal disorder, a feeling of predictability and memorable experience (and the stability that flows from a conviction of these two) and a belief in the existence externally of a similar situation—one that is felt to support experience remembered and to develop in a manner that is predictable. The second class of conditions belongs to what common sense declares to be a world independent of the observer which has characteristics of its own, notwithstanding any that may be attributed to it by the observer or any that might, through oversight or otherwise, be

substracted from it. Amongst these characteristics there may be relatedness of one element to another, either of the kind adumbrated in the so-called scientific law or of some other to which the scientific law is an approximation.

But here I have introduced the idea that there might be kinds of relatedness, and this will certainly need very thorough investigation by anyone whose work is so closely concerned with relationships as is the psycho-analyst's. It is a matter I shall investigate further when I discuss the function of words as hypotheses. For the present I wish to emphasize the significance of the two classes of conditions to which the scientific statement must apply: its significance as a member of the class of elements associated with the mentality of the beholder, and as a member of the class of elements assumed by common sense to exist independently of the observer. It is this that leads me to say that there is a sphere of human thought and activity that can be embraced by the title, 'The Science of Psycho-analysis and the Psycho-analysis of Science'. It is within this area that this discussion finds its subject. The subject has no beginning or end, and it is therefore accidental that I commence by stating two hypotheses, both possessing the high degree of generalization common to high-level hypotheses that are being employed as premises in a scientific system.

In accordance with my aim to attempt to conduct a psychoanalysis on scientific principles, I propose the following hypotheses, which are to be the premises for further hypotheses.

Hypothesis 1. No cure can be permanent or have the qualities essential for permanence unless it is based on what reason and common sense alike tell both analyst and analysand is the truth about the personality and mental mechanisms of the analysand, and so make it possible to attempt a scientific view or truthful view of external reality—partly because a false view leads to mistakes potentially fatal, but also because a false view, e.g. psychotic, needs a great expenditure of effort and the construction of elaborate social apparatus.

Hypothesis 2. The truth about the personality and mental mechanisms of the analysand, as demonstrable by the analyst to the analysand, leads to a permanent cure—as that would be understood by analyst and analysand taking a common-sense view of the results of such a demonstration.

From these premises it should be possible to deduce secondary hypotheses of such a kind that they lend themselves to verification empirically in the way that is familiar to all those who employ scientific methods, no matter what discipline they pursue.

This, however, is not my aim here. The introduction of these two primary hypotheses is a part of my attempt to demonstrate how the general principles of all sciences can be particularized when applied to psycho-analysis. Therefore, though I may find it necessary to deduce hypotheses that are empirically verifiable from the primary hypotheses, I shall do so not with a view to verifying the hypotheses, primary and secondary, but for the purpose of psycho-analysing the unsolved scientific problem that this scientific procedure brings in its train.

Thus: suppose that I have, in the course of my work with the patient, deduced certain lower-level hypotheses, which, in the manner of such hypotheses, are of decreasing generalization. As a result, I am now in a position to test and verify these hypotheses.

The patient comes into the room, sits on the couch and . . . I have already carried my description far enough for present purposes. I have said that we are concerned to establish the truth, but the philosophers who concern themselves with the validity of perception, and psycho-analysts who have an intensely practical interest in this matter, will already have their problems. How do I know it is a patient? Or a room? I have no doubt about these sense impressions, but they are private to myself. How can I claim that my senses have, in the world of external reality, a factual counterpart—a real room, a real patient?

It is perfectly legitimate to deal with this as Braithwaite has done by limiting the discussion to a problem that (even excluding the problems of the phenomenalists) is, as he says, quite enough for one book. And for the time being I shall follow his example. But only for the time being. I shall therefore assume that I may use such data for my investigation as common sense tells me are facts in the world of external reality. By these means I limit the area of discussion to that part of the subject which is concerned, as Braithwaite says, with 'the relationship of public scientific laws to public facts of observation'. By this he means that he is excluding all problems that arise through the fact that sense impressions, on which all scientific work ultimately comes to rest, are private to the beholder and cannot become a matter for scientific investigation until they are made public, i.e. undergo transformation in the observer that enables them to be communicated to another. As will be seen later, this process, which I call public-ation, is in my opinion no different from the process involved in the individual who has to transmute pre-verbal into verbal thought if what is implicit is to become explicit, or what is unconscious, conscious.

In the psychotic, what is unconscious is not the material ordinarily associated with the repressed, but the ownership of the material. He remains unconscious of this by virtue of continuous projective identification, which takes the place of repression. But the projective identification *is* unconscious; therefore the material remains conscious, but the projection of it is unconscious.

[Undated]

Disorder of thought

To call an affliction a disorder of thought is to shift the emphasis away from what is thought—the content of the thought—to that which contains the thought; on the other hand, from the architecture to the theme is to shift the emphasis from the container of what is thought, to the content of the thought.

* * *

Envy contributes to the belief that external objects are the patient's thought. Since he cannot admit dependence on an external object, he claims (in order ultimately to escape feeling envy) that he is, like the breast that feeds itself, the producer as well as the consumer of that on which he depends for this life.

How to keep awake

Since it is essential that the creative worker should keep his α-function unimpaired, it is clear that the analyst must be able to dream the session. But if he is to do this without sleeping, he must have plenty of sleep. The need for this now becomes apparent as a way by which α-function can be preserved for the sake of analysis, i.e. neither for waking up nor for going to sleep, but for a special and entirely new function, and not—as has hitherto been supposed—because the capacity for judgement is peculiar in being easily and rapidly fatigued. It is because α-function is by nature intended to make sense impressions or an emotional experience available either to the unconscious or to the conscious, *or* to make wakefulness or consciousness available to the emotional experience—as, for example, in learning a skill, from walking to fighting. Making oblivion available is not the same as repressing, but if the analyst has not had enough sleep, α-function may produce oblivion.

Time, cause, and Oedipal situation

Provenance: guilt related to the Oedipal situation. The idea of cause belongs to criminal investigation. In its simplest form there are:

(1) feelings of guilt, passive and active—i.e. I am guilty of . . . You are, or someone is, guilty of . . .;

(2) someone must have done something, i.e. caused it;

(3) the person or thing that caused it must be antecedent to it;

(4) the denial that the guilt caused it.

In other words, these ideas (of causation + time) derive from very early experiences, just as 'foot' derives from early references to the body in the exploration of what we call space. In 'time', one thing is before (antecedent), the other after (subsequent); but in 'space', does the infant have a left or right, before or after, or what? If it sees its foot and then its hand, does it feel its foot caused its hand?

31 January/1 February 1960

Narcissism and social-ism

These two terms might be employed to describe tendencies, one ego-centric, the other socio-centric, which may at any moment be seen to inform groups of impulsive drives in the personality. They are equal in amount and opposite in sign. Thus, if the love impulses are narcissistic at any time, then the hate impulses are social-istic, i.e. directed towards the group, and, vice versa: if the hate is directed against an individual as a part of narcissistic tendency, then the group will be loved social-istically. That is to say, if A hates B, as an expression of narcissism, then he will love the society. "I hate B because he is so harmful to the society that I love", might be an assertion symptomatic of what I would call a state of narcissistic hate of A for B. I maintain that in a narcissistic statement there is always implied a social-istic statement. The two *must* go together: if one is operating, so is the other.

It follows that if narcissistic hate is felt for A, then social-istic love is felt for B. If A is one person, then B will become a *group* of people all possessing the admirable characteristics that distinguish B from A who lacks them. Put in still other terms: if one group of impulses is dominated by narcissistic trends, then the remaining impulses will be dominated by social-istic trends. Let X be a person: if his hate impulses are social-istic, his love impulses will be narcissistic. But suppose his impulses towards himself, say love impulses, become narcissistic, then all his other impulses will become social-ized, and he will split himself up into a 'group'. Love of self need not be narcissistic; love of the group need not be social-istic. At one pole is one object: at the other pole an infinitude of objects. At one pole there will be one object to which one group of emotions will be directed: at the other pole a number of emotions will be directed to the infinitude of objects that owe their numbers to a splitting of one object.

6 February 1960

Beset as he is by the examples in history of the many occasions on which men of great ability and integrity have been unable to maintain a grasp of the truth about the phenomena that they wish to investigate, and made further aware of the pitfalls attending his search by the fact that his study is itself an investigation of a most serious source of errors in human judgement, the analyst's problem is to find a method—if there is one—by which he can be aware that he is falling into error, and even (if possible) of what kind of error he has become the victim. The search for this method constitutes for the psycho-analyst the search for a scientific method. For him the scientific method is that procedure, or series of procedures, by which error is made to declare itself.

As we have seen, one area in which a solution might be sought is in situations in which common sense can be brought to bear. One of these situations is in analysis itself in so far as a personality is observed in changing conditions of mood, circumstances, and time. Features that appear constant amidst the changes may be accorded a certain degree of probability. What meaning we are to give such constant features, what use we are to make of them, and how we are to use them, must be debated further.

It must be noted that unfortunately it may not be the features that are remarkable for their constancy amidst change that are the analytically significant ones; it is likely that it is those phenomena we most wish to investigate (and are therefore associated with the observations, the truth of which concerns us most) that least lend themselves to the check of common sense. The other situation in which common sense is brought to bear is in the situation produced by public-ation. As we have already seen, this involves recording and communication, both of which are consequently seen once more to be matters that deserve serious study and constant work devoted to their improvement. Presumably no safeguards exist against the eroding effect of connotation and communication that is exerted by changes in the cultural atmosphere of the group, but the fact that these changes render communication precarious adds force to the need for elaboration of rigorously accurate methods of record. Furthermore, the fact that the communication that Bach wished to make when he inscribed his score may not be that which his audience received, and the fact that the communication that his audience received may not be that which some present or future audience may receive, need not be inimical to the search for truth by the group in history. For the continued existence of the communication, its preservation by the group may be interpreted as a sign that the group continues to receive something from the communication. What is it that inheres in the communication that causes it to be meaningful in what appears to be so many different ways to so many different people?

11 February 1960

Compassion and truth

1. Compassion and Truth are both senses of man.
2. Compassion is a feeling that he needs to express; it is an impulse he must experience in his feelings for others.
3. Compassion is likewise something that he needs to feel in the attitude of others towards him.
4. Truth is something man needs to express; it is something he needs to seek and to find; it is essential for fulfilment of his curiosity.
5. Truth is something he needs to feel in the attitude of others towards him.
6. Truth and compassion are also qualities pertaining to the relationship that a man establishes with people and things.
7. A man may feel he lacks a capacity for love.
8. A man may lack capacity for love.
9. Similarly, he may feel he lacks a capacity for truth, either to hear it, or to seek it, or to find it, or to communicate it, or to desire it.
10. He may in fact lack such a capacity.
11. The lack may be primary or secondary, and may diminish truth or love, or both.
12. Primary lack is inborn and cannot be remedied; yet some of the consequences may be modified analytically.
13. Secondary lack may be due to fear or hate or envy or love. Even love can inhibit love.
14. Applying (8) and (10) to the Oedipus myth, the death of the Sphinx is a consequence of such lack, as the question posed

was not intended to elicit truth, and consideration for itself could not exist to erect a barrier against self-destruction. Tiresias may be said to lack compassion less than regard for truth. Oedipus lacked compassion for himself more than he lacked regard for truth.

12 February 1960

> All our ideas are reducible in the long run to the data of sense-experience.
>
> F. Copleston, *A History of Philosophy*, vol. 6, p. 8

Montesquieu's theory [ibid., p. 11] is not simply an empirical generalization but deals with ideal types of government. This raises an interesting possibility: if there are theories, e.g. quantum mechanics, in which there is no level of empirically verifiable data but a level of statistical hypotheses that take the place of empirically verifiable data, could one have a theory in which the place of empirically verifiable data was taken by hypotheses of ideal types analogous to statistical hypotheses? And if so, what is the relationship of the hypotheses of ideal types to premises or high-level hypotheses of increasing generalization? Are generalization and idealization the same thing? If not, in what way do they differ? There may be a place for three types of hypothesis that need to be distinguished:

(1) high-level, generalized and not empirically verifiable, therefore

(2) statistical hypotheses, taking the place of empirically verifiable hypotheses and embodying a probability statement. This involves the question: *how* does the scientist use these probability statements?

(3) ideal-type hypothesis, which says that in a given state (which in fact will never be found) there does exist a state of ought-to-exist-ness of whatever it is that the hypothesis is referring to. For example, take the statement that 'excessive

> splitting and projective identification lead to a disintegration of the personality'. 'Excessive projective identification' is an ideal state and not an empirical generalization. The hypothesis asserts that in so far as this ideal state is realized, a disintegration of personality ought to be found. Is this a probability statement in a statistical hypothesis? No: but I suspect it is a statement that is 'understood' when a statistical hypothesis is used, and this is the clue to the problem posed by Braithwaite (*Scientific Explanation,* p. 124) as to *how* a scientist uses a probability statement in a statistical hypothesis. The ideal-type hypothesis may be regarded as a primitive non-mathematical probability statement, what Braithwaite would call 'reasonableness' (ibid. p. 120). It should not, as far as I can see, ever embody in itself a probability statement. In any case, I consider the probability statement is often employed as an assertion of a measure of certitude. But if I do not regard the ideal-type hypothesis as identical with a statistical hypothesis, I also cannot regard it as a high-level generalization, for clearly it is used in psycho-analysis as a low-level hypothesis.

In place of the level of empirically verifiable data, there is no step as yet between the statement, 'excessive projective identification leads to disintegration of the personality', and perception of sense data in the empirical experience of analytic treatment.

If this is so, then in psycho-analysis the hypotheses of a scientific deductive system may be hierarchically arranged, not with high-level hypotheses of increasing generalization and low-level hypotheses of increasing particularization, but with high-level hypotheses of increasing idealization and low-level hypotheses of increasing realization. Or it may be a special kind of scientific deductive system in which generalization and idealization are combined, and realization and particularization are combined. How does this compare with the realizations of mathematical formulas?

Before attempting an answer to this, we must consider certain similarities and contrasts that emerge by comparing mathematical formulas with dreams. The elements of a dream, by being used as the starting point for a series of free associations, can be made to yield thoughts and ideas coherent with each other and displaying in their integrated form a construct (Freud's latent content of the dream) that seems to show a great expansion of meaning compared with that displayed in the dream from which it has been derived. Certain algebraic formulas, treated according to rules laid down in advance—not free associations—similarly yield an expansion that is coherent within itself and, like the latent content of the dream, is often found to be applicable to data of an empirically verifiable kind that, in the coherent form that the mathematical expansion has revealed, provide a realization for the system of formulas that make up the original algebraic calculus. By analogy, the latent content of the dream is employed by the psycho-analyst to 'interpret' empirical data presented by the patient, and so reveals a coherent form that may be regarded as a 'realization' of the latent content of the dream.

In both these instances the 'realization' has been sought in the domain of phenomena considered to exist independently of the observer. In some sense the algebraic calculus, like the latent content, may be regarded as an attempt on the part of the individual to produce a mental apparatus as well adapted to comprehension of his environment as the visual sensory apparatus is well adapted to sight of his environment. The latent content of the algebraic calculus can so far be treated, for purposes of comparison, as parallel. It is necessary to observe, if confusion is to be avoided, that the latent content is being used to achieve comprehension of data deemed to be independent of the observer, even though the latent content is a product of the mind of the observer and the data to which it is being applied are facets of the observer's personality. This independence would be challenged if the latent content was applied, or deemed to be applicable to, the problem associated with the production of itself—in short, if it were felt to be a latent content relating to a dream of which it was the latent content. Similarly with the algebraic calculus: the selected fact of Poincaré would ordinarily be expected to apply to data independent of the observer and to be designed to give order and coherence to these phenomena. But I have suggested that the selected fact—latent content, or algebraic calculus in this instance—is itself an attempt to deal with the internal psychic incoherence (shown in the Kleinian theory as the paranoid–schizoid position), at least by an externalization in which, and through which, the individual is able to offset internal feelings by a sense of external achievement. Is it possible that there could be a latent content relating to a dream of which it was the latent content? Is it possible that there is an algebraic calculus, or that in any algebraic calculus there is a facet, such that the coherent whole expressed by the calculus found its realization in the realm of elementary mental phenomena from which it originated, as well as in data independent of the observer?

14 February 1960

Fundamental, basic, inborn character disorder

There are occasions when it is important to know what are the fundamental characteristics of the patient with whom we are dealing. By this I mean that there are certain qualities of personality—a capacity for loving is one—which are of great importance in determining the nature of the person and of his behaviour. We would like to know what are thc patient's fundamental characteristics, but curiosity on this topic is hampered because the questions that are the tools of curiosity are often ill-suited to the investigation we have in mind. The vocabulary that we employ to frame our questions has been elaborated to serve purposes that are often very different from those of the psycho-analyst; we are hampered, in a manner with which we are already familiar, in our attempts to frame theories and solutions of problems. But we give insufficient attention to the obstruction of the formation of the question. For example, I have said we would like to know the fundamental characteristics of the patient, but this question as it stands does not provide the emotional experience of the analysis with sufficient precision to admit of an answer. I do not suggest there is any question that does, and if I now propose some elaboration of my question it is not to solve a problem but to propound it. The question, 'What are the fundamental characteristics?', I shall replace by two others:

1. What are the characteristics that are inborn and irreducible by any means (short of a physical disaster of the kind experienced in certain forms of physical illness or brain damage) that have been shown to be associated with character change?

2. What are the characteristics, which an answer to the first question would specify, that occupy the dominant executive position in this man's psyche? That is to say, if a capacity for love is one of his main inborn characteristics, does it in fact inform his outlook and behaviour?

It now becomes clear that the two questions multiply. Thus, taking question 2, what is the 'executive position'? Is there such a thing? Or does it simply depend on how strong are his feelings of love? And if so, is 'How strong?' a question we can ask, or is there some other more apposite? And so I could continue the elaboration of questions. But that fact itself shows no useful purpose is served by an attempt at abstract systemization, and at the same time that such elaboration is necessary at some time and somehow. I shall show that the essential point is that such questions should be given a chance to proliferate in the analyst's mind, and that this chance should occur in the analytic session itself. If induction means anything, it should mean 'producing questions'. This and α should be the supreme mental activities of the analyst—not theorizing, though he must express theories. The interpretations themselves, which are acts, must not be confounded with theorizing; theorizing must not become an activity of the analyst when analysing; it is, as Darwin pointed out, inimical to observation.

17 February 1960

Animism, destructive attacks and reality

In the earliest phases of development objects are felt to be alive and to possess character and personality presumably indistinguishable from the infant's own. In this phase, which may be considered as anterior to the development of the reality principle as Freud describes it, the real and the alive are indistinguishable; if an object is real to the infant, then it is alive; if it is dead, it does not exist. But this 'it' that does not exist and is not alive—why is it necessary to talk about it or discuss it? The problem is to give an answer *verbally* about objects in a *pre-verbal* state. The difficulty will constantly crop up in what I have to say, and my solution of it will constantly demand indulgent understanding from the reader.

In this instance it is necessary to talk about this object which should be non-existent and therefore impossible to discuss. Its importance lies in the fact that the infant, if enraged, has death wishes, and if the object is wished dead, it is dead. It therefore has become non-existent, and its characteristics are different from those of the real, live, existing object; the existing object is alive, real, and benevolent. (I propose to call the real, alive objects α-elements; the dead, unreal objects I shall call β-elements.) In order to distinguish the distinction between real and unreal that I am making here, from the distinction between real and unreal which is appropriate to Freud's description of the interplay between pleasure principle and reality principle, I shall call these objects proto-real objects belonging to the domain of proto-reality. The infant, in all the early phases of its life, is dominated by the pleasure principle. It is therefore, in so far as it feels pleasure, surrounded by these proto-real objects felt to be real and alive. But should pain supervene, then it is surrounded by dead objects destroyed by its hate, which, since it cannot tolerate pain, are non-existent. But ordinarily they continue to exist because the sense impressions still operate. Should intolerance of these objects grow beyond a certain point, then the infant commences attacks on the mental apparatus that informs it of the reality of these sense impressions and of some object that is felt to be beyond the sense impressions. The existence of the real objects can be denied, but the sense impressions persist, e.g. after the eyes have been shut. It is therefore felt that the real objects have now forced their way into the personality. The next stage, imposed by yet more powerful intolerance, is the destruction of the apparatus that is responsible for the transformation of the sense impressions into material suitable for waking unconscious thought—a dream-thought. This destruction contributes to the feeling that 'things', not words or ideas, are inside.

Excess of death instincts for whatever reason or duration, in addition to contributing to an excess of dead objects—painful and proto-unreal—means that animism (an animistic view) cannot develop. The need to placate contributes to a complex state in which the dead object has to be re-animated and worshipped. These objects are then not so much gods and idols that are believed to be alive and endowed with human attributes, as objects chosen specifically and precisely because *they are dead*. Contrary to common observation, the essential feature of the adored or worshipped object is that it should be dead so that crime may be expiated by the patient's dutiful adherence to animation of what is known to be inanimate and impossible to animate. This attitude contributes to the complex of feelings associated with fetishism.

The breakdown in animism affects the capacity of the individual to transform sense impressions into material suitable for use in dream-thoughts. Objects sensed are felt to have life and personality, to be capable of combination and interaction. Thus dream-thoughts and dreams become possible, thereby making it possible to learn from experience.

The dead, non-existent objects are products of murderous hate; guilt invests them with attributes akin to those associated with conscience, omnipotence, omniscience, but not the qualities necessary for employment in dream-thoughts.

18 February 1960

α

The occasions when the patient expresses a number of feelings verbally—"I am anxious, I don't know why." "I am feeling a bit better, I don't know why."—may be an expression of an experience such as I suggest takes place when he has a dream. That is to say, he has an emotional experience on which dream-work-α is done so that the emotional experience can be made available, stored for use in consciousness. Ordinarily α operates to enable a conscious emotional experience to be stored in unconsciousness; it just occurs to me that this may be very like the function performed by logic in the elaboration of a scientific deductive system in which premises and derived hypotheses are so arranged that they follow each other.

But how is α related to logic? There are logical dreams, but on the whole they would seem to be rare. Yet the ordinary dream has a logic; it is narrativized. The patient today said he had had a dream, but in fact could only report disjointed fragments in a way not unlike the ordinary session. (He said, incidentally, that in twenty years' time a new patient might be cured by psychoanalysis in half the time that he is.)

But what else can one say about the construction? Freud assumed that the interpretation, the latent content, was the origin of the dream, and that it had been worked on by the dream-work to produce the dream. I say that the origin is an emotional experience—perhaps even an experience that is emotional and nothing else—and that this is worked on (rationalized?) to produce the dream, the manifest content as we know it, and that it is the *analyst* who then does the *interpretation* to produce the so-called latent content. Then what validity or significance is to be attached to this product, the latent content?

20 February 1960

Attacks on α

The patient has the capacity to exact an emotional relationship from the analyst, and to reject it. A state is produced in which one cannot 'remember' what has happened in the session. Some points are clear: (1) The patient denies information to the analyst. (2) The patient arouses 'inevitable' emotion and denies any material that would allow α to operate and therefore the analyst to profit by the experience for the patient's benefit. Is this not unnecessarily elaborate? Why not just deny information? Because it is essential for there to be an *experience* from which no benefit is to be obtained. (3) The patient has the occasional vivid experience, e.g. he is loathed by his family. (4) The patient denies α and so loses a sense of reality, e.g. he is not able to see the irresponsibility of continuing the analysis. The prevention of visual imagery makes the experience not storable or usable either in conscious waking thought, unconscious waking thought, or in dream-thought.

February 1960

Displacement

Painful feelings related to a situation that has immediately arisen are displaced—for example, feelings of rejection, i.e. of rejecting and being rejected. The true self is felt not to be wanted nor yet to want the other true self; something must be done with these feelings. They are entertained, but the subject of the thoughts is no longer felt to be the person, someone in the past, who has immediately stimulated them, and around that person there is spun out a web of hostile reverie. Such past objects are carefully preserved; maybe they are specifically created for that purpose in the first instance. Note that the painfulness of the feeling is largely increased by the feeling that the rejection is of a true self and cannot therefore be assumed to be capable of resolution.

What seems to have happened is that the immediate cause is suppressed, perhaps before it has become clear to the patient that he has been stimulated at all. And at once the old 'memory' is substituted for the awareness of the current event. The subject of the early story becomes the main character, after the patient, in the current day-dream, which has been drawn across to shut out the thinking proper to the immediate reality situation. Is not this account sufficient?

Another version: the feelings of rejection and hate are split off from the personality and are felt about someone absent in time and space.

To what extent are the mechanisms of dream-work evident elsewhere? For example, can all cruel and hostile feelings be displaced into a stammer? Or are they all condensed? In short, is it not possible that the mechanisms that Freud describes as peculiar to dream-work are in reality found to be operating over a wide area of the psyche and in a great number of different functional fields?

* * *

(I need to work out displacement condensation etc., and the relation to context and therefore changes in meaning.

Also need to work out relations of bizarre objects to animism; in particular the fact that they have character only because they are ghosts. In this way they differ from inanimate objects that are felt to have life and independence—the ordinary characters associated with an animistic view.

Also work out the theory that interpretation is an attempt to relate an individual's peculiar and particular characteristic to the social group, because the analyst who makes it is a member of a group and so associates the individual with himself, and because interpretation is into the language of the group.)

22 February 1960

It is curious how much anxiety I feel about following up my views. Today's session with X made me feel more than ever that not only my theories but my practice also are on the right track.

Why cannot X wake up if he cannot 'dream'? It must be for the same reason that you cannot let something become unconscious if α is not done to that something. The inability to have visual images of what is taking place means that the emotional experience cannot be preserved either in the conscious or the unconscious. (In this I have equated α with having visual images—this is not so, I think.)

How important is attention? And is it the same, as I think it is, as 'dreaming' what is going on?

Paying attention to what is happening here and now involves:

(a) respect for the truth,

(b) respect for myself,

(c) respect for my objects.

But

(1) I have just displaced this by thinking I was giving a paper to the Society.

(2) I have emotionalized it by making it an occasion where I am loved and admired.

(3) I have replied to a hostile criticism from X with a moderation that does me credit.

(4) In short, my mind is wandering, and I am transforming the task, which I have already put off for an hour, into an event that is pleasing and successful.

Is this not very like a dream, wish-fulfilment and frustration-evasion and all? (And may not all this be 'digestion', a way of fixing an experience in mind?)

I am not in bed asleep and a prey to emotions, but I am sitting up at a table on a not-so-soft seat. The experience I am having is perhaps painful, and pleasant only in so far as I am able to transform it—Freud's idea that the dream preserves sleep. What is the painful fact I am denying? That it is difficult to write, that no one loves me, and that I have to work? Perhaps my denial of these painful emotions has the effect that I then have a painful sleeping emotional experience on which I then again have to do α dream-work to produce the manifest content of the dream.

If this is the case, the dream-work-α may have as its function the exclusion of material that would otherwise distract from the main task in hand—the actual conscious object of my writing. But my idea is not that—it is that the dream-work-α transforms this experience so that I can store it and remember it. This may be too simplified, and yet it seems to fit some important facts with X.

24 February 1960

α

There are the following states that need to be distinguished:

(1) genuine 'dream', but carried on with the analyst for fear of annihilation if 'dreamt' elsewhere (this is an attempt to make a current emotional experience available for dream-thought and conscious thought; it is a definite and desperate attempt to make external reality and internal psychic reality available to thought, and therefore to usher in an ability to learn from experience);

(2) hallucination of a dream, forced by the inability to dream and incapable of yielding associations (no associations, as with hallucinating the breast that yields no milk; starvation of reality means there is nothing to set against phantasy);

(3) artefact; a try-out but inevitably failing to yield associations of any value or reassurance against the dread of hallucination, the super-ego and annihilation (related to fear of annihilation);

(4) confusion due to excessive projective identification (not relevant to this situation).

* * *

"I feel there is something I have forgotten. It's a ridiculous idea and no grounds for it that I know of, but there it is. My apparatus is not working properly. Dr C thought it should be ten times more efficient; only doing one tenth of one in the States, but he forgets it is quite a difficult matter. But it's very interesting having to do it. I think it is a half only. Dr C is a very clever man, but he is wrong about this. The Z-chamber—it holds me up a bit." (This apparatus is what you feel you have forgotten.) "It is a matter of research; it holds me up. Letter from D. I was delighted to have it." (Stammering very badly all the time.) "Kept thinking about it all day. She's a nice person; not very interesting and a letter really just like a man. Keep having lots of dreams but I can't remember them." (Lack the apparatus that makes it possible to 'remember' and to do research.) "A dream that was horrible, though I can't really see what was horrible about it. A woman—and I was in an old-fashioned bus in which there was a lot of woodwork. The windows were shut. I asked if we could have them open so as to have more air. A surly kind of man who reminded me of you was very hostile, and I don't remember what happened next." (Inability to remember and feeling you have forgotten, associated with feeling of not being able to emerge from a state of mind—inability to get 'air'.) "Had lots more dreams." (Either none or I'm to be overwhelmed by them. Inability to dream.) "A dream without associations is not very much use." (Like the research, it reveals disjointed bits that have 'no associations'.) "Another dream in which I was stammering and it made it difficult to talk to the girl." (Not really felt to be dreams at all, and this feeling goes towards producing a feeling of 'impotence'—inability to dream.)

This session increasingly gave me the feeling that he was having, or is about to have, a psychotic breakdown. Everything pointed to the idea that he felt as if he could not breathe, that some man was refusing to let him get air in; and he was swearing and attacking the man with his oral flatus—the stammer. His attitude was euphoric, perhaps megalomanic. I drew attention to what seemed to be evidence that he felt unable to learn from the experience he was having with me.

The session seemed to be very important because it bore out my theories. It is evident therefore that I should want it to bear out my theories, and that I should regard it as important if it appeared to do so. So far, so obvious. Other sources of distortion involve deeper and deeper analysis for their discovery. He said something about research always leading to an infinite number of unknowns. But I cannot be sure how he phrased it. But how he 'phrased it' is very important; what did he *say*? I am pretty certain that that was what he meant, but when I interpreted it I was saying in effect that he felt that whenever he learnt anything, it revealed by that very fact the great number of disjointed elements that remained incoherent.

What I have said is that I do not know precisely what he said, and that I do not know precisely what my reply was. I thought he said approximately *Y*, and that I replied that what I thought was approximately *Y* had a meaning that was approximately *Z*—which I now assume I have rendered approximately. Well, either this means that in my view and with my personality it is impossible to have any but the most tenuous contact with someone, or that for some reason much fuss is being made about an experience—contact with another—which is quite ordinary and taken by most people in their stride.

No: it may also mean that the ordinary view, or lack of it, is not good enough for psycho-analysis. But the view I am putting forward can hardly be regarded as an improvement on the ordinary view. It is destructive and only suggests that we cannot 'know' what happened in an analytic conversation. What I am trying to say is that I can give a description that pulls together all the scraps of ideas that I associate with the session, and make them cohere in a way that gives them meaning. I can then feel the session was a meaningful experience. But I am also wanting the analysand to say it was meaningful. He might say it was, and that for him its meaning was that he had a psychotic breakdown. This would not satisfy me; I need to believe that it was meaningful for him in a sense that he has 'felt better' for it. And *I* want to be able to 'feel better' for being a psycho-analyst, i.e. for having such experiences. This means one wants to believe that everyone, including one's self, feels better for attempting to 'understand' one's self and others. But 'understanding' here means being able to do dream-work-α, to allow α to operate during one's emotional experience of another person. This reminds me of 'reality starvation' in the extreme case of the psychotic. The need to know the truth then becomes a matter of psychic need. And the α operations need to be investigated to see what they are—the mental 'digestion'.

This seems to throw light on the function of the intellectual leader. He is someone who is able to digest facts, i.e. sense data, and then to present the digested facts, my α-elements, in a way that makes it possible for the weak assimilators to go on from there. Thus the artist helps the non-artist to digest, say, the Little Street in Delft by doing α-work on his sense impressions and 'publishing' the result so that others who could not 'dream' the Little Street itself can now digest the published α-work of someone who could digest it. Vermeer was able to digest the facts in a particular way, or perhaps they were particular facts. The same presumably is true of the scientist. But why did the work done by Aristarchus not have any impact for close on two thousand years? And why did Kepler's work succeed relatively quickly? It may be that it was less a matter of concern at the time of Aristarchus. Is opposition necessary? Must the reality view be opposed before it can flourish?

Note the difference between the leader who is to show the *way* to thinking, and the 'mother' on whom the psyche is to be allowed to be parasitic—projective identification, psychotic dependence.

27 February 1960

Mathematics

1 + 1 = 2. But suppose we sexualize the plus sign: then 1 + 1 = 3 presents no difficulty. But it does not mean that 1 + 1 *must* = 3. For that, it would be necessary to do more than sexualize the plus sign. It would be necessary to make it at least ♂ + ♀ = 3. It would probably be necessary to make the plus sign mean 'sexual intercourse with intent to procreate children in adequate conditions between adequate people'.

What is happening here is that the plus sign is being treated as a variable as well as the terms of the expression. What mathematics can evolve if all the signs and terms in an expression are variables? There would seem to be nothing but chaos possible, but it is not so. For example, 1 + 1 = 3 has a meaning if I say 1 = a man, and 1 = a woman. In this case the 'value' of the plus sign has been affected 'contextually'. This reminds me of 'contextually' contingent propositions (Braithwaite, *Scientific Explanation,* p. 112).

28 February 1960

The scientist's mistrust of human intellectual effort tends to make him look longingly at the machine that can so often be made to appear the ideal recording instrument, a matter of rigid scales, pointers, unchanging weights, and so on. This attitude, which has something to commend it, yields matter for speculation if one considers it as betraying suspicion of anything that possesses life. How are we to find the truth, to gain knowledge, if facts can be recorded only by an object incapable of judgement or anything we regard as thought on the one hand, and on the other if thought is possible only by an object incapable of recording facts?

The difficulty may not be real in any significant way, but seems so because the method of formulation, in terms of knowledge, truth, and reality, leads to fallacious exaggeration of some elements of the problem, to the exclusion of others. Progress is less impeded if we consider 'know' to refer to a relationship, and reality and truth to refer to qualities of mental phenomena necessary to sustain mental health.

[Undated]

Need for a scientific method

Preoccupation with the psychology of the philosopher might lead to disregard of the truth or falsity of his ideas taken in themselves (F. Copleston, *A History of Philosophy,* vol. 1, p. 9). Similarly, it is presumably true that in addition to distortion produced in the analyst by his own conflicts, there must be other elements that might contribute to his failure to be scientific, e.g. insufficient knowledge of the subject. We may too easily assume that *all* difficulties can be dealt with by more analysis. The subject of this discussion is how to determine, elaborate, and display the procedures that constitute correct analysis, or that conform to standards that at least avoid methods that could not possibly be scientific in any circumstances. And, reciprocally, how to see that findings allegedly psycho-analytic cannot possibly be scientific even if true.

The first requisite is a means by which one could tell that one was going wrong; the second, a means by which one could rectify the mistake.

I think I was wrong with X. I object to this after years of experience. My objection is based on a feeling that I have tried hard and made endless efforts to be on the right tack. But this is my avowal. I know the criticism and can be critical because I have a picture of myself as a sulky man, feeling very sorry for myself in the plight in which I have been pleased to depict myself. The view that I have 'tried hard' and 'made endless efforts' is flattering to my esteem, but it is a view set in a moral outlook in which 'trying hard' is a virtue that will be rewarded. And if it is not, I have a right to be annoyed with someone—fate or X perhaps.

It occurs to me that I may be going wrong because I don't please myself. That is to say that it is a sign I am going wrong if

I am not pleasing myself in the sense of making myself pleased, and in the sense that I am not pleased with and by myself. But am I stating a symptom or a cause? And doesn't this mean that I believe something has caused 'this', or that 'this' is causing something? I am caught in a web of my own devising.

It means that I have not the ability, character, or personality that I conceive to be pleasing. But who is the 'me', the character who thus passes judgement on whether or not such characteristics as I have are 'pleasing'? And to whom are they, or are they not, pleasing?

I have a picture, a visual image of someone who is loved by all. But this also sounds like a state I once believed to exist, say when I was a baby, and it further sounds as if I had never got over it. This would mean that the ambition is not suitable to my present age, just as my capacities are not suitable to or matching my ambition—which may also have been true of infancy or childhood.

It looks as if the need was to reconcile my awareness of my character—that is to say, my character as I think I know it—with my conception of a desirable character. But 'desirable character' is merely meaning a character that would be desired. And the character that is desired turns out to be a character that is desired. In short I must feel loved by myself and others.

Here I think I see I have linked up with the discussion of socialism and narcissism [*see* 31 January/1 February 1960, p. 122]. I wish to feel that when I love and admire myself I am also loved and admired by the group. Well, why not?

I now have a picture of myself called on by the chairman to say something in the Society. But I decline, as I have nothing to say. And everyone thinks how modest I am—except a few people, who are puzzled. This is probably what is called a day dream, but it might be called a night dream with greater approximation to descriptiveness of its content. In fact I think this is what I mean by an α-element. If this is so, and the visual images and pictures I have mentioned so far are examples of them, then the dream-work-α may be a more stately process than I realized, and the α-elements are more slowly produced.

But I think there may be more. I noticed just now that I had a vision of Mrs A unable to have visual images while doing her auto-analysis; I might easily have failed altogether to notice it. In that case, the α-elements may be produced far more rapidly and incessantly than I realize. I wonder if dreams, i.e. the actual emotional experiences, are not the emotional experiences I do not have, or cannot allow myself to have, during wakefulness. They then have to be retained, if I am to learn from the experience, by being converted through dream-work-α into α-elements, and then these α-elements are combined according to certain rules to make them approximate to what in daytime wakefulness would be narrative of the event in which I am participating and which I need to record.

I could schematize it thus:

Emotional experience → dream-work-α → α-elements → rationalization and 'narrativization' → dream
Sensation of waking event in which personality is participating as in an unfolding narrative → dream-work-α → α-elements → dream-thoughts

A comparison of the two levels suggests that some kind of approximation is being attempted between an awareness of an external event and an internal process of manipulation, 'digestion', of the same event. In the first case the origin can be taken to lie in an emotional experience, associated with dream-thoughts, leading to an awareness that then has to be dealt with (like any other emotional experience, no matter what the origin) by dream-work-α which converts it into α-elements; these then undergo a process of narrativization to make them approximate to the emotional experiences of waking life in which the personality is participating in a temporal sequence that accordingly has a narrative quality, so that the emotional experience originating in dream-thought is rendered suitable for storage and waking conscious thought. In the second case the emotional experience in which the personality is consciously participating as a temporal sequence in which one event succeeds another (thus having a narrative quality) is being worked on by dream-work-α to convert the sense impressions of the external narrative experience into α-elements that are capable of storage and lend themselves to use in dream-thoughts; these, though unconscious, proceed equally whether the personality is asleep or awake. One of the reasons why sleep is essential is to make possible, by a suspension of consciousness, the emotional experiences that the personality would not permit itself to have during conscious waking life, and so to bring them into reach of dream-work-α for conversion into α-elements and a narrative form, consecutive and dominated by a causation-theoretical outlook, suitable for being worked on by conscious rational processes of thought. Dream-work-α, and its product of α-elements, is therefore an essential link between dream-thought and conscious rational thought, and the raw material on which both have to work.

Free-floating attention, regarded as necessary in analytic work, might then be described as that state of mind in which the analyst allows himself the conditions in which dream-work-α can operate for the production of α-elements. The psychotic patient knows this and sets himself out specifically during the sessions to attack anything and everything that makes the production of α-elements possible either in himself or the analyst, or, for that matter, anyone else.

[Undated]

Need for study of scientific method

> Though we are aware that any knowledge at which we arrive is the result of a process on our part, we do not reflect on the nature of the process—at any rate in any systematic way—and make it the object of a special study. But sooner or later knowledge of our mistakes and the desire to be sure that we are getting the genuine article, i.e. something that is really knowledge, lead us to reflect on the process. We do so, prompted by the hope that we can discover the proper process, i.e. that in which we shall be safe from error, or at least to determine within what limits we can carry out such a process. But in the end we find ourselves having to ask whether we are capable of knowing at all and are not merely under the illusion of thinking that we can know.
>
> Prichard, 'History of the Theory of Knowledge', from *Knowledge and Perception*, 1932

Prichard points out that in ordinary life when we are seeking knowledge, our interest is chiefly absorbed in the nature of what we are trying to know, and not in the process by which we try to get to know it. It is probably true that most psycho-analysts are similarly absorbed in psycho-analysis rather than in the process by which we arrive at a knowledge of psycho-analysis. This preoccupation with the subject, to the over-shadowing of the study of the process by which it is learned, is excusable; for the subject is vast and there is much to learn. And yet one may permit oneself some surprise at this imbalance, for psycho-analysis itself may be seen as born of a doubt about the realities of the knowledge we have, and of the processes by which we obtain it. The central feature—the analysis the aspirant has to undergo—is imposed because it is supposed that without that experience the candidate's inadequacies relate to and prejudice the mental processes by which he acquires knowledge of his patient. Furthermore, psycho-analysis is itself a technique for the investigation of the human mind, and it can be said to have discovered—in the course of the work that culminated in Freud's paper on the 'Two Principles of Mental Functioning' [1911b, *SE 12*]—the origin of the elaboration of psycho-analysis itself, namely the pressure of inner needs that demand more than hallucinatory gratification. [Marginal comment added later: The demand is for the *reality*. A parallel quotation from Freud to balance Prichard would help.]

Nevertheless there has not yet been much work done relating psycho-analysis to the general body of scientific history, or its methodology to the elements common to the methodologies of all scientific discipline.

Criticism of psycho-analysis also applied to other sciences

It has been a common criticism of psycho-analysis that its methods are not scientific. It is therefore with some surprise that the student of psycho-analysis who turns to the study of scientific method in order to learn of the respects in which psycho-analysis, and his own method of practising it, falls short in scientific rigour and precision, finds that the scientific defects that are charged against psycho-analysis are observed by the more self-critical scientists in the practice of their own disciplines. It might be said that the history of mankind is full of instances of the kind of experience described in the quotation from Prichard [ibid., p. 151]—instances, that is to say, of the falsification of a theory followed usually by the questioning of the theory, but sometimes by the questioning of the methods by which the supposed knowledge was obtained. Plato's well-known description [*Republic, Book VII*], in which he likens mankind to men in a cave seated with their backs to the light, is a famous instance of overt expression of suspicion of the validity of knowledge based on the perceptions of men held in the cultural framework of a group. In more recent times, Hume's attack on the idea that the scientific hypothesis is based on anything other than the tendency of the human mind to associate various elements, did much to prevent the growth of an almost mystical belief that a 'natural law' was the statement of a truth that various elements were constantly conjoined because their conjunction was a function of some linking force parallel with, but independent of, the human tendency to see them as conjoined. Despite the somewhat wayward approach that Hume made to the problem, his insistence on the part played by association as a function of the human mind carried enough weight to be disturbing, notably to Kant, who felt impelled to refute him. Yet despite the vulnerability of Hume's attitude it is doubtful, in the opinion of some philosophers of science, whether Hume has ever been really answered (cf. Bertrand Russell, *History of Western Philosophy*).

At the moment I do not wish to go into this subject further than is necessary to indicate that historically there are two elements in what we now call scientific methodology that have a very considerable ancestry. One is recognizable today as the philosophical problem of perception centring on the difficulty of knowing what validity is to be attributed to our belief in the real existence of an entity that in fact can only be seen to be a deduction from sense data. The other is the belief in a contribution made to any hypothesis by some force variously though vaguely adumbrated, yet having enough precision to make a not wholly hazardous guess at its nature—as I hope to show. It is these two elements that make it appear to me to be worthwhile to approach phylogenetically a subject of which the psycho-analytic discussion by Freud provides the ontological counterpart. A further reason for making this twofold approach will, I hope, become apparent in my discussion of narcissism and the social component of the individual's instincts; for I want to show the great importance that the political nature of man (in Aristotle's sense) plays in all scientific methodology and in human personality problems as they are investigated through the agency of psycho-analysis in its operational conformity with scientific methodology.

This is perhaps the appropriate moment to draw attention to the fact that this discussion may be regarded throughout as the scientific methodology of psycho-analysis *and* the psycho-analysis of scientific methodology; my preference, in the interest of accuracy, is for it to be seen as both simultaneously.

I shall commence by making the phylogenetic approach. I prefer the term, 'phylogenetic', because I wish to avoid any suggestion that this is a historical summary. What it is will emerge in the course of the exposition, but I may say that my main object is to point to certain phenomena in the social history of the subject because they are germane to my argument, and not for any other reason.

The fate of the heliocentric theory

First I must draw attention to the uncertain fate of various ideas often well expressed and established in their time. Such a one is the heliocentric theory of the earth's movements, which was put forward by Aristarchus of Samos and attested by Archimedes and Plutarch. It appears to have 'disappeared'—as far as any practical influence it had—until it was put forward again nearly two thousand years later by Copernicus. This fact merits attention by any scientist: here we have a hypothesis that we now suppose to be true because it is attested by the correlation of many findings. It could have been verified by observation, yet it was completely displaced by another hypothesis. It is true that the equipment did not then exist for any profound verification, but this does not explain the establishment of a geocentric theory unless we assume the importance of a phenomenon to which I shall draw attention later, but which I shall not anticipate now. (The observational equipment lacking telescopes meant that verification was carried out by techniques that favoured the geocentric view and did nothing to support the heliocentric view in a way that made public-ation possible, and so denied the heliocentric view the support of 'common' sense.)

Relationship between cosmology and phantasy

The lack of means for establishing the reality of the earth's movement round the sun as a factual counterpart of the heliocentric theory meant that there was freedom to entertain views that appeared to be supported by the observations available to the ordinary individual, and at the same time enabled those observations to correspond with certain classes of internal phantasy, and for certain classes of internal phantasy to be externalized to the exclusion of others. Or I should say that certain phantasies could then be externalized by virtue of the geocentric cosmology, leaving others to be given some different outlet. This state of affairs is common to all cosmologies and not simply to those existing during the dominance of a particular school of thought. I wish to emphasize that while it is true that internal phantasies play a very big part in supporting a given scientific view, or even in precipitating its adumbration, the traffic is two-way, and the view that the community holds on what it quite reasonably regards as scientific grounds dictates what phantasies are to be externalized in the prevalent cosmology, and what phantasies are to achieve some other outlet. A little thought will show the seriousness of this situation.

Consequences

Let us suppose—and what follows is only intended to be a postulate—that the geocentric view makes it easier to externalize a phantasy of the superiority of the all-providing breast or mother. Then the phantasy of the dominance of the male would need to find a means of externalization in some activity—scientific, political, aesthetic or religious—that lent itself to such externalization.

My object in making this postulate is not to establish a hypothesis that lends itself to particularization and thence to formulation in terms that make empirical verification possible; the time is not ripe for that. My object is to indicate that in addition to the obvious importance of establishing correct methodology—because only in that can we approximate to confidence in the kind of knowledge our methods win for us and so achieve a corresponding and proportional freedom from errors that might be disastrous—there is the fact that our methods are prey to forces derived from a class of phenomena of which little is known but which it is very much the business of psycho-analysts to study. I refer to the phenomena associated with the need to establish a particular scientific view for the greater ease in externalization of one particular class of phantasies, and the further associated phenomena that derive from existent cosmology—the phantasies to which it allows an outlet in externalization, and the phantasies which its existence compels to seek some other outlet of externalization. I suggest that there is a vested interest in the maintenance of an existent cosmology, or for that matter any existent scientific deductive system, which derives from manifold sources but with only two of which I wish to concern myself here. One is scientific and realistic—as for example that seen in the maintenance of Newtonian Laws even after the behaviour of Mercury's perihelion had shown them to be inadequate, but there was no Einstein to propound a relativity theory to take their place—and the other is emotional and relates to group and individual phantasies. It is notorious that there is the strongest resistance to the upsetting of an established scientific deductive system, even though that system was itself feared, hated, and opposed at its inception.

The meaning of 'scientific deductive system'

By the term, 'scientific deductive system', I mean any system of hypotheses in which certain hypotheses occupy a high level in the particular system, and are used as premises from which lower-level hypotheses are deduced. Lower-level hypotheses are of decreasing generalization until the lowest level of all, which have a degree of particularization that makes them suitable for verification by empirical experience such as scientific experiments, or, in the case of psycho-analysis, clinical experience. Although it is not a matter of immediate moment, I consider it of great importance that there should be established a calculus that represents the scientific deductive system, and in all cases where the scientific deductive system is represented by the associated calculus I include calculus and scientific deductive system as essential to each other; unless otherwise stated, I wish it to be assumed that when I speak of a scientific deductive system I refer to it and the associated calculus that represents it.

[Undated]

Commentary on the scientific deductive system

(1) Destruction of the capacity for assimilation of sense impressions is not total in any analysable patient. The non-psychotic part of the personality is associated with the continued functioning of the capacity for assimilation of sense impressions.

(2) The word, 'assimilation', is not employed as a technical term.

(3) 'Sense impressions' here bears the ordinary meaning, but without the implications that the term carries in everyday use, and which will be seen to be specifically excluded by the theories concerned with the psychotic part of the personality.

(4 & 5) 'Phenomenon' and 'thing-in-itself' are terms used in the Kantian sense to mean things as they appear to the observer, and things as they might be supposed to be in reality without an observer. 'Things-in-themselves' has much the same meaning as Bradley ascribes (in *Principles of Logic*) to the term, 'things in actuality'.

(6) The term, 'object', is chosen partly because it carries a sense of concreteness, partly because it is sufficiently abstract to allow me to invest it with a special meaning. Yet this special meaning is difficult to convey. The patient uses a word, but his word does not name the same thing as is named by the same word used by the analyst, or even as used by the non-psychotic part of the patient's personality. He appears to feel that the word is not the name of a phenomenon nor yet the name of the thing-in-itself, but is *identical* with the thing-in-itself. Unfortunately, this is further complicated by the fact that the thing-in-itself seems to be regarded by

the patient with the same expectation that we entertain for an idea. Thus, if someone moves a table, it is to him as if someone had interfered with his mind. It is for a word thus used that I reserve the term, 'object'; it is identical with bizarre objects, but I mistook their origin (*see* 'Differentiation of the Psychotic from the Non-Psychotic Personalities', 1957).

(7) The essential point of this hypothesis is made by the words, 'as words are ordinarily articulated'. The statement can be made to appear almost tautological if it is remembered that the words are, as I have said, objects and therefore do not lend themselves to procedures appropriate to the ordinary use of words. The essence of 'articulation', as used here, is that it is a name for the process of bringing elements together, integrating them, so that the combined parts form a complex whole. The meaning I attach to the word will be clearer if its use is contrasted with that of 'agglomeration', which I discuss below. The further problem of the justification for such a view will also be discussed in the usage of the term, 'agglomeration'.

(8) The words used as those objects that are ordinarily called feelings are those terms employed in ordinary speech that the mathematical logician, J. H. Woodger (in *Technique of Theory Construction,* p. 10), calls 'statement-forming assignatory functors' and includes amongst the class of logical constants. But the mathematical logician is attempting by abstraction to gain in precision a method of communication that is more exact than that of ordinary speech. This hypothesis, on the contrary, is concerned with a method of communication and thought that is quite different from that of ordinary speech and employs words incidentally, not essentially.

(9) Intensity is expressed proportionately to the violence of the muscular movement. Verbal expression is incidental to the central feature, which is the change of musculature evidenced by the tongue and vocal cords in movement; for this reason a stammer cannot be interpreted without reference to

the muscular movements that give rise to the sounds. The sounds are important, but they are incidental to the movement of tongue, lips, and vocal cords. For this reason the analyst is well advised, in attempting to interpret a stammer, to intuit the muscular movements involved and to ask himself what they portend; he should not be misled by the sounds made into devoting his exclusive attention to them. The whole topic of muscular movement under the dominance of the pleasure principle, as it is described by Freud (motor discharge), is apposite in this discussion.

(10) The use of the term, 'agglomeration', is liable to give rise to misunderstanding, unless it is remembered that it is appropriate to a particular situation when that situation is viewed by the light of a particular hypothesis and during the time it is so viewed. For since the analyst is concerned to find a fresh standpoint that affords him a hypothesis giving meaning to the phenomena presenting themselves to his scrutiny, in so far as he is successful in doing this he will be successful in making what (from one point of view) seems to be an agglomeration into what (from the point of view of his new hypothesis) is seen to possess a kind of integration. This in fact is what happens if the theory I am here propounding is applied to this very phenomenon of agglomeration.

11. The emotions and feelings may appear to have a direct relationship to the analyst. An angry patient mentioning the words, 'train' and 'policeman', may at a superficial view be angry with the analyst. In fact the anger joins the 'train' and the 'policeman'. The relationship with the analyst is as described in (9) above.

12. Projective identification is the name given by Melanie Klein to her discovery of a mechanism by which the patient splits off a part of his personality and projects it into an external object. The part may be regarded as good or bad; it retains its identity in its new habitat and is felt to control the person or thing into which it is projected; the part thus rejected by the patient is felt now to be persecutory to him. At the

same time the mechanism—in so far as it is felt to be actual and not an omnipotent phantasy—leads the patient, being still identified with the split-off part, to feel confused with the person or thing into which he has projected this part of himself. This very brief summary is intended to be a reminder only: the full meaning of the term can only be sought by reference to the totality of Melanie Klein's work in which the theory and its implications are worked out.

* * *

Unassimilated sense impressions (Phase D)

i. The destruction (1) of capacity for assimilation (2) of sense impressions (3) does not impair retention of the sense impressions. They are stored and are available; but they are felt by the patient to be indistinguishable from phenomena (4) or things-in-themselves (5). They are devoid of relatedness to other retained sense impressions.

ii. The stored unassimilated sense impressions appear in the patient's communications to the analyst as objects (6) which are given a name, the name usually being a word in common use.

iii. These objects cannot be articulated (7) as words are ordinarily articulated.

iv. The intensity of the patient's feelings appears in the analysis as muscular movements, changes in mien, changes in posture, attitude. The feelings are contained in words; the words are not names of the feelings, but are felt to be the feelings themselves. The words employed for this purpose are those in articulated speech to suggest relatedness, such as 'and', 'with', 'in', 'outside', and all verbs (8).

v. Changes in musculature and varied expressions discriminate intensity of feeling, but not one feeling from another (9). They are intended to effect evacuation of accretions of stimuli.

vi. The feelings are objects no matter in which guise they appear in the analysis.

vii. What appears to be an articulated sentence is an agglomeration (10) of objects, and is therefore not to be distinguished from the agglomeration manifest to the analyst as apparently inarticulate or incoherent speech.

viii. All emotion, however expressed, whether in words or changes in musculature—such as is evidenced by a smile or stammer or attitude—is the link (11) between other objects, and has no reference to an external person or thing.

ix. The analyst remains as real and not an aspect of the patient himself, only as a necessity demanded by the exigencies of projective identification (12).

x. The agglomeration (itself a whole object but differing so fundamentally from what is usually subsumed under the term, 'whole object', that it is undesirable to use it in this context) is intended to be a vehicle suitable for conveyance by projective identification and is correspondingly amenable to the process of return to the personality ejecting it, either because he wills it or because the person or thing intended to harbour it forces it back into its owner.

xi. The objects formed by the process that excludes assimilation are amenable to the usages of a personality employing projective identification and its introjective counterpart, but do not lend themselves to any function other than evacuation and return.

xii. An object is useless except for its employment in projective identification.

xiii. Evacuation of emotion, evidenced by the absence of all connections that *are* emotions, leads to disintegration of the patient because that which holds the objects together is no longer available. This differs from splitting in that it is a passive falling apart of the objects.

* * *

Repair of capacity for contact
(Phase L)

1. Increasing strength of the ego leads to an increase in strength of the imprisoning capacity of the word which is the manifestation of the object that is a part of the ego contained in the word.
2. Because of 1, objects cannot fuse.
3. Because of 1, objects cannot link.
4. Owing to dominance of 2, objects cannot be agglomerated or articulated.
5. Failure of agglomeration and articulation increases sadism and thus initiates Phase D.
6. Phase D is suffused with frustration modification so that Phase L is reactivated.
7. Objects can now link.
8. The links are Death instincts and Life instincts.
9. Objects join destructively.
10. Objects join in sexual intercourse.

* * *

Repair of capacity for assimilation
(Phase A)

a. Repair of the capacity for assimilation is manifested in analysis by verbal statements that appear superficially to be disjointed free associations.
b. Though expressed verbally, they are a method of communication of visual images, auditory impressions, olfactory impressions, emotions.
c. The verbal statements are evidence of the production of material suitable for employment in dream-thought by a process analogous to dream-work in reverse.
d. The material for which these statements are the evidence has the character of the objects of Phase L, but they are capable

now of articulation with each other to form complete wholes, of storage and the concomitant notation, and of reproduction. They are consequently not suitable for projective identification.

e. These verbal statements are devoid of any element of personality; thus they contrast with the objects of Phase D which are indistinguishable from parts of the personality with which they are impregnated.

f. These verbal statements are transformations, still in the process of further transformation, of immediate sense impressions of immediate events. In this respect they are similar to the objects of Phase L, but differ in that they are in process of change associated with assimilation, whereas the objects of Phase D are in process of being ejected unchanged, or destroyed by splitting.

g. The dream-thought material represented by these verbal statements may be distinguished from the objects of Phase L by the fact of their integration one with another.

h. The integration is betrayed by the emergence of feelings of hate and fear of the analyst as super-ego, and trust in and affection for the analyst as a loved object.

j. Projective identification is seen to be employed in the conveyance of whole objects—not simply fragments.

k. The dreams that are reported carry associations that the patient can communicate.

* * *

A. The destructive splitting of the super-ego involves destruction of the capacity for assimilation of all phenomena of internal and external reality.

B. The projective identification of the phenomena leads to an impoverishment and weakening of the personality to a point at which annihilation of the personality is felt to be imminent.

C. The destruction of the capacity for assimilation leads to a deprivation of the personality of all elements necessary for development, thus producing a mental state analogous to the physiological state of starvation, and an augmentation of fears of imminent annihilation.

D. Dread of annihilation forces an attempt at repair of the capacity for assimilation and, *pari passu,* an increased impulse towards destruction of the capacity for assimilation, since such increased capacity is associated with the production of material for dream-thought (Phase A, b. & c.) and therefore of awareness of the super-ego (Phase A, h.).

E. Predominance of life instinct over death instinct leads to dominance of the impulse to repair the capacity for assimilation (Phase A).

F. Similarly, should death instincts predominate, the destruction of the capacity for assimilation becomes dominant (Phase D, i.).

G. In so far as life instincts predominate, Phase A comes into operation.

H. In view of the fact that Phase A involves the restoration of the super-ego (Phase A, h.), the attempts at repair of the capacity for assimilation only take place in the presence of the analyst who, as the trusted object brought into view by the presence of predominant life instincts, is felt as a barrier against annihilation—despite fear of him induced by reparation of the super-ego associated with the sub-dominant death instincts.

I. Following H., the phenomena of Phase A, f. become evident—that is to say, the transformation of the patient's sense impressions of the events currently taking place in the analysis.

J. A. and C. lead to an inability to dream.

K. The dominance of life instincts (E.) forces the use of dream-thoughts (D.) for the production of dreams.

L. For the reasons given in H., the patient is able only to dream in the presence of the analyst, and so there come into operation sessions that are indistinguishable from dreams from which a person is unable to awake; or, alternatively, sessions in which the patient resorts to the forced rationality of wakefulness.

M. Should the patient's fear be too intense, or his capacity for tolerating it be too small, he will compromise (K.) and produce, instead of an actual state of dreaming, either a consciously contrived dream or a hallucination of a dream.

N. The contrived or hallucinated dream is a compromise between K. and c.

O. The contrived or hallucinated dream can yield no associations, in this respect appearing to be defective in the domain of mental life in a manner analogous to the defects of the hallucinated breast in its inability to supply what the real breast supplies.

P. In contrast with the dream of L., the contrived or hallucinated dream of O. can be interpreted to display its qualities but not its content, for it has none that can be elicited.

Q. In contrast with the contrived or hallucinated dream of O., the dream of L. can be interpreted to display its content as well as its characteristic peculiarity distinguishing it from non-psychotic dreams.

R. Both the dreams of L. and O. must be distinguished from dreams reported as such by the patient.

[Undated—1960]

Analytic technique

More than one patient has said my technique is not Kleinian. I think there is substance in this. I would put it as follows: I consider that the behaviour of the patient is a palimpsest in which I can detect a number of layers of conduct. Since all those I detect must, by that very fact, be operating, conflicts are bound to occur through the conflicting views obtaining contemporaneous expression. In this way, the conflict that is so important to the patient's sufferings and to theories of dynamic psychology is, according to me, accidental and secondary to two different views of the same situation.

Winnicott says patients *need* to regress: Melanie Klein says they *must not*: I say they *are* regressed, and the regression should be observed and interpreted by the analyst without any need to compel the patient to become totally regressed before he can make the analyst observe and interpret the regression. But by itself my theory will not do. That is to say that the patient feels he gains by being able to say, for example, "I am only a junior analyst". It seems to me that stated as I have stated it, it does not give due weight to the transference—and this is the objection that would be made. But it could, I think, easily prove only to be a matter of adjustment.

27 March 1960

Technique: meaning and interpretation of associations

There is a value, when listening to the associations, in making a mental distinction between the *meaning* of the associations and their *interpretation*. The patient says, "I went on Hampstead Heath yesterday and did some bird-watching".

Taking the meaning first:

1. Does he mean he was scrutinizing their sex life?
2. Or is it an attempt to describe getting into the hands of the police by behaving in a suspicious way?
3. Or does he mean he has at last taken some exercise?

And so on with other speculations. Then, having decided that point, what is the interpretation?

In conjunction with the rest of the analysis together with current transference, the preceding associations and the meaning as decided above, you finally produce the interpretation.

[Undated—1960]

Scientific deductive system

How would a s.d.s. be produced for analytic theory? Can there be anything analogous to the 'law of gravitation'? It seems possible to produce a series of formulas that might succinctly express schizophrenia. Let us try it in the way that Braithwaite did it:

First, I think, must come the rules of the 'game'. But do the rules then come from the nature of the subject? Yes: that would seem to be the common sense of it. What are the rules of psycho-analytical schizophrenia? I jot down a few at random as they occur to me.

1. The patient always attends at the stated time and place. Analyst like-wise—or is it so? Sometimes it sounds as if that is not so. Perhaps in this respect the analyst is free to do just what he chooses.
2. The patient pays his fees regularly.
3. Analyst and patient are freely interchangeable.

These seem adequate for a start, but I could add two more.

4. The patient can do what he likes.
5. The analyst must give only strictly accurate interpretations.

But these are rules of the psycho-analytical game. We want rules of a s.d.s. Are they the same? Should the rules relate instead to Kleinian theory? There is no reason why they should not relate to any or all of these things.

[Undated—1960]

The painful component

The solution of any problem must be regarded as having been faulty in the first instance if the consequence is neurosis. And yet the solution was a victory for right, moral right; and the victory consolidated the 'rightness' and morality of the part of the personality that triumphed. The triumphant part is included in the super-ego; it is the morality of the super-ego that is challenged, just as it is the 'id-ity' of the id that is challenged by the super-ego. The pain of readjustment consists in having to admit that the 'unworthy' part of the personality was right. The 'wicked' triumph—but make things worse by triumphing on the home ground as it were, in the realm of morality itself. The victorious aspect of the personality writes the history books, but the victorious side varies considerably from time to time. Unsaleable books, unreadable and unread papers do not constitute a social component; the thinker *must* be a man of action. The physical act of writing and carrying through all the other acts, up to and including public-ation, constitutes being a man of action *for the writer*.

[Undated—1960]

The synthesizing function of mathematics

If a formula, or rather a calculus, is available, it may bring order to events that otherwise appear to lack any relationship. Thus a patient makes two remarks, and then makes two more; they appear to be entirely without any connecting link. It could be said that the two remarks, together with the other two remarks, make four remarks, and therefore that these facts could be seen to be related to each other in that together they made four facts. But it would be very unlikely that the mathematical application had served to effect the illumination of a relatedness of any consequence. Nor is it easy to see how, as things are at present, any calculus that has been constructed, or is likely to be constructed in the near future, would illuminate the relatedness of a series of disjointed associations of the kind with which we are familiar in analysis, particularly perhaps in the analysis of a psychotic patient. Moreover, it has to be remembered that we are always concerned with seeing the relatedness of the apparently disjointed and unconnected aspect of the elements in the analytic situation; the observation that two remarks and two other remarks make four remarks produces no flash of recognition because it effects no illumination of the point of intersection between paranoid–schizoid and depressive positions.

I use this phrase deliberately so as to emphasize a peculiarity in the use I am making of these two Kleinian concepts. I am here regarding them as comprising classes of events, and I am suggesting that no interpretation is of value unless at the moment at which it is given it involves, partly through the element of contrast which is inseparable from the juxtaposition, the illumination of the disorder of scattered, familiar, and apparently unrelated elements, and the order, cohesion, and relatedness of those same elements. Furthermore, this interpretation is not psycho-analytically effective unless, when given, it is common sense, i.e. one that involves agreement in two or more senses in the analyst and the patient, and between the analyst and patient in whom these senses are in accord. Judged by these criteria, the suggested 2 + 2 interpretation can be seen to break down because it is so unlikely that it will serve the function of intersection between the two classes represented by the paranoid–schizoid and depressive positions.

* * *

Causation

The cause is that fact which is selected to give coherence to elements whose relationship to each other is either not perceived, or else seen to be such that it is irrelevant or inimical to the scientific deductive system of the beholder. In particular, the hypotheses that act as premises to the system, together with the beholder's common sense and the elements for which a cause is to be found, are brought together so that time is shown to link the elements to each other and not to separate them. It is intended to refute or deny the idea or possibility that time separates one element from another, just as in other contexts it may be desired to find a fact that demonstrates the coherence of elements that otherwise might be supposed to be separated rather than linked by space.

It is not, therefore, that there are many different opinions as to the cause of a certain event, but many different scientific deductive systems and therefore many different elements that can be selected as the intersection of the class, 'cause', and the class, 'effect'.

[Undated]

Communication

I Importance of communication as a link between related objects

> Knowledge of modern discoveries relating to logic would dispel a good deal of the prevailing confusion (which shows itself from time to time in controversies that disfigure the pages of Nature) concerning . . .
>
> [J. H. Woodger, *International Encyclopaedia of Unified Science*, vol. 2, No. 5, p. 3]

The complaint is as old as the story of the Tower of Babel, and so is the wish that the problem might be solved, if in no other way, by divine intervention (as in the 'Acts of the Apostles', II, v) or by simultaneous translation (as at international congresses), or by a discipline of rigorous mathematical logic (as is proposed in the article from which I have taken my quotation).

Psycho-analysis does not allow one to suppose that the mechanics of communication operating through a universal language—whether that language is a universally known natural language, or an artificially produced language such as Esperanto, or the formulations of mathematicians, or the notation of musicians, or even the 'universal linguistic' of art itself, the content rather than the vehicle of the content—will be likely to rid us of disfiguring controversy in our attempts to co-operate in scientific achievement. But psycho-analytic experience shows that even the attempt to deal with individual tensions has not been, and is not likely to be, successful in abolishing this controversy.

If the major problem were only the 'disfiguring' nature of controversy, the matter would be painful and worth investigation, but in fact far more serious issues are involved than the emergence of phenomena that disfigure the image that men wish to have of those of their number set apart as leaders of scientific and intellectual ability and integrity. So many controversies are wasteful and manifestly, from the outset, unlikely to issue in any clarification of the matters in dispute; the feature of almost all scientific controversy is the impotence of the disputants who show an inability to meet each other's contentions because they cannot communicate thesis or antithesis.

Language has been invented; translation can be achieved; musical and mathematical notations exist; men compose and paint. And now psycho-analysis attempts to elucidate the barriers and links that hinder or promote the relationships that require a capacity for communication. Nevertheless, the success of psycho-analysis lies so far not so much in bringing communication nearer, as in showing unmistakably the feebleness of our methods of communication even in the communication of disagreement. But this does not touch a yet graver issue, namely the problem of communication with our successors, for it would appear on the surface that if we cannot communicate with our contemporaries, we are even less likely to be able to communicate with our successors. If this communication cannot be made, the future development of analysis is imperilled and the successful discoveries made so far could be lost to the world. That this can happen is evidenced in the fate of the heliocentric theories of Aristarchus which seemed to be so clearly propounded that there could be no reason for their disappearance. As surprising and as inexplicable is the apparent disappearance of the meaning of a whole culture when the Bulgar state was captured by the Grand Duke of Moscow in 1431.

I hope I have made clear the central importance of communication in scientific method, and why there is prima facie reason to approach scientific method by this channel; the investigation will involve discussion of the psychology of the individual as an individual and as a member of a group. It will also involve appeal to many facets of human endeavour with which I am not competent to deal; but I hope that I may make sufficient headway to indicate the nature of a problem that others may be able and willing to investigate.

II *Does such a link exist in mathematics or music? The problem created by change of environment*

How is it that mathematics and music are able to find a method of communication? Or is it illusory in the sense that we can reproduce the sounds the composer intended to hear, and yet do not in fact experience what he and his contemporaries experienced when they heard the same sounds, so that the disappearance—through inability to record the essence, only its outward trappings—is as complete in the music of Bach as it is in the culture of Byzantium or in the recorded history, say, of Hubert de Burgh, of whose actions and sayings we may know all we need, but of whose thoughts and spirit we know nothing? [Powicke, *King Henry III and the Lord Edward.*]

It seems hardly possible: at least one feels that even if such a loss is admitted, the mathematician and musician yet preserve far more than the psycho-analyst is able to do, or likely to be able to do, unless he can effect some radical change in his methods of communication.

It may be that the difficulty lies in a failure to grasp what are the features it is essential to communicate. Even if the analyst is fully possessed of material that he wishes to record because it is to him essential, it may be true that the material he fails to record, because to him it is obvious and axiomatic, is in fact only so because it is a part of his cultural climate and is therefore taken for granted. But suppose the cultural climate changes; then what he has recorded may well become meaningless because the key to it has gone with the change that has overtaken his civilization; regarding the cultural atmosphere of that civilization as permanent, he will have failed to pass on any record. Theoretically, I suppose he could record something that in his epoch was essential and meaningful, but which would be banal and unimportant to his successors. Suppose the god of the Christian religion came to be explicable—in all the manifestations attributed to him—as some perfectly satisfactorily demonstrable phenomenon of physical science, without the need of any mystical suppositions: would it be possible for those living under dominance of such cosmology to understand the religious music of Bach? In what sense could it be said that a Bach cantata had been adequately recorded and transmitted to the members of the new culture and civilization? It is clear that we may gain something from studying the means by which mathematicians and musicians and artists communicate, but not all that we could wish.

III What should be the content of the psycho-analytic communication?

Such vicissitudes as are secondary to unpredictable changes in culture we cannot guard against, but there still remains the lesser but important obligation to be sure that we are recording and communicating the essentials of our work, and not simply peripheral or accidental elements that we have mistaken for the essential. And here arises the problem: what in fact does happen in correct analysis? What is correct analysis, and what is the essential germ without which we have recorded virtually nothing? This is a grave problem and one that probably requires a concept of methodology to which science is a stranger. All existing concepts of methodology are already shaken by the advances of quantum mechanics, and it appears certain that methodology will in future have to reckon with a lowest level of hypotheses in a set—that is to say, a level formerly occupied by empirically verifiable data which consists of statistical hypotheses. I think it very doubtful that such a revolutionary change in outlook is revolutionary enough to meet the needs of scientific psycho-analysis. The only course open to us is to pursue the inquiry and see where it leads.

The first point to be decided is what it is that the psycho-analyst is to communicate, i.e. to embody in a notation that is precise and permanent. (I am not here considering the communications that are made in a session by the analyst's interpretations.)

Two people are in a room together, usually for fifty minutes at a time and for five sessions a week. We are concerned here with the account that is to be given of these proceedings by one of them—the analyst. What ought he to report? Can he know to whom the report is to be made—in the sense that he will have to vary his exposition to suit the needs of his audience and therefore should know what those needs are? Or is it possible to make a communication that will have value (by presupposing an abstraction, a conventional formulation that remains constant) for those to whom the communication is addressed? In the analysis of the psychotic it has been found valuable to suppose that all interpretations are addressed to a non-psychotic part of the personality even though there may appear to be little or no evidence for the existence of such a part. The navigator is able in certain circumstances to make use of an artificial horizon; can the analyst, communicating to other individuals, do the same? And if so, can he give a scientific description of the artefact that he proposes to use in this way? The artefact should be such that the formulations that are stimulated by a belief in its existence are lifted out of the vicissitudes suffered by any communication through the changes in convention and culture to which I have referred. This artefact (receptor) must be composed of characteristics that we assume to be immutable and outside the play of forces such as changes of civilization. I believe this artefact receptor will be found to be not very different from the 'non-psychotic part of the personality'. Certainly it would save trouble and confusion if it turned out to be the fact that the same hypothetical construct could be used in analytic practice as in a communication to an extra-analytic audience, and vice versa. For the present it is necessary only to consider such a constant in order to realize that the answer to the question, 'What is to be communicated?', cannot be considered without reference to such a construct. Superficially this can look like a demand for an answer to a question that depends for its answer on another question that has to be answered after reference to the answer to the first question. But this kind of dilemma is one to which we shall have to grow accustomed until a methodology is produced which releases psycho-analysis, and probably all other sciences, from the restrictions of a classical scientific method that is as inadequate to psycho-analytic needs as classical wave mechanics are to the needs of the quantum mechanical physicist.

IV What is the content to be?

Let us suppose that the receptor characteristics have already been elaborated and are known to us. (I shall later educe arguments showing my justification for such a procedure when I describe the α-function of dream-work, and the way in which α-elements are employed in dream-thought.) What is to be recorded and communicated? The answer is deceptively simple: the analyst must record and communicate what he has recorded and communicated. That is to say that if my intention is to record and communicate, then I have no choice in my subject matter; any departure in my report from what I have recorded and communicated makes my report a link in a relationship that is not scientific but belongs to some other category—not what I later call a K-link, but one belonging to a different class. Furthermore, it is addressed to the psychotic part of the personality by the psychotic part of the personality, however much this fact may be disguised by the employment, or the apparent employment, of non-psychotic mechanisms. Even a verbal statement that bears the stamp of rational persuasiveness will be found to be the vehicle for projective identification and to obtain any force and significance it has from its being so employed, and none—save deceptiveness—from its rational form and characteristics.

I am aware that my statement of content for the communication and record must seen to be either question-begging or platitudinous, but I believe that this will be seen not to be the case when we have penetrated more deeply into the subject.

Suppose now the receptor *and* the content of the communication: how is the record, and communication of the record and communication, to be effected? Before attempting any answer to this, we must note an ambiguity that has crept in. 'Record' has two different meanings: in one sense it means 'to receive a communication', and strictly speaking should refer to the way in which this is done; but it also means 'to store the communication received' in such a manner that it is available first of all when I want it, and secondly when (in this instance) the reader is ready to receive it.

V α-element

But I seem to have involved myself in some kind of contradiction. This is intended to be a scientific communication, and I have already expressed the view that as such it should be addressed to a hypothetical concept, the non-psychotic part of the personality which is endowed with certain unspecified immutable characteristics. I feel I am addressing it to an actual person—intelligent, friendly, engrossed in what I am writing and, to be frank, quite warmly appreciative of my effort. Analytic experience tells me this is really myself and that I shall be in for a rude awakening when I find out the real response. 'A rude awakening': am I then asleep? By no means. But this figure, these characteristics with which I have endowed it and you, might very well exist in a dream.

I propose to call this image an α-element. (This does not refer to its function as part of a phantasy; it applies only to the visual image itself.) The hypothetical concept, the 'non-psychotic part of the personality', I consider to be a version of the α-element which belongs to a level of increasing generalization in the hierarchy of hypotheses that form the theory to which both the α-element and the hypothetical concept belong. Conversely, the α-element approximates to a level of decreasing generalization, or increasing particularization, thus having a relationship with the hypothetical concept somewhat similar to that which exists between the level of empirically verifiable data and the hypotheses of the scientific deductive system related to it.

Can the relationship of the α-element to the hypothetical concept be described as more than 'somewhat similar' to that which exists between empirically verifiable data and the generalized hypotheses representing them? Could it be described as identical? For the present I think we are justified only in noting a certain similarity. The same similarity must likewise be noted, but left for later treatment, in the resemblance that the relationship between the α-element and the hypothetical concept of the non-psychotic part of the personality bears to the relationship between the hypotheses of quantum mechanical theory and the statistical hypotheses that appear, in this theory, to take the place of empirically verifiable data.

We must consider the possibility that in a scientific deductive system the appearance of bi-polarity that is presented by the hierarchical arrangement of a theory (with premises and high-level hypotheses of high generalization at one end, and low-level sets of empirically verifiable data of high degree of particularization at the other) must be replaced by something far more complex in which what I later call 'a selected fact' has grouped about it a constellation of elements in sets that are determined only by the nature of the link and its characteristic of being attached to the selected fact. In such a system the scientific deductive system would form only one set of elements, linked by the logic of the deductive system, and possessing the selected fact as one of its elements. But I feel that we must not attempt to proceed further before examining in greater detail some of the statements I have made, and the concepts that I have been compelled to introduce without adequate explanation.

VI Dream-work-α

Psycho-analysts, and Freud in particular, have described how the dreamer compresses, distorts, displaces and disguises the dream-thoughts in such a way that the manifest content of the dream bears little apparent resemblance to what he calls the 'latent content' of the dream, namely that content which is revealed by interpretation. This transformation of dream-thought into manifest content is, Freud says, brought about by dream-work. I wish now to employ this term to describe a related but different series of phenomena. To avoid confusion with the concept already established in psycho-analytic usage, and to avoid inventing a term that introduces—by virtue of its penumbra of already existing associations—implications I would prefer to exclude, I propose for my purposes to modify Freud's term by calling it 'dream-work-α'. What I propose to designate by this term I shall now relate.

In the state of mind of relaxed attention necessary in making observations, the individual is able through his senses to establish contact with his environment. He is aware of his sensations and could, if required, describe what they are—as I, for example, can describe the colour of the paper on which I write, my hand holding the pen, and so on. Similarly you, the reader, can make observations of your experience as you read the word printed on the page. I shall not in this inquiry consider the individual who had a defect that prevents his experiencing even this degree of contact with his environment, but I shall consider the individual who is able to make sensory contact and yet seems quite unable to learn from the experience; for such a patient enables me to observe, by contrast, a more usual chain of events of which I might otherwise remain unaware. This chain of events, as far as I am able to tell, is something like this: suppose I am talking to a friend who asks me where I propose to spend my holiday; as he does so, I visualize the church of a small town not far from the village in which I propose to stay. The small town is important because it possesses the railway station nearest to my village. Before he has finished speaking, a new image has formed, and so on.

The image of the church has been established on a previous occasion—I cannot now tell when. Its evocation in the situation I am describing would surprise no one, but what I now wish to add may be more controversial. I suggest that the experience of this particular conversation with my friend, and this particular moment of the conversation—not simply his words but the totality of that moment of experience—is being perceived sensorially by me and converted into an image of that particular village church.

I do not know what else may be going on, though I am sure that much more takes place than I am aware of. But the transformation of my sense impressions into this visual image is part of a process of mental assimilation. The impressions of the event are being re-shaped as a visual image of that particular church, and so are being made into a form suitable for storage in my mind.

By contrast, the patient might have the same experience, the same sense impressions, and yet be unable to transform the experience so that he can store it mentally. But instead, the experience (and his sense impressions of it) remains a foreign body; it is felt as a 'thing' lacking any of the quality we usually attribute to thought or its verbal expression.

To the first of these products, that of dream-work-α, I propose to give the name, 'α-element'; to the second, the unassimilated sense impression, 'β-element'. It may be wondered why I should need to consider β-elements at all in an inquiry into scientific method if they are a characteristic of a disturbed personality. My reason is that while I have been led to observe β-elements through treating disturbed patients, their occurrence is by no means restricted to their use by disturbed individuals—as I hope I shall presently show.

If my contention is correct, the production of α-elements is of the first importance: on an adequate supply of these elements depends the capacity for what Freud calls 'unconscious waking thinking', the ability to entertain and use dream-thoughts, the capacity for memory, and all the functions of the apparatus that Freud tentatively suggests come into existence with the dominance of the reality principle ('Two Principles of Mental Functioning' [1911b, *SE 12*]).

The β-elements are characteristic of the personality during the dominance of the pleasure principle: on them depends the capacity for non-verbal communication, the individual's ability to believe in the possibility of ridding himself of unwanted emotions, and the communication of emotion within the group.

The α-elements may be presumed to be mental and individual, subjective, to a high degree personal, particular, and unequivocally belonging to the domain of epistemology in a particular person. The example I have given of the visual image of the church is to a high degree particular, and must be regarded as belonging to the lowest level of empirically verifiable data. In the context in which I have cited it, it is not even a symbol, although once the individual has experienced such a visual image there is nothing to prevent its appearance in other contexts fulfilling the functions usually associated with symbols. What I wish to emphasize is that its character as an α-element is its suitability for employment in dream-thought and unconscious waking thinking, and not the way in which it may be employed. I may have more to say about the characteristics of the α-element that make it suitable for use as a symbol or an ideogram, but for the present I emphasize its character as an element—an irreducibly simple object.

I may make my point clearer by drawing attention to the last sentence in which I have had to call an α-element an irreducibly simple 'object'. The term, 'object', carrying with it the association of a subject, and being in any case a word referring to a word, is more complex and less elemental than the α-element. It is as if, in order to state how simple, lacking in complexity and elemental (not elementary) an α-element is, I had to say it was something far more complex which is derived, through a process in the mind, from α-elements. The impasse is similar to that of the quantum mechanics physicist whose knowledge of elementary particles depends on methods too gross to detect them. In this instance the verbal description perforce employs terms that are too complex and refers to ideas when the discussion is of something altogether simpler.

The function of dream-work-α is to produce something that bears a relationship to an idea that is analogous to the relationship an elementary particle bears to an atom in physics. The function of the α-element with which we are concerned in a discussion of scientific method, is its key position in the apparatus by which the individual learns anything. Similarly, the function of the β-element which concerns us is in communication within a group.

Without α-elements it is not possible to know anything. Without β-elements it is impossible to be ignorant of anything: they are essential to the functioning of projective identification; any unwanted idea is converted into a β-element, ejected from the personality, and then becomes a fact of which the individual is unaware, though he may be aware of feelings of persecution stimulated by it.

I reserve the term, 'knowledge', for the sum total of α- and β-elements. It is a term that therefore covers everything the individual knows and does not know. As I use it, the term must not be supposed to imply the existence of a thing in itself called 'knowledge'; it is a name for a postulate that has no actuality; there is no corresponding 'realization' in the sense that abstract mathematical systems may have one or more concrete realizations. 'Knowledge', in my sense, will thus be seen to appertain purely to the realm of epistemology. In my use of the term it is nonsensical to talk of knowledge of astronomy, or of there being any actuality corresponding to a term, 'astronomical knowledge', other than in the sense of α- and β-elements employed by the individual in his relationship with a domain of facts.

We have now approached this difficulty: the α-elements are, by definition, indispensable to the apparatus that enables the individual to know something. But they are also what he knows in that they are elements of assimilated sense data; they are his knowledge. This may not appear to be a difficulty if we state it in some such terms as, 'We use our knowledge and experience to gain more knowledge and experience'. But there is a difficulty that I wish to make apparent, and I can do this best by supposing a phase to exist—if we go back far enough in the individual's life—in which there is no knowledge, i.e. no α-elements or β-elements.

It may well be that this early learning, or first stage of any learning, is effected by dream-work-α on the one hand, and the mechanism of projective identification on the other. This supposes that the β-elements can be employed when α-elements do not exist, and the α-elements are a later stage of β-elements—that is to say that dream-work-α operates on β-elements and not directly on sense data. There is also evidence to support a theory that β-elements are employed, or felt to be employed, as projectiles so that they are planted in an object which perhaps submits them to a transformation by its dream-work-α apparatus before the projecting personality re-introjects them. But although these possibilities offer a way out of the difficulty—and indeed are, I believe, more than possibilities—they do not cover a mechanism in which the α-element is used to explore the emotional experience in which the person finds himself.

August 1960

α

It is advisable to revert to the patient's dream over and over again—elaboration 1, 2, 3 . . . *n*; but not simply as dreams to be interpreted and related to a stimulus. *They must be related to the dream-work that the stimulus has stimulated.* How is this to be done? It may be easiest with the psychotic patient, for with him there is more chance of being able to see the stimulus, i.e. the consulting room scene itself, and his dream-work reaction to that situation. In particular it would seem necessary at first to make a distinction between α and projective identification—or at least to show that 'excessive projective identification' means projective identification to the exclusion of other methods of dream-work-α. The methods of dream-work-α are not the same as those of dream-work which is related to interpretation of dreams, but are the *reciprocal* of dream-work and are related to the capacity to dream, i.e. to transform into dream, events that are grasped only on a rational, conscious level. In this way α is the reciprocal of dream-work. Furthermore, it suggests that the element of 'resistance' in dream-work, as elucidated by Freud, is a compound of two elements: resistance, as described by Freud; and a felt need to convert the conscious rational experience into dream, rather than a felt need to convert the dream into conscious rational experience. The 'felt need' is *very* important; if it is not given due significance and weight, the true dis-ease of the patient is being neglected; it is obscured by the analyst's insistence on interpretation of the dream.

[Undated—1960]

α
and paranoid–schizoid position

To what extent is the constant transition from paranoid–schizoid to depressive position and back again the essential mechanism of learning throughout life? As I listen to a patient, am I not all the time thinking that I see 'the point', and then rejecting it to reassume paranoid–schizoid? And is this not a kind of regurgitation? A chewing of the contemplative cud? Should that not be the visual image—a cow, milk-and-calf producer, chewing the cud? It means then that in the chaos of unconnected incoherent facts I see 'the point'—the selected fact. If I am wise, I reject it and reassume chaos. I select another fact, or the same one. I reject it and reassume paranoid–schizoid position. And may not this also give rise to situations in which the patient appears enviously to reject an interpretation that he accepted the day before? (Melanie Klein, *Envy and Gratitude,* p. 69.) That is to say that as well as envy it may be an example of failure to return to paranoid–schizoid, and a wish to make the *analyst* do so; *he* has to feel that the whole of the mass of discrete objects has again lost its coherence and cohesion.

The difficulty that the schizophrenic patient has in extricating himself from a state of mind means that he tends to have great difficulty in the rapid change from Ps to D that is necessary for α. This contributes to the analyst's impression of lack of progress because the slowness of oscillation hinders realization of oscillation. That is to say that the successful interpretation brings relief but takes the patient into the depressive position and confronts him with yet wider vistas of uncoordinated elements. In the next session he starts where he left off—he can do nothing towards returning to Ps and back to D. In other words, he is displaying a slowness of reaction comparable with the slowness of change at the beginning of analysis when the same mood may remain unchanged for months.

Dream-work-α

To what extent is myth-making an essential function of α? It may be that the sense impression has to be transformed to make it suitable material for dream-thought, but that it is the function of dream-thought to use the material put at its disposal by α, the units of dream-thoughts so to speak, in order to produce myths.

Myths must be defined; they must be communicable and have some of the qualities of common sense—one might call them 'common non-sense'.

Dream-work and α

The episode of the rain storm has emerged at different times in fragments. Rain—without a raincoat—taking the only taxi—pneumonia feared for me—self in rain at my house.

Then there was his account of the baby with a horn on its nose—some cowl on its head—his wife and blood—shambles.

There was his dream of his other self. This was coherent and might be an account of what I had said to him in a session. If so, it is almost accurate, but I am his other self and it is called a dream.

What do I know about all this? Virtually nothing. It is hardly even true to say that I know he said it, because although I was present and heard him talking and saw him lying on the couch, there is little I can do to digest it. In other words, I do not *know* what took place—I *suspect*. The conditions do not exist for me to have the experience of knowing, but the conditions do exist for me to be suspicious. I can only pile one hypothesis on another. Taking the view that I need to be able to operate α, I find in fact that I cannot.

The obvious explanation is that I know of no theory and can find no selected fact that makes the facts cohere. What theories are there? The following occur to me:

1. He is aware of reality and delivers splitting attacks on it so that the elements appear as elements.
2. These elements are scattered in time.
3. The elements are sometimes conjoined, e.g. my house and my being wet through. But these elements were not thus joined in the episode.
4. Usually the elements are widely separated, and the matter intervening seems intended to isolate each element from another. It might be said that a kind of mental faeces links, or separates, the elements.

In all this I have described some facts (2, 3, and the first line of 4) as theories; this gives a measure of the uncertainty. Can any scientific theory be produced to meet such a position—a theory of improbability? An uncertainty principle perhaps?

[Undated]

Splitting of the breast enables the infant to take the milk without understanding its dependence on the breast and the indulgence it extends to him. Such understanding involves hate and envy, and these impel attacks on the apparatus of understanding to prevent the stimulation of envy—envy thus destroying envy. The attacks mean that *in effect* the breast as a source of understanding, the 'mental' breast, is felt to be destroyed since no apparatus to understand it means no understanding of it, and so no 'it' to understand. That leaves the sucking breast only as a 'thing' incapable of loving and understanding, and incapable therefore of endowing something else with understanding.

[None of the entries on pages 188–283 was dated, but it can be assumed that they were written between 1961 and 1967.]

[Undated]

The problem of perception: common sense and group polarity of instincts

Berkeley says the stimulus may be God; so does Descartes. I shall maintain there is truth in this and that amongst all the objects that any given hypothesis at any given moment asserts to be constantly conjoined there is always the element that is that aspect which 'God' presents. Thus if I say I see a table, I am stating that this is an empirical experience in which my hypothesis that certain elements are constantly conjoined—those elements in fact whose constant conjunction I have decided to call, 'a table'—are again conjoined; furthermore, that amongst these elements, hardness, shape, etc., is an element that is 'God's' contribution, a presenting in me the awareness of certain sensations. In this context I regard God, or Descartes' evil spirit or Demon (in his first 'Meditation') as being interchangeable views of the same thing.

What is this God or Demon? In my view it is none other than the social component, '*Vox populi, vox dei*', of the instinctual equipment. Or, looked at from another point of view, it helps to convince me that these conjoined sensory experiences are, or are proof of the existence of, a table. In the instance of the table this may not be of moment, but throughout the history of scientific endeavour we find evidence of acceptance by the scientist of beliefs that are supposed by him to be ideas corresponding to an objective reality, but which, in the light of later knowledge, we can see to correspond to that special or particular reality that we now see to be the common sense of the time. Such evidence is not proof but is at least not incompatible with the view I am proposing: that certain perceptions of the individual are not so much qualities under investigation as impositions on the individual's outlook by common sense (in my terminology) or God's idea (in Berkeley's) or the deceptions by God and Demon (in Descartes').

[Undated]

Ultimately, a science stands or falls in proportion as it is a valid technique for discovery, and not by virtue of the 'knowledge' gained. This last is always subject to supersession; indeed, supersession of findings by new findings is the criterion by which vitality of the subject is judged.

Induction

A generalization is induced from many (number not specified) instances—until presumably we get, 'All men are mortal', as our premise. But this seems to me to be a hypothesis like any other: a hypothesis that is then used as a premise in a deductive system no doubt, but a hypothesis none the less. And it derives from other hypotheses; for example, 'men'. But are any words that are not nouns hypotheses? All? Mortal? Are? If sounds can be combined to make words, then words can be combined to make further hypotheses.

The statement, 'All men are mortal: Socrates is a man; therefore Socrates is mortal', is supposed to be a deduction from the premise, 'All men are mortal'. But the premise is supposed to be arrived at by a process of induction. That is to say that a great number of people are known to have died, and from this, inductive reasoning leads to the generalization that 'All men are mortal'. It is my contention that this is false. I do not believe anyone has ever thought that a lot of people have died and then have begun to suspect that men die, until the suspicion begins to harden into a conviction and at some given moment the generalization flashes into existence—all men are mortal.

My theory is that contact with reality induces questions, and that the process of induction gives rise to questions. The hypothesis is inspired by the need to deal with—not necessarily to answer—the question. It may still be true that the hypothesis does answer the question, but that may only be because in a particular instance there is an answer that would deal with the question.

The question may be of little social significance. That is to say it may, like instances of sense impressions that constitute purely 'private' knowledge, be a purely private question. Such an instance would be someone who fears that he has been responsible for the death of a particular man. His doubts and questionings could then be dealt with by the hypothesis, 'All men are mortal', and from this he could establish a deductive system of which 'All men are mortal' would be the premise, and so arrive at the conclusion that the particular man had died because of his mortality and not through any action on the part of the man who felt guilty. Such an inductive process is not, perhaps, as socially valuable as that of another whose induced questions had a bigger social or public component analogous to the 'common sense' of the man whose knowledge, the facts of which provided him with the material for his scientific observations, might be regarded as 'public' knowledge for public communication.

Any contact with reality leads not to the collection of facts that common sense would regard as material suitable for empirical observation and testing, but to the induction of a series of questions, or an amalgam of the series of questions—what? why? how? where? The statement, 'All men are mortal', is a response to that *private* question, and the problem of induction that has troubled philosophers is really not so much, 'How is that premise arrived at?' but, 'What was the question to which this hypothesis-turned-premise is the reply?'.

[Undated]

Mental health

The man who is mentally healthy is able to gain strength and consolation and the material through which he can achieve mental development through his contact with reality, no matter whether that reality is painful or not. This view may owe its origins to experience in no way metaphysical, but such as might be achieved through failure to admit the existence of a physical hazard to physical progress and the resultant fall. The reciprocal view is that no man can become mentally healthy save by a process of constant search for fact and a determination to eschew any elements, however seductive or pleasurable, that interpose themselves between himself and his environment as it really is. As a psycho-analyst I include the man's own personality as a part, and a very important part, of his environment. By contrast it may be said that man owes his health, and his capacity for continued health, to his ability to shield himself during his growth as an individual by repeating in his personal life the history of the race's capacity for self-deception against truth that his mind is not fitted to receive without disaster. Like the earth, he carries with him an atmosphere, albeit a mental one, which shields him from the mental counterpart of the cosmic and other rays at present supposed to be rendered innocuous to men, thanks to the physical atmosphere.

[Undated]

I have said that the inchoate mass of incoherent, or apparently incoherent, elements can, by selection of the appropriate fact, be made to appear to the observer to come together as a whole in which the elements are now seen to be related to each other as parts of the whole. When time is essential, this selected fact is known as the cause, but this fact is otherwise no different from other facts that are selected for their apparent ability to bring these elements together as a whole. Such facts do not necessarily possess intrinsic significance; that depends on what fact the observer lacks, and that clearly depends on the observer. The acceleration of the falling body could not be 'understood' by Galileo till he had selected the fact that the fall was proportional to the time through which the body had fallen, and not the distance (is this an instance of asking the right question: 'when?', not 'where?'). This fact is not a scientific fact unless and until it can be communicated and then found to be (or not to be) a fact that fulfils this function of integration for a large number of people, or a society or a group, 'in common'. But at first it is a private fact and is chosen because it fits into a scientific deductive system or calculus of immense complexity, for it is co-extensive with the entire mentality of the person.

In the instance of acceleration of falling bodies, it was Galileo who required a fact that would give coherence and meaning to the facts already known to him but felt to be devoid of coherence. But the environment, the world of external reality, was for all practical purposes no different for all Galileo's contemporaries. The majority of mankind, we may be sure, were unaware of any lack of coherence in the facts that they perceived to be associated with falling bodies. Yet it is not to be believed that the individual lacked preoccupations then, any more than he does today. Every individual is in a state of mind in which he is aware of elements of a world independent of himself. A contemporary of Galileo might be as well aware as Galileo of the facts that bodies fall, but, as is the case with the majority of individuals today, those facts presented no problem.

It is at this point that we touch on the problem of induction that has given rise to so much confusion for the philosopher of science. It has always been felt that induction is very important. Even today Bertrand Russell considers that no scientific method is possible without induction, and even goes so far as to suggest that induction is the foundation of all scientific knowledge. It is evident that he is not happy in the consequences that follow from this belief, and he expressly states his conviction that Hume's arguments (against the supposition that something additional to constant conjunction is a purely psychological phenomenon arising from the tendency of the human mind to associate ideas together) have never really been met. I hope to show that, thanks to psycho-analysis, we are now in a position to see why the philosophers who argue in favour of induction are led into an impasse from which they have so far found no escape; and also why philosophers who are not satisfied by Hume's dismissal of constant conjunction as adding nothing extra to a pure phenomenon of the human mind—namely its tendency to associate one idea with another—cannot propose any alternative that will at once express the nature of their dissatisfaction *and* fill the gap that they feel Hume's theory leaves in the structure of scientific method.

I think the fault lies in the belief that the inductive method consists of the collection of data and the inference, from the data observed, of generalizations such as are commonly embodied in a hypothesis. I believe the hypothesis is not based on what is commonly supposed to be observation, but is essentially a statement that such-and-such is a fact. This supposed fact has invariably the following features, which are essential to it as a hypothesis.

1. It states that certain elements are constantly conjoined.
2. It states that these elements are conjoined in a particular way.

When one of the elements is time, the elements are always stated to be related to each other as cause and effect. The word, 'cause', is applied to the selected fact that, for the particular individual observer, gives coherence to certain elements that have, to him, been mentally present as incoherent and demanding coherence. Essential amongst these elements are (externally) time, and (internally, and peculiar to the individual) feelings of guilt. We shall see later the importance of this description of the nature of a scientific hypothesis, but for the moment I want to turn to the problem of induction.

I believe that philosophers are correct in expressing the need for some theoretical concept, such as induction, to represent a verifiable fact that plays an essential role in the scientific method. I also believe that the process of induction—whatever that might turn out to be—is and must be related to a sensory awareness of data of external reality. But the function of induction is to extract from the data that have been collected via the sensory apparatus, not a hypothesis but a question—preferably the right question. By 'right question' I mean that which is dictated by common sense (in the sense in which I have defined it); for any other question is a matter of private concern, and all scientific matters are of public knowledge of public facts made public—the scientific work consisting of public-ation.

I suggest then that the process is one of awareness of incoherent elements and the individual's ability to tolerate that awareness until such time as induction leads to the formulation of a question. (Of the nature of those questions I shall speak later.) The question once formulated gives rise to an inspiration, the selection of the 'fact' or, as I would suggest, the sophisticated fact or hypothesis. From this follow the steps by which a scientific deductive system is built up: from the high-level hypotheses acting as premises, through the intermediate derived hypotheses, through decreasing generalization to the lowest-level hypotheses, we reach the particularizations that are open to invalidation by empirical testing.

It will be noticed that I have done away with the suggestion that the hypothesis is derived from observation that certain elements are constantly conjoined; I have substituted for it the theory that the hypothesis invariably maintains that certain elements are constantly conjoined and that it is the function of the hypothesis so to do. This substitution may at first sight seem to be of very little consequence, and indeed even to be a merely arbitrary alteration in the accepted order of events. But in fact, as I shall now demonstrate, it is an emendation that, like so many in the history of science, is apparently trivial in itself but effects a change that is of an importance apparently out of proportion to its seeming insignificance. For, once it is accepted that an essential feature of the hypothesis is to state, together with whatever it states, that certain elements are constantly conjoined, then it becomes possible to see something of the history of the hypothesis as a development in the human mind in its change to the phase that Freud calls the dominance of the reality principle. Furthermore, it becomes possible to make a new approach to the difficulties that have been raised by the philosophers of perception to the discomfiture of those philosophers who feel that a place should exist for the exercise of common sense, and that common sense and the objections of the phenomenologists could not really be brought together in anything more satisfactory than a head-on collision.

I suggest that the elements of scientific method to which I have drawn attention, namely the relationship between the psychological needs of the individual, the demands of the reality principle, the demands of reality on the individual for recognition as reality if he is to survive, the hypothesis as an assertion of constant conjunction of elements and a statement that the elements are conjoined by different forms of relatedness that may be distinguished from each other, the social component that is discerned in the fact that public-ation is an essential and not an accidental feature—all are present at an early stage in the history of the individual and the race, and are associated in particular with the development of verbal thought. Here again I think the problem is simplified if we ignore for the time the characteristic of words which has so far dominated the picture—namely their characteristic symbols—and consider each word to be by way of what at a later stage we call a hypothesis.

Regarded in this light, I suggest the individual seeks by the emission of selected sounds, later to be distinguished by words, to convey that certain elements in his surroundings are constantly conjoined. Thus the individual may express by some sound, such as 'da–da–da'; that certain sensory impressions are always conjoined; the 'da–da–da' being conjoined with them is a method of public-ation of the hypothesis, and at the same time a reduction of the hypothesis to terms that can be verified by empirical tests. "Da–da–da", says the infant. "Yes", says the perceptive mother, "That's right; it's Daddy". And the scientific method, high-level hypothesis, generalization and verifiable statement, together with public-ation, has been born.

I do not suggest that this is going to meet the objections of the philosopher of perception who may still feel that the problem of how the private knowledge of sense impressions is ever to be translated into public knowledge, or how the individual is ever to be assured that any phenomena lie beyond the sense impressions of which he is aware, is insoluble. I can only reply, taking a leaf out of the hypothetical book of my hypothetical infant, by public-ation—that is, speech. This problem, which appears to many philosophers to be a matter of dialectic, cannot be regarded as unimportant by the psycho-analyst who may be treating a patient whose sense impressions appear to give him information that does not correspond with what the analyst ordinarily considers to be the appropriate external facts.

* * *

When is the private fact made public? In the individual, when it has become a matter of common sense; that is, all his senses combine to give the same information. But amongst these elements of personality, in which I include the sense perceptions, I wish to include also that aspect of the senses which is held in common with the group. Private knowledge becomes public knowledge when the common sense of analyst and analysand agree that the perceptions of both indicate that some idea corresponds to an external fact independent of both observers. I shall later suggest that it is the moment of public-ation that is the point at which a mental phenomenon—a thought, an idea, a hypothesis—becomes an action in a psycho-analysis. When the psycho-analyst gives an interpretation that is a public-ation of private knowledge, he is translating thought into action, word into deed, just as much as the physicist conducting a laboratory experiment.

[Undated]

In my papers, 'Differentiation of the Psychotic from the Non-Psychotic Personalities' [1957] and 'Attacks on Linking' [1959], I was concerned with the effect on the patient's capacity for communication with himself and others of the minutely destructive fragmentation—originally described by Melanie Klein (*Notes on Some Schizoid Mechanisms*)—which the schizoid inflicts on these methods of communications as a part of his destructive attacks on all links. At the moment I am not concerned with the destructive attacks nor yet with the attempt, implicit in the psycho-analysis of such a patient, at reparation of the destruction and synthesis of the fragments—except in so far as it might be possible to deduce from these experiences some tentative hypotheses to illuminate the normal process of development. The elements with which we shall be concerned are hallucinations associated with intense deprivation (whether caused by the blockading effect of the patient's own envy or for any other reason, e.g. destruction of all links, murderous super-ego, predominance of death instincts), dreams, speech and its disorders (e.g. stammer), painting and drawing, and reports of difficulty with musical execution.

I shall commence with the description of a clinical experience. The patient gives virtually no information in terms of ordinary conversation. But he is able to create an impression. In my attempt to understand him I am successful in that I receive an impression, but I am unsuccessful in that the impression I receive cannot be evaluated. The patient speaks: "Well, I don't seem to have anything to say . . . I say I have nothing to say . . . it doesn't seem to me that I have, anything at all . . . I suppose I've done something wrong . . . of course I did go . . . no, it's no good."

These statements are made as if they were addressed to me. Each group of words is followed by a pause, as if I were invited to reply. My silence prompts the patient to repeat himself in a tone that betrays his sense of being disregarded by me. The phrase, "I suppose I've done something wrong", is an expression of grievance at the utterly unreasonable treatment to which he is being subjected in being made to feel guilty when in fact he has nothing with which to reproach himself. The total episode must have occupied ten minutes, and up to this point bears the stamp of a contrived situation.

The remainder of the session, after appropriate interpretations, took on an entirely different stamp and consequently becomes irrelevant for my present purpose. I propose, therefore, to dwell on certain aspects of this fragment, ignoring subsequent developments and the work that preceded it, except to say that the main characteristic was the same as that of this fragment, namely envy. Even so, the fragment expressed only one facet of the operation of this emotion. Envy in one form and another dominated every session for months on end, and the essential feature of the envy was its disastrous efficacy in cutting the patient off from every—or what seemed to be almost every—source of vitalizing influence.

The isolation of the patient was effected by the severance of his means of communication with the vitalizing influence. This is the true significance of the attacks on linking to which I have drawn attention; these attacks and their effect are clearly manifested in the destruction, namely projective identification, ideogrammatic expression, sound (as the matrix of that specialized form which in its maturity we recognize as music), and indeed the ideational counterpart of all the senses.

But in addition to these there is an attack on the Positions because they are a vital factor in the conversion of the unknown to the known. That is to say, the individual's capacity for learning depends throughout life on his ability to tolerate the paranoid–schizoid position, the depressive position, and the dynamic and continuing interaction between the two. The Positions are not to be regarded simply as features of infancy, and the transition from paranoid–schizoid to depressive position as something that is achieved once for all during infancy, but as a continuously active process once its mechanism has been successfully established in the early months. If, therefore, this is not established at the outset, then its operation remains defective throughout life (in varying degrees of intensity), and the patient cannot reap the benefits that accrue through smooth operation of the to-and-fro between the two positions that should, for a full and healthy life, be always available to him.

As I attempted to show in my paper on the attacks on linking, this means that the two main routes by which the patient can maintain communication with the sources essential for healthy development are both obstructed with degrees of thoroughness dependent on the severity and duration of the attacks on the links. I shall discuss this in detail later, but for the present pass it by to consider what these vitalizing sources are from which the patient is isolated.

I must make it clear at the outset that I cannot pretend to anything but a shadowy idea of these sources; I do not doubt that they will need psycho-analytical investigation for many years. But, broadly speaking, I believe they are sources that betray their presence and activity in the Oedipus myth.

We are accustomed, thanks to Freud's discoveries, to attribute great significance and importance to the Oedipus complex, and consequently it has come to be regarded as if it were the starting point of a dynamic process.

* * *

I wish now to regard the Oedipus myth, the Sophoclean version of that myth, and Freud's own discoveries as all being attempts at the resolution of a developmental crux. I hope to show that these attempts at resolution are far more widespread in time, and far more various in the form and method of resolution adopted, than has hitherto been realized or even suspected. One such attempt can be discerned in the issues involved in the production of a scientific deductive system and the calculus that represents it.

With this end in view I propose to examine Euclid's elements. This brings me back to the point at which I said a search must be made for the intersection of processes analogous to those which we ordinarily see in dreams, with the processes we ordinarily associate with mathematical logic. But before doing this I must give a warning: it is inevitable that I should appear at certain points of the discussion to be seeing sexual, and particularly Oedipal, symbols in certain Euclidean propositions. As I shall make clear, there is nothing new in this: in fact insights date back at least to Plutarch. But in some respects it would be putting the cart before the horse to think that Freud's Oedipal discoveries elucidate the Euclidean theorem, for I wish to propound the hypothesis that the Euclidean theorem and Freud's discovery of the Oedipus complex, together with the Oedipus myth and the Sophoclean version of it, are alike in that they are both attempts to resolve the conflicts and problems of which they are at one and the same time the manifestation and the attempted solution. I further wish to show that the problems involved in the interplay between the Positions have also prompted attempts at resolution analogous to those to which I point as associated with the matrix or matrices of the Oedipus myth.

I have previously pointed out that the Oedipus myth itself embodies the problem of knowledge in that a question is posed, demanding an answer. One point on which I shall dwell is, what was the question posed by the Sphinx? To this I shall suggest a solution. I shall also suggest that envy plays a role in the fundamental problem, which has not been appreciated although it is of first importance. This envy is directed against the capacity of the individual that makes him able to negotiate the Positions.

To start with the Sphinx and her question—I stress, *her* question—tradition has it that the question was: what walks on four feet in the morning, on two at noon, and on three in the evening? And the answer was: man crawls on all fours as a baby, walks upright in the prime of life, and uses a staff in old age.

I shall propose a different answer. But I must first draw attention to an aspect of Euclid's Fifth Proposition in his first book. We are so accustomed to regard his use of the term, 'isosceles triangle', as bearing only the meaning that we associate with a mathematical term, that it is difficult to realize that the Greek term could be translated as, 'a three-kneed thing with equal legs'. R. B. Onions has shown—and he cannot be accused of any tenderness to Freud's theories of sexuality—that the knees, in early Greek literature, are very frequently associated with the genitalia [*Origins of European Thought,* p. 174]. This has made me look at Euclid's Fifth Proposition in a new light. It also makes one inclined to attempt a revaluation of the question traditionally attributed to the Sphinx. But for the moment I shall rest content with bringing together Euclid I.5 and the Oedipus myth.

[Undated]

The Oedipal chain

The fate of the primal scene:

1. There may be an actual sensory experience. This would correspond to the lowest-level hypotheses of empirically verifiable fact.
2. The scene assumes the character of a hieroglyph or an ideogram.
3. The ideogram becomes (a) formularized, or (b) abstract. If abstracted, then it becomes a figure constructed out of the 'elements' (of Euclidean geometry).
4. An intermediate phase derived from another context—the invention of Cartesian co-ordinates.
5. The further abstraction of the scientific deductive system that is Euclidean geometry, to produce the algebraic calculus representing the scientific deductive system that is Euclidean geometry. Thus is established algebraic geometry.
6. Further calculi.

Reverse the direction

Now the algebraic calculus has to be returned to the lowest-level hypotheses of empirically verifiable data; it can then find its 'realization' in 'space' from which Euclidean geometry supposedly springs. But in fact the calculi that have been produced are many and diverse, including those of non-Euclidean geometry. Some of these calculi are applicable to study of astronomical space. But in so far as inappropriate calculi may be used, they tend to betray their origin, and the space that is explored by virtue of these calculi is given characteristics that are markedly reminiscent of the empirical data from which the calculi were originally derived. Are these characteristics then actual characteristics of space? Are there actualities or realities corresponding to the *ideas* of reality that the calculi have enabled the astronomer to achieve? Or are the ideas only reflecting the origin of the calculi and the scientific deductive system, Euclidean geometry—namely the space of the primitive individual from which the scientific process sprang?

Unfortunately astronomy is based on data derived from one sense, sight, so 'common sense' may be hard to achieve. Furthermore, the actual elaboration of calculi, in the way I have described it, is a kind of expanding mental universe—from primal scene to nebulae—and this fact may colour the theory of the universe which is being produced, so that it is supposed that there is an expanding universe rather than an effect of an expanding mental universe that is produced through minute and excessive splitting, and explosive ejection of the apparatus of perception—the ego. This would mean that the sense of an expanding mental universe is itself illusory and related more to megalomania than a development of apparatus for achieving knowledge.

Thus two possibilities are opened up: one is that, thanks to the elaboration of scientific methods, we are learning more; the other is that, thanks to the impulse to escape from Oedipal material, calculi are produced which are impregnated with the impulse to escape and the archaic remnants of that from which escape is sought.

But even in the original elaboration there is clearly an attempt at more than escape. Therefore there may be presumed to exist an element conducive to an accurate assessment of space which is to be as overwhelming to the man as the space, apparent to his infant capacity, was to him in infancy.

The attempt to escape will tend to betray the corresponding attempt to discover that from which escape is sought in the expanding concepts of space as the individual travels from infancy to adulthood. The psychotic shows a desire to occupy a very small space.

Can the calculi produced yield equipment suitable for investigating the problem from which they sprang? Can the calculi, which represent an attempt at abstraction as escape from an Oedipal situation, be made to explore that situation? Do calculi already exist which do just that? Can Oedipal conflicts be resolved by a *mathematical* experience? The internal universe would then be explored by a calculus turned back on its origin.

Exploration of space

In paintings of the nude we have another approach to exploration or 'discussion' of space—the earliest space of all. And Kenneth Clark shows the wish to bring mathematics to bear on it. Is it to control or to further the exploration, or to escape by mathematics?

One would suppose that painting is a kind of representation of that which becomes an ideogram, hieroglyph, diagram, or figure of geometry in another situation and in another discipline. There may be counterparts of the scientific deductive system in activities other than scientific activities. What are these counterparts? In the arts it is sometimes said that the artist is concerned with a particular aspect of truth. He must then, like the scientist who looks to his methodology, have to question his methods of achieving it. What does the artist question? Surely not simply his technique with a brush? Or with his musical instrument? The composer's tools are scales, harmonies, etc. Are there significant places in his schemes for intervals of thirds, fourths, and fifths? In short, is there a musical counterpart of the theorem of Pythagoras? And is there an 'algebraic calculus' that represents the B Minor Mass? Are the following ideas, linked by the double arrow, related?

(1) B Minor Mass ↔ scientific deductive system

(2) scientific deductive system ↔ musical score

[Undated]

Theorem of Pythagoras
—Euclid I.47

The side subtending the right angle: the sides containing the right angle. How much can be obtained by ignoring the figure, the diagram, except in so far as it serves a function—like that of the material of a sculpture by Henry Moore—in framing the place where there is *no* material? To act as a boundary to the open space, that is to say the part where the figure is *not*.

Then the squares on the sides containing, and the squares on the side subtending, the right angle serve to enclose the triangle—the 'three-kneed thing', but also the right angle.

The construction is a trap for light.

Pons Asinorum + Positions

Euclid I.5 marks the point at which the 'elements' of geometry are left behind when the student crosses the Pons.

[Undated]

The relationship of Ps and D positions to the Oedipus complex

Paranoid–schizoid and depressive positions will from now on be called by me, 'the Positions', as a matter of convenience.

The Positions are emotional experiences intrinsic to work. All anxiety is related ultimately to The Anxiety, which has two roots:

(1) the contents of the Oedipal situation, which has as its scientific deductive system (s.d.s.) the Theorem of Pythagoras and as its calculus the relevant portions of algebraic geometry;

(2) fear of the Positions, which have as their s.d.s. the Pons Asinorum, Euclid I.5, and its associated algebraic calculus.

Both theorems have always engaged the attention of mankind and have been confused with each other by name, e.g. the French call I.47 the Pons Asinorum (*see* Heath, *Euclid,* p. 417).

The I.47 Oedipus and I.5 Pons Asinorum belong to different axes in human knowledge, but they intersect: one is related to content of knowledge (I.47 Oedipus), the other to acquisition of knowledge (I.5 Positions).

The Oedipal situation may occupy different positions in the hierarchy of hypotheses in different s.d.s.'s. In some it may be an initial formula; in others, a derived formula according to the function which the associated calculus is intended to fulfil.

There must be a counterpart to this in non-scientific discipline, and the same difference in hierarchical positions will be observed.

The s.d.s. associated with Euclid I.5 and the algebraic calculus associated with it are all associated with the Positions.

The Oedipal situation is associated with Euclid I.47 and its associated s.d.s. (if different from the theorem itself) and its associated algebraic calculus.

The scientific deductive system and calculus via Euclid

What are the scientific deductive systems that could be used in psycho-analysis? What form would a calculus take? Can it be found in Euclid? That is certainly what I suspect. That is to say that the problem would be associated with the three-kneed thing with equal legs; and this would provoke the search, as described by Poincaré, for the harmonizing fact to be selected. What then?

If this is correct, then one would suppose that the scene described by 'blood everywhere' might be formalized, say, as 'the looking-glass murder'—rather like a film being projected end first so that the scene of bloodshed would depict itself as one in which the 'blood everywhere' was being reabsorbed through the original route. Cubism might be a kind of attempt to geometrize a scene: in this way the looking-glass murder would need to be formalized—but how? Do Lewis Carroll's chess rules for *Alice Through the Looking-Glass* give a clue?

The clue is in the translation of an isosceles triangle as the three-kneed thing with equal legs (A. D. Ritchie, *Studies in the History and Methods of the Sciences,* p. 28) and then the astounding fact—and yet I expected it and was looking for it—of the popular names for the Euclidean propositions, and in particular for I.5 and I.47, the Pons Asinorum and the Theorem of the Bride (Heath, *Euclid,* vol. I, p. 415).

The question that arises at once is that which I have already formulated about Poincaré's statement of a need to find a fact that harmonizes as a method of coping with the intolerable paranoid–schizoid position (Poincaré, *Science and Method,* p. 30). Is the mathematical discovery reassuring by virtue of its being an external creative attempt that can be set against the internal stress of depressive or paranoid–schizoid positions? Or is a formula produced which itself brings into being a calculus (and the s.d.s. it represents) that is of 'importance in various branches of science', including in particular the relationship of paranoid–schizoid to the depressive position? Certainly Poincaré describes the former experience, that is the reassurance, the therapeutic reassurance, obtained by being able to do something creative and harmonizing externally, which can then be used as an external fact to set against *internal* depression. And yet it is a description that does not exclude the possibility of some internal adjustment by virtue of which he now possesses a capacity for seeing wholes. Are I.5 and I.47 externalizations of the Oedipal situation? Is that all? Or are they s.d.s.'s that make it possible to investigate the Oedipal situation? This point would be clinched if one found that I.5 or I.47 reached a conclusion that could then be translated into terms of lowest-level hypotheses—or, rather, into terms of empirically verifiable data—which could then be seen to have carried the theory of Oedipal conflict to a point further than any yet reached in psycho-analytical discovery.

It is possible that a s.d.s. and calculus produced under pressure of Ps ↔ D might be important in other branches of science, or even in other branches of the same science, namely analysis, rather than in the investigation of Ps ↔ D itself. Similarly, the s.d.s. produced under pressure of, say, the Oedipal situation might be of no use in investigation of the Oedipal situation, but of service in the Ps ↔ D situation. In either case we know the s.d.s. to have been important in astronomy, i.e. in an entirely different branch of science. It may be only now, after this excursion into outer space, that it can be brought back after two thousand years to its own sphere.

[Undated]

An interpretation

An interpretation should not be given on a single association; a single association is open to an enormous number of interpretations. But two associations, like two points that determine a line, determine an interpretation. Not quite. What do they determine? A direction; a trend of thought perhaps. And does this mean that it is at a point of this kind that one might find the intersection or meet a logical product of the psycho-analytical interpretation with the s.d.s. known as Euclidean geometry? Is the statement that two points determine a line really an abstraction from an empirically experienced fact that two ideas, taken together, determine a trend in the speaker's mind? If so, then it is possible that the s.d.s. that is Euclidean geometry is of great importance in the science of psycho-analysis (Braithwaite, *Scientific Explanation,* p. 27) and can be used to establish calculi, e.g. algebraic calculi, to 'fix' certain psycho-analytic theories and expose fallacies in others, as was the case in mathematics when nineteenth-century mathematicians tried to represent the mathematical 'proofs' of certain eighteenth-century mathematicians in an adequate calculus.

I have noticed that something that seems clear when I write it appears to have lost all meaning when I come back to it freshly on a subsequent occasion. The words are all there and are as likely as not clear enough, but I find that I no longer know what they are about. It is like the disappearance, apparently, of all knowledge or understanding of Greek literature in Byzantium, or of astronomical or other ideas that are clearly grasped by one generation but then seem to be completely lost by subsequent generations, e.g. the heliocentric theory of Aristarchus. Is it possible that one of the great functions of abstraction is to 'fix' an element, *the* element, of empirical experience, which without abstraction is lost? Is there something permanent and indestructibly precise about the formula of a scientific deductive system that renders it peculiarly fit for the preservation of ideas? Is this a function of logic—logically necessary propositions? Would a s.d.s. give a permanence to Melanie Klein's paranoid–schizoid and depressive positions?

How does one *find* the appropriate calculus? Or invent it if it does not exist? Galileo had to get on without the differential calculus in solving the problem of the freely falling body.

[Undated]

Probability

The statement or belief that something is probable is related to prediction. Even when it appears to refer to the past, as in a statement that something probably happened, it means that at a future date it is likely that something will be discovered which proves that such-and-such event took place.

It has been supposed that there are universal hypotheses, so-called deterministic hypotheses, which state validly that 100% or 0% of things are A; and these are contrasted with statistical hypotheses, which state that a certain proportion of things, between 0% and 100%, are A (Braithwaite, *Scientific Explanation,* p. 115). Psycho-analytical hypotheses mostly belong to the latter class, which now includes the hypotheses of any scientific deductive system relating to quantum mechanics.

Braithwaite cites, by way of example, the statement: '51% of children born are boys.' He points out that there can be two statements of probability involved thus: it is probable that the hypothesis—that it is probable that 51% of children born are boys—is true.

This at once raises the question whether any hypothesis says any more than that something is probable, unless it is a definitory hypothesis; even the universal hypothesis, unless it is definitory, only states (as I have already pointed out) that certain events are constantly conjoined. But this means that all hypotheses are really definitory hypotheses; that is, that in the view of the person using a particular s.d.s. (which for the time being expresses the view he holds) such-and-such phenomena are constantly conjoined.

What then does the rational number express? Does it express a fact that 51% of children born are boys, or that he wishes it to be understood by himself and others that he is in a state of mind in which he has a 51% feeling of certitude? If the latter, then he is also expressing the view that he is 51% liberated from the Ps position; or that 51% of the potentially unrelated facts (Poincaré, *Science and Method,* p. 30) in the area of his mental activity have now been harmonized by the ideational counterpart of a fact he has selected.

What deductive system is this fact supposed to fit? Or for what system does it provide a lowest-level hypothesis? Any statement made by an analyst as a statement of fact about an event in analysis should be regarded as a statistical hypothesis, for it must be more obviously an approximation to the truth (rather than the truth itself) than is the case with most other disciplines. Even if we assume that an electrical recording could be made of the events in a session (which is in fact not the case in the kind of analysis with which I am acquainted), there remains the fact that at best such a recording can only bear the same relationship to fact as a pointer, reading from a piece of apparatus in a laboratory, bears to the facts it purports to indicate. Indeed, the comparison is extremely flattering to the supposed analytic record. The apparatus in the physics laboratory is, say, designed to record one comparatively simple fact—the wavelength of an electro-magnetic wave; the analytic record, though it is restricted to phenomena perceptible to hearing only, is nevertheless called on to record very complex sounds—two people talking.

But if quantum mechanics has to rely on statistical hypotheses as its lowest-level hypotheses and can thrive on them, as manifestly it does, the same may be true of psycho-analysis. The essential point would seem to be to establish the nature of the lowest-level hypotheses in a psycho-analytic deductive system. By that I mean the nature of the statement that has to be made if the investigator is to be presented with what he can regard as empirically verifiable statements of fact on the one hand, and on the other, if he is to know what kind of phenomena he has to deal with in his attempt to produce a s.d.s. and its representative calculus.

I propose to ignore for the time being statements made by other analysts and to consider only the problem involved in an attempt to produce a s.d.s. and its associated calculus, which will serve as a generalization that will be an epitome of experience on which I can draw in my analytic work, and which I can use to communicate my experience to the patient—and if possible to other workers in the field.

I propose to limit the sphere of experience on which I draw to two main areas: the totality of my own life, or such part of that experience as is available to me; and the psycho-analytic situation as it obtains when I see a patient five times a week for an indefinite period. I shall not for the time being attempt to define this sphere with any further precision.

My experience in analysis will mostly be restricted to one part of this situation, namely the part described by Poincaré (*Science and Method,* p. 30), and one that is therefore analogous to the paranoid–schizoid position. In practice, what this means is that at the beginning of the session I shall not burden my mind by attempting to remember what the patient has said on previous occasions. There may be a time and place for attempting such a recall, but that time and place is not at the commencement of a session. Nor shall I burden my mind with attempting to recall what others, or even I myself, may have said or thought about such a patient as I am about to see. I shall not even consider what kind of patient he may be.

The reason is simple: I am concerned in a session with what I do not know. The session is the only time when I can have contact with what I do not know; at any other time I can only have contact with, or think about, phenomena which I believe—rightly or wrongly—that I have already observed. But in the session I can have contact with phenomena that I have not so far observed, or have observed only partially. It is an opportunity that is not to be missed, for if it is it can never be repeated. It therefore merits as precise a description as I can find to delineate the emotional experience to which I attach such supreme importance. It is the emotional experience appropriate to the observation of a series of apparently unrelated facts that the analyst believes are related to each other and to him in a significant manner [*see* 'Notes on Memory & Desire', 1967].

At first sight it seems obvious that this emotional experience must be akin to that of the paranoid–schizoid position. But kinship must not deteriorate into identity because that would preclude the possibility of synthesis, which is essential to the analyst's work. 'Our mind . . . would be obliged to forget each of these details before examining the next because it would be incapable of taking in the whole', as Poincaré describes the state preceding the discovery or selection of the harmonizing fact. Nor is it wholly satisfactory to postulate a state of mind akin to the depressive position unless it is made equally clear that it must not be *identical* with the emotional experience associated with the depressive position.

Freud has described the value of a state he calls benevolent neutrality, a kind of free-floating attention. Poincaré would appear to desiderate an absorption in logical mental processes that, if not in themselves mathematical, at least issue ultimately in mathematical formulation.

For convenience I propose to call this state, which is neither the paranoid–schizoid position nor yet the depressive position but something of each, the Positions. I shall further suggest that the process of discovery or selection of the harmonizing fact or, as I should prefer to regard it, its ideational counterpart, cannot be initiated or maintained without the mobilization of the mental processes of dreaming.

It must not be supposed that I am setting this up in contrast with, or as an alternative to, what I conceive to be the logical or mathematical absorption that Poincaré had in mind; nor am I suggesting that the analyst should go to sleep. But I believe that the analyst may have to cultivate a capacity for dreaming while awake, and that this capacity must somehow be reconcilable with what we ordinarily conceive of as an ability for logical thought of the mathematical kind.

[Undated]

The attack on the analyst's α-function

I have pointed out that it is essential to mental efficiency to be able to 'dream' a current emotional experience, whether it is taking place while the person is awake, or while asleep. By this I mean that the facts, as they are represented by the person's sense impressions, have to be converted into elements such as the visual images commonly met with in dreams as they are ordinarily reported. Such an idea will not seem strange if the reader considers what happens in reverie—the word itself, chosen to name the experience, is significant of the widespread nature of the experience. Certain conditions are necessary for this work of conversion to be carried out, but these conditions, as we shall see later, may be denied, so that α is made either impossible, or at least difficult. The analyst needs to have these conditions in his work, for smooth working of α-function is essential. He must be able to dream the analysis as it is taking place, but of course he must not go to sleep. Freud has described the condition as one of 'free-floating attention', but it is a state that is of value in many tasks besides analysis, for, as I have said, α-function is essential to proper mental efficiency, no matter what the task.

Clearly it would be helpful to establish in some detail what goes on in α-function; an examination of the conditions required for its fulfilment might give some clues. Indirect evidence is available from the psychotic patient who appears to be sufficiently aware of the analyst's need to be able to set out to deny him it—presumably as an extension of the patient's own attempts to destroy his links with reality, and in particular that which links live objects to each other. It is well known that in many sessions the patient is at pains to behave in such a way that the analyst is given no information at all—in so far as this lies within the capacity of the patient. Frequently he will do this by being mute, but on the occasions to which I refer, the patient is not only loquacious but is most insistent that the analyst should follow every word he says and will constantly inject comments that are intentionally evocative or even provocative. The analyst is to be so treated that he cannot stay awake, and so interrupted and importuned that he cannot go to sleep.

This is clearly a much more positive attack on the analyst than mere mutism or other forms of withholding information. It also bears a striking resemblance to the state produced if the patient cannot wake up or go to sleep—not through lack of α-function but artificially induced.

Can it be dismissed as a somewhat ordinary exercise in sadism, or should some significance be attached to the resemblance of the analyst's predicament to the state in which the patient finds himself when incapable of α-function? The resemblance may be fortuitous and not therefore of significance. It may be the repetition, this time against the analyst's α-function, of the attack that has been previously made by himself or another on his own α-function—in which case it may help us to understand how the α-function is destroyed and what vicissitudes we may anticipate in the patient's development. More probable than either of these is an attack on α-function made through the agency of projective identification, partly because projective identification is so consistently employed that it is difficult to imagine without very good reasons for the supposition that its use would be in abeyance, and partly because any other view leads us into unnecessary difficulty in explaining the skilled nature of an attack which implies the existence of a high degree of well-organized sophisticated destructiveness quite out of keeping with what we know of the patient's condition. The operation of projective identification, if we could assume it, would go some way towards resolving a contradiction that makes a supposedly insane patient behave with the organized efficiency that the diagnosis precludes. I do not mean by this that resolution of this contradiction is a matter of major consequence, but that it needs to be resolved because this would help investigation of something that *is* a major problem—the nature and operation of the non-psychotic part of the psychotic patient's personality.

The analyst's Odyssey

The patient comes to the door and looks away so as to avoid my eyes. He is dirty and unkempt; he wears gloves but they are not a pair. His face expresses almost physical pain. He holds out his hand limply to allow it to be shaken, but he seems almost to dissociate himself from the act physically as well as mentally. He lies down on the couch. "Well", he says, "I don't seem to have much to say." There is a pause of two or three minutes. "Funny, I seem to be feeling anxious." He is tense and lies still in a posture that might, but for his tension, be described as limp. He examines his hand with detachment, as if he were witnessing a hallucination or some event from which he wishes to detach himself because he is so frightened by it. He turns his head slowly to follow the movements of his hand. He folds his hands on his chest. The operation is complete; he composes himself for slumber.

I have good reason for anxiety about this patient; I know him to be violent, and I know his fears that he may commit a murder are not groundless—or so I think. Thinking over the matter, I am not so sure. I have occasion for the same kind of misgivings about his finances; and the same kind of misgivings about my misgivings. My experience of him makes me feel reasonably sure that if I allow my attention to wander, he will quite happily—if one can apply such a word to him—let his wander too. But I decide to wait.

I may adjust my position in the chair, or even make some sound or movement much less obtrusive. At once the patient starts violently, as if I had frightened him beyond endurance, or maybe even struck him. His attitude expresses intense pain. Slowly, reproachfully, he subsides. The session has begun.

"I forget what I said", he presently announces. After a further pause, "Funny", he says, puzzled. Later on he says, "There is something I meant to say". The session gradually peters out. The tension, apparent earlier, slowly ebbs away.

I indicate it is time to stop. "Yes. Thank you", he says. And he goes out, leaving me to wonder if he seemed to be slightly shamefaced, or if I imagined it.

The session may take a different form. He may start talking to me softly, confidentially. "They are cutting the grass. Of course", more confidentially still, "I could hardly protest; the tea was awful, really awful". There is a sudden sharp mocking laugh, stifled almost as it is uttered. "Well", he goes on in matter-of-fact tones, as if to suggest he is going to get down to business, "there it is; no home, tea all over the place. I simply will not stand it." The last sentence is uttered with a kind of desperation, as if he were attempting to break through a restraining barrier formed by an inability to express himself in terms that would link him with another person. "I will not stand it", he whispers.

On the face of it there seems to be no reason why such sessions should ever come to an end. Let us see what can be said about them.

First, I do not feel able to communicate to the reader an account that would be likely to satisfy me as correct. I am more confident that I could make the reader understand what I had to put up with if I could extract from him a promise that he would faithfully read every word I wrote; I would then set about writing several hundred thousand words virtually indistinguishable from what I have already written in my account of the two sessions. In short, I cannot have as much confidence in my ability to tell the reader what happened as I have in my ability to do something to the reader that I have had done to me. I have had an emotional experience; I feel confident in my ability to recreate that emotional experience, but not to represent it.

Another session: "I don't seem likely to do much." After a pause, "No. It seems very unlikely but . . . just *hark* at it!" He stumbles over some words, artificially, I thought. "Aah . . . just listen to me. I went to the art galleries in the end and the waitress said, she *said* it wouldn't be long. I was furious. I just broke the place up . . . oh, shut up. *Shut* up, I say. Shut *up* . . . I must have done something wrong." This is said reproachfully as if to indicate that as usual I am bad-tempered and hostile and trying to make him feel guilty. "Oh well, I suppose I must say something." He then becomes sulky and examines his quite remarkably filthy nails. "Another session going to waste. . . . I know I had something very important to say. . . . In the end I just had to get up. Oh shut up." He whispers, "Shut up: shut up".

There are many interpretations I could give, and have given in the past. They are apparently quite ineffectual; there seems to be no particular point in repeating them. What, I wonder, can have happened to them? Years of analytic interpretations, and the patience and knowledge that go with them, have been swallowed up by him, or poured into him by me, without apparently leaving the slightest trace. He might simply be a gaping hole or mouth, with nothing beyond it. He is taking up time and space and analytic experience that another patient might use to some profit. He might acknowledge some of the effort on his behalf, but it is simply as if his mouth gaped ever wider for more and more, all swallowed without discrimination of any kind. He requires more. And all through the session he interrupts, often saying he does not want to interrupt, breaking in in a manner to which my powers of description cannot do credit, with futile, hostile commentary on his futile, hostile comment—if such disjointed phrases can be called comment. What is he commenting on? He is commenting on a relationship between two people, or on what links them. What in fact links us is endurance, fortitude, patience, anger, sympathy, love. Is the task in hand, the analysis itself, a link? It seems hardly possible because it rarely comes to a point where it might be called analysis.

Yesterday he felt it was hardly to be justified—the time, expense and effort to analyse him. He was lucid—almost—and I am reporting far more what he said than what I understood him to say. Ordinarily I have to interpret what I have understood him to say; this may be significant. It means that I am forced to have an emotional experience, and that I have to have it in such a way that I am unable to learn from it. I have consciousness, a sense organ enabling me to perceive the psychical qualities (as Freud puts it in *The Interpretation of Dreams* [1900a, *SE 4, 5*]), but I am not to be allowed to comprehend it. Then I cannot learn by the emotional experience, and I cannot remember it.

* * *

Take now a different patient. Out it pours—masses of semi-whispered, disjointed stuff, name after name, some of which I know, some I may be supposed to know, some presumably I cannot be expected to know. They are mostly doing something that the patient sees: "It didn't occur to him . . ."; "I asked him, he did realize . . .". It does not require interpretation so much as loud cries of, "Help! Help! I'm drowning, not waving."

What is it all? Can anyone stem the flood? What interpretation, when there must be so many millions? He may be proving and feeling how superior to me he is, how much further he can see than I can; it may be a modernized urination, or flatus, or defaecation. It might be, as this might be, a book by Sacheverell Sitwell in which virtually nothing is done with the material. The overburdened mind just deposits it in the lap of the analyst and says, "Here, *you* do it!"

This is really an abstraction technique. This is what I am doing here in this writing, and hoping that I shall then be able to make head or tail of it. But I can't. The essential feeling is that nothing can be made of it—there is no selected fact, nothing to make it all cohere. If this is so, then perhaps the essential thing is an emotional situation in which the following features can be distinguished:

(1) feelings of persecution,
(2) a mass of apparently unrelated facts,
(3) an inability to find a selected fact, or perhaps to believe it would be any good if one could,
(4) an inability to see any value in the facts, to regard them as dead particles, bits of faeces.

But surely the point here is a lack of capacity for integrating? Is it that the content is significant? Or is it the cement—narrative, logic, selected fact? It can be content *and* . . . [breaks off here]

[Undated]

Freud described the conscious as 'the sense organ for the perception of psychical qualities'. If the patient, thanks to deficient α, cannot be awake or asleep, conscious or unconscious, can he have a conscious or an unconscious? His attacks on α-function make it impossible to become conscious or unconscious, but he can have a conscious and an unconscious, so he is able to perceive psychical qualities. But he cannot transform them into α-elements. This is where I do not accept Freud's description of the conscious as *comprehending* psychical qualities, but do accept his description of the conscious as *perceiving* them.

It is evident in my clinical experience that the patient *can* perceive psychical qualities in that he says he is anxious, or frightened, or depressed. He must then be able to perceive that, but he seems unable to learn from the experience of being anxious, or frightened, or depressed. It may depend on what he expects he would learn if he learned anything. But as I have shown with the emotional experience of having emotions in sleep, this kind of patient cannot 'dream' it and so cannot learn from the experience. Exactly the same thing is true of the emotional experience when he is awake: he cannot become unconscious of the emotions, and he cannot become conscious of them. What, then, is the position in analysis when the analyst gives an interpretation drawing the patient's attention to an emotional experience that the analyst can deduce from the patient's behaviour? At least we should expect to run into great difficulties in so far as an analysis is to be regarded as an emotional experience, for we cannot regard it as anything less and yet suppose it has some kind of reality.

It is tempting to suppose that the patient fears that if he learnt anything from his emotions, he would learn that he is alive, and from that, that his parents had had sexual intercourse; he then fears that this would release murderous envy and hate towards them and towards himself as the result of such intercourse. In one case it was clear that the patient feared just such an attack, for those reasons, from the analyst and an elder sister. "I don't know what I mean" had this situation as one of its backgrounds—he feared that he himself was a sign that could be read to mean that his parents had had intercourse. But though we may suppose that he has other fears of what he would learn, such as that he is insane, it is wisest at this point to suppose only that the patient hates emotions and concurrently cannot 'digest' them, i.e. bring α-function to bear on them. And this must affect the analyst's attempt to interpret.

If the patient cannot have a conscious because of lack of α-function, how comes he to have sufficient of one to perceive his emotions, to act as a sense organ for the perception of psychical qualities? He *can* have a conscious; he merely cannot *become* conscious.

Let us suppose now that the patient *is* capable of the process of the formation of a presentation or idea. Is that to say that the patient is capable of α-function and can transform the sense impressions, be they what they may, into α-elements? No: it means that he can have visual images on which, as Freud says, ideation depends ('Two Principles of Mental Functioning' [1911b, *SE 12*]).

I shall include the capacity to have visual images amongst the factors in α-function, but it is only one factor—though an important one. It makes storage possible because visual images are a kind of notation. One patient talked of lines and dots making up the film cartoon; it sounds like the elements of geometry (Euclidean). But before dream-thoughts are possible, it is necessary to find the selected fact and to use it for initiating the paranoid–schizoid and depressive position interplay. This means that α-elements cohere, separate, cohere again, separate again, converge, diverge, and so on. It is an experience in which coherence and separation are never observed; at one moment the α-elements are coherent, and then they are incoherent. It is similar to the experience of watching reversible perspective—at one moment one thing, and at another, another. It is similar to the dream—at one moment it is remembered, and at another there is no trace.

In distinction to this method of employing α-elements are two others: they can be strung together temporarily, in time, in a narrative sequence (as is the case in dream); and they can be connected logically, which is linear as in Euclid.

[Undated]

Curiosity, and fear of socialized super-ego

The story of the Garden of Eden and the story of Oedipus each contain a character whose attitude to knowledge is hostile—or perhaps I should say, 'two-faced', since the Sphinx demands the answer to a question and may therefore be supposed to be favouring a search for it, and God of Genesis plants the tree of knowledge of good and evil in the garden. Psycho-analysts have concentrated attention on the sexual pair and have left discussion of the attitude to knowledge on one side. Yet in man's search to know, few disciplines have penetrated so far in illuminating that source of his difficulties that lies within himself. This adds significance to the neglect of the material that might be compacted in the roles attributed to Sphinx, God and Devil (also Tower of Babel—verbal thought attacked).

But my concern here is not to elucidate these myths. I wish to clarify the similarities and differences between psycho-analysis and scientific method as it is understood and employed in spheres other than psycho-analysis. Nevertheless I believe the reader would find it rewarding to refresh his memory of these stories and to bear them in mind as he reads this; their effect thus used could be restorative during the arid passages that must be traversed in this investigation.

[Undated]

Tower of Babel: possibility of using a racial myth

Can we, at such a crisis as this, fall back on a racial myth on the offchance that it is a tool that has not yet outlived its usefulness? Let us interpret, for *our* purposes, the story of the Tower of Babel. I propose to use this story in a manner analogous to the use to which a scientist might put an already existing formula of mathematics. The mathematical construction may have been invented without any intention that it should be used as the scientist proposes to use it, or indeed without any intention that it should be used at all. Yet the scientist, despite the mathematician's avowal that his formula has no meaning at all, may decide that he has found a realization that is the counterpart of the mathematical formulation and will use the formulation accordingly. This I shall now do with the story of the Tower of Babel.

First, I decide that the story is formulated in *Genesis,* but I might as easily decide to write my own version. This story I do not interpret: I use it to interpret a problem of mine. When I say I might decide to write my own version, I do not mean that the basic elements of the story can be altered. Some transformation is necessary which is not an interpretation of the story, nor yet a sophistication. It is not an operation such as Freud proposes for the elucidation of a dream: it consists in a recognition first that the story is a social version of the phenomenon known to the individual as a dream—it even has some resemblance to the consciously sought selected fact; it is an emotional experience that has been subjected to α-function.

There must be many such myths that are not recognized at all, except in a pejorative sense in which some unlikely story, or one that the listener does not wish to believe, is dismissed as a 'myth'. We cannot now say how they started, nor are we able to observe the process of myth-formation, if any, at work in our midst. If an individual, some anonymous genius, invented it, then we may suppose that the process is one marked by the following steps: the individual has an emotional experience; it is transformed by α; it is published. In almost every instance nothing further happens, for the emotional experience is of too particular a nature to be at all widely significant. It might then be regarded, by analogy with scientific method, as a hypothesis, not false in itself, but applying to events of such extremely rare occurrence as to make it pass unnoticed, in the way that a mathematical formulation (Poincaré, *Science and Method*) might be perfectly sound yet never be employed because no realization had yet been perceived to which it might be applied as the algebraic system corresponding to its representative scientific deductive system. This must be the case with virtually all so-called dreams; they express, thanks to α-function, the stored and communicable version of an emotional experience. To this extent the narrator of his dream has been able to render the experience communicable, and has even published it, but the emotional experience itself—and consequently its α-formulation—has small social value because of its extreme particularity.

But there are others that might be grouped on an ascending scale of generalization until we reach, through myths of national significance, those, such as the Oedipus myth or the story of the Tower of Babel, which are felt to be of so nearly universal significance that their publication spreads over wide areas of racial and national thought and is also repeated in time. The individual who is able to transform such an emotional experience, by virtue of his α-function, into material that can be stored, communicated and finally published must belong to the category we loosely call 'genius'. But my point is that we must regard these stories (and later I shall consider actual historical events too) as being parallel with the algebraic calculus produced by the mathematician not simply to represent a specific already-existing s.d.s., but as a mathematical formulation that has not at the time, but may at some future date turn out to have, an actual realization to which it is applicable.

This being my view, I return to our chosen myth of the Tower of Babel. How are we to determine what the basic elements of the story are, without simply laying ourselves open to the charge of tampering with a text that, on my own showing, should be treated with respect? The theory of α-function may give us help. I suggest that we assume that the story is intended to deal with an emotional situation; further, that the visual images verbally conveyed have to be considered as α-elements. The narrative form we regard as being a method of imposing an appearance of coherence and integration on these elements whose coming together might otherwise demand explanation. The narrative, like the words 'as if', etc.—which Freud thought could not be expressed in dream language—seems to be a method of expressing the emotion that has to be stored. I propose we ignore, for the time being, the narrative and other forms of conjunction, except for one very important point: these elements unequivocally mean that the α-elements, the visual images, are constantly conjoined. The function of the narrative form is to enable the individual and the race to observe and to maintain this constant conjunction.

This brings me to the application of our myth to the problem that it is to interpret. The scientist must know enough mathematics to understand the nature and use of various mathematical discoveries and formulations, such as the differential calculus or the binomial theorem: the psycho-analyst must know his myth. The scientist must also know enough to have an idea when he is confronting a problem to which a particular mathematical procedure would apply: the psycho-analyst must know when he is facing a problem to which a myth would provide the psycho-analytic counterpart of the algebraic calculus. This, one might say, is precisely what Freud did; he recognized, as a scientist, that he was confronted by a problem to the solution of which he would have to apply the Oedipus myth. The result was the discovery, not of the Oedipus complex, but of psycho-analysis. (Or is it man, or man's psyche, that is discovered when these elements are constantly conjoined?) It is in this sense that I believe that the myth of Babel, or Oedipus, or Sphinx must be used as a tool comparable to that of the mathematical formulation.

Before proceeding further with the investigation of the myth as a tool for investigating emotional problems, I must point out that already this inquiry has reached a point that has implications for the use of dreams. I have said that most dreams are of very low-level generalization, but this fact, which is a disadvantage if the matter at issue is the mental life of the group in space and time, is an advantage when the issue is something so idiosyncratic as the mental life of a particular individual patient in analysis.

The dream of the individual must be taken to mean that certain α-elements are constantly conjoined. The α-elements in themselves, and their constant conjunction as shown by the dream, must be regarded as of equal significance. The α-function has then served the purpose of making storable, communicable and publishable an emotional experience that is constantly conjoined and has made it possible to record the latter fact. How does this relate the ordinary, apparently non-recurrent dream to the recurrent dream? If myth and manifest content of a dream are to be regarded as the group and individual versions of the same thing—and that thing an assertion that certain α-elements are constantly conjoined—to what use are we to put this statement? If we are to regard it as analogous to $(a + b)^2 = a^2 + b^2 + 2ab$, then presumably we need to know how the statement has been constructed and what the rules are that have to be obeyed if we are to use the statement correctly. At first sight the mathematicians appear able to do this; we can say something about the way these letters, *a* and *b*, are being used, and we can explain the rules by which their manipulation is to be guided. We can also show that certain problems can be solved if we recognize that the elements of the problem can be adequately represented by this algebraical formula. Furthermore, we can be taught how to recognize that a given problem would be aided by this particular formula rather than another, and we can pass on that information. There is, nevertheless, a gap: some individuals are more easily able to understand the explanations and to grasp when and how such a formula can be applied to advantage than others who are thought of as being mathematically ill-equipped. It is not only the mathematically ill-equipped who have difficulty in accepting the mathematical explanation of fundamentals of procedure, as mathematicians and philosophers show by their discussions of these problems, which are inseparably bound up with the nature of mathematical ability itself. But nevertheless there is no doubt that mathematicians have formed a method of recording and communicating their formulations which makes teaching of the formulations and their use assume an enviably uniform and stable discipline—at least to me who proposes that myth and dream should be regarded as corresponding to algebraic calculi and therefore as capable of yielding, after scrutiny, the tools that can interpret, through their suitability to represent a problem, the problem itself, and so open the way to its solution.

I propose now the task of establishing the fundamental rules for the use of dream or myth. The first point is that all dreams have one interpretation and only one—namely, that α-elements are constantly conjoined. The second is that every dream has a corresponding realization, which it therefore represents. This realization may be of such insignificance or rarity that it is never observed to occur, although potentially it might do so. Sometimes it is observed, and its resemblance to the dream that represents it is so nearly conscious that the dreamer has an illusion that he expresses by saying he had a dream that came true. This usually means that the dreamer believes the facts of the realization were correctly foreshadowed in a dream in which the same or similar facts occurred in a similar narrative. This is an illusion in which the similarity that exists between an emotional experience (as it is recorded and stored through the agency of α-function) and an event (to the understanding of which the stored emotional experience is essential) has been transferred to what are believed to be two narratives. In fact, one narrative serves to mark the conjunction of α-elements required to store two different but related emotional experiences: one, that which was experienced in sleep or the waking state known in *déjà vu* phenomena; the other, that which was experienced in the course of actual events in the individual's life. Since the same dream would serve as the product of α-function operating on the two emotional experiences, it is believed that the supposed events of the narrative of the dream, and the events of the emotional experience to which the dream serves a function analogous to that of algebraic calculus to empirical data, are the same. The third point is that certain factual experiences will never be understood by the patient, and therefore will never be experiences from which he can learn, unless he can interpret them in the light of his dream or the myth in which the group has enshrined both the dream and the belief in the dream's validity for all members of the group. In psychoanalytic practice this means that what the analyst has to interpret are certain facts that befall the patient in the light of a dream that has stated that for the patient certain α-elements are constantly conjoined. Thus, if the patient reports a dream that he was seated in a railway train and gave the signal usually given to indicate an intention to stop when driving a car, and that his arm fell off, it must be assumed that certain elements are conjoined.

The following are a few of the points known to me that are relevant to understanding what the elements are that are conjoined: the patient was not responsible for driving the train; he wanted to be helpful and warn the traffic against a possible accident due to ignorance of the train's movements; this, from his point of view, worthy behaviour did not meet with success because his arm behaved as if it were having a tantrum and fell onto the grass, where it lay unhelpfully. The patient was bewildered that such unexceptionable behaviour should provoke such a hostile response and that he should find himself vulnerable to criticism because of the behaviour of his arm which apparently was quite independent of him. The dream indicated that for this person any attempt to be cooperative or creative led to independent action by the appropriate part of his personality, that is, to thwart his creative and helpful intentions. The helpful intention was in itself good because it meant that the patient was in an agreeable and therefore rewarding state of mind. It is this rewarding state of mind that is denied to him by the independent action of his arm. This potentially pleasing state of mind is further attacked because disapproval was drawn to him from the remaining passengers by the behaviour of his arm. These were the most obtrusive elements.

At first sight it may seem that this is an interpretation, though a superficial one, of the dream. I would make a distinction between two kinds of interpretation by calling one the 'meaning' of a dream or any other kind of association, and the other the 'interpretation'. I consider the 'meaning' to be that aspect of the communication which, if it were made extra-analytically, is what the speaker consciously wishes to convey. Failure to interpret the dream is the most potent contribution the analyst can make towards producing acting out; failure to dream through lack of α-function is the patient's main contribution. But before a dream or association can be interpreted, its meaning must be established. Though it is fairly easy to say that the meaning of an association is that part of a communication that the patient consciously wishes to make, it is not easy to say what part of a dream is the communication that the patient consciously wishes to make. For, assuming the theory of α-function is applicable, the manifest content of the dream is a verbal expression of visual images that have been joined together because, being joined together, they record that certain elements of an emotional experience are constantly conjoined and, by recording it, make it available for unconscious waking thought (as in the example of the establishment of walking as a skill that can be exercised without further intervention by consciousness) or for conscious waking thought, as when the individual repeats the dream to himself or someone else, thereby making it accessible to the correlations that are the basis of the rationality of common sense, and to the criteria of common sense that are the establishment of correlations without evidence of contradictions. From this it follows that the publication of the dream is a request for knowledge often overtly posed as such in the form of a wish to be told what the dream 'means' or predicts. At first sight this would seem to be a reasonable request to make of an analyst. In fact it is not reasonable to make it, nor is it reasonable for an analyst to feel called upon to say what a dream means. The problem is not the dream but the emotional experience of which the dream is the irrational counterpart of the algebraic calculus. And about this emotional experience the patient feels much as an infant might feel about bumping its head on the floor—it wants to know what it means. An emotional experience, then, is in some respects like a physical experience in that it can be felt to have a meaning; that is to say, it is felt to be an experience from which something can be learnt. The α-function is the first step (without which nothing can be learnt) in turning the emotional experience, or rather the data associated with it, into material from which it is possible to learn; that is, material suitable for dream-thoughts (Freud's unconscious waking thoughts) or for correlation with common sense, which implies not only conscious waking thought, but also awareness of individual attitudes and outlook, which are a part of the individual's endowment and equipment as a member of a group. This brings me to the essential feature in the conscious communication of the individual reporting a dream: it is an overt expression of curiosity. It is exposure for test by common sense of a hypothesis, as Hume would understand such a term, namely as an assertion that certain associations are constantly conjoined. As an expression of curiosity we may regard it as suitable for investigation by the application of myth, using myth as the counterpart of an algebraic calculus.

We have now arrived at this position: the core of the dream is not the manifest content, but the emotional experience; the sense data pertaining to this emotional experience are worked on by α-function, so that they are transformed into material suitable for unconscious waking thought, the dream-thoughts, and equally suitable for conscious submission to common sense. Freud clearly thought that this material was equally suitable for more than correlation with and by common sense, and attempted to apply to it the methods of scientific investigation, as if what I am calling α-elements lent themselves to that kind of procedure. This is to assume that the α-elements can be used for purposes other than simple correlation—one of the most rudimentary of scientific procedures. The manifest content, as it would be called if we were discussing dreams in Freud's terms, is a statement that these α-elements are constantly conjoined; that being so, it is in every way analogous to the selected fact, the function of which is to display the constant conjunction of elements characteristic of the paranoid–schizoid position, and some of which it has the property of showing to be related. We shall have to consider later how the manifest content of a dream (a narrativized collection of visual images) and a mathematical formulation such as an algebraic calculus can come to be fulfilling an apparently identical function when they are in every other respect so different from each other. For the moment I must point out only that the hypothesis, the word regarded as a hypothesis, and the manifest content of a dream all share the characteristics of the selected fact in being able to bring coherence to facts previously known but not previously seen to be connected. Since the core of the problem that awaits solution is an emotional experience, we must make a distinction between this and the emotional experience that is secondary to a problem that awaits solution. We have hitherto supposed that every problem, of whatever kind, is, when reduced to its abstract basic elements, the task of finding the selected fact that harmonizes elements previously known by showing them as related to each other in a way that was not apparent before the discovery of the selected fact. I have shown that this is a description that is so close to the description in Kleinian theory of the interplay between paranoid–schizoid and depressive positions that speculation must be aroused about the nature of this description, which, as a hypothesis itself, is an example of a selected fact, and about the nature of the phenomenon to which it applies. Are there in fact elements? And if, thanks to some selected fact, they are seen to be related to each other in a particular way, does this mean any more than that—the human mind being what it is—the individual from time to time has this experience of observing the harmonious inter-relatedness of these elements, whereas in fact there is no reason to suppose that any such relatedness exists? Elements and relatedness alike are aberrations of the observing instrument.

Suppose that this last is the fact: then we would be in the position of being able to observe that our observations consist of elements that we believe to become synthesized by some mental event which corresponds with a fact. But this statement is a supposition based on a supposition. It is evident that, no matter how I attempt to state this problem, we are involved in an absurdity. This I believe to be a peculiarity related to those problems in which the emotional experience is primary. It is for this reason that I say a distinction has to be made between the experience that consists in attempting to understand an emotional experience that is secondary to the attempt to solve a problem, and the experience that consists in trying to solve a problem in which the emotional experience itself is the problem. In the first, it is possible to regard the problem as one of unrelated objects requiring synthesis; in the second, there is probably no way of regarding the problem 'as' anything at all. It is possible that there are external problems of which it is true to say that there is no way of regarding them 'as' anything at all; it may be that it is from precisely such a situation and its accompanying emotions that the selected fact extricates the observer by appearing to reveal the relatedness of some of the elements. In short, there are situations that are felt to be problems that either have no solution, or to which no solution can be found with the equipment at the disposal of the individual experiencing them. Such situations are not absolute: they may be fairly common and of short duration, but such an experience, if it lasts, itself becomes a problem that makes demands on the individual's equipment of intelligence and personality.

The essentials of this situation depend, as far as the individual is concerned, on his appreciation of the environment (that is on what he thinks are the facts of his environment) and on his appreciation of himself (that is on what he thinks are the facts of his personality). As far as the external observer, the analyst, is concerned, the situation may be regarded as limited to the following elements:

(1) the environment,
(2) the personality of the individual,
(3) the relationship between (1) and (2),
(4) the belief that the individual himself entertains about (1) and (2).

Even if we restrict the field in this way, and even supposing years of psycho-analysis, we know little about all four. The difficulty is increased because comparison is not possible; terms such as 'little' seem to say something, but under scrutiny appear to be expressions of feeling and not statements of fact. Even so, the problem has been simplified in some of its aspects by the introduction of the external observer, the analyst. For it is legitimate to believe that by transferring the problem of the relationship between an individual and his emotional state to an external observer, we at least make the investigation approximate to the situation that obtains in scientific investigations of objects by trained observers. This raises two questions.

First, in what respects has the problem been simplified? In view of my discussion of the possibility that the belief that a scientific discovery has been made is really an expression of feelings that are a product of the transitions between paranoid-schizoid and depressive positions and back again, it would seem likely that the problem has not been simplified so much as altered in kind. Even in a discipline such as physics, in which scientific method has been rigorously pursued with apparently gratifying results, it is clear that there is no justification for any assumption other than that the facts discovered are simply a selection from the sum of knowledge of those facts, or characteristics of facts that lend themselves to comprehension by human mathematical and logical faculty, human perception, human tool-making capacity, human capacity for interpretation of the behaviour of the tools employed; they also lend themselves to adequate representation by the constructs which α-function contrives from the sense impressions supposedly related to these external objects.

The second question raises the doubt about simplification to a higher pitch still. In psycho-analysis the observer is not an external force, except in the sense of not being the analysand, because he *is* an important part of the environment. What is being investigated, as the physicists also have discovered, is not an object *in vacuo* but a relationship between the object and its environment. (As also in mathematics—*see* Semple and Kneebone, *Algebraic Projective Geometry,* p. 3). The alternatives may be set out in a formula:

> Suppose A to be the person concerned with his own emotional experience, a,
>
> and B to be the psycho-analyst,
>
> and C the environment less A and B.

Then

(1) self consciousness would be: A knows $a + B + C$,

(2) analysis would be: B knows $A + C$.

But (1) can be seen to be complicated by the fact that A may not recognize that a appertains to himself and not to his environment.

This setting out of the problem shows that analysts have not really decided if what needs to be investigated is a, or $A + B + C$, or $A + a$. Let us assume that this is not a material point and that *all* combinations, until it is proved to the contrary, need to be known. Let us further assume that in psycho-analysis, what A needs to know is, A knows $a + B + C$; to know that would be to know all that needs to be known of other combinations.

Let us fall back on the idea that, to make progress in *this* investigation, what is needed as our tool is not an algebraic calculus but a myth. The myth, or myths, we require must serve to elucidate the problem of learning, and must elucidate this problem when it is associated with investigating or learning about an emotional experience that is felt to be primary and not secondary to some other investigation. Since I know virtually nothing about this subject beyond the tentative suggestions I have been making, I shall not be disturbed by the fact that the choice of myth I make would not be the choice someone else might make. As I know no rules, I do not have to obey any, but will make up some as I go along, thus following the precedent of the King in *Alice in Wonderland.*

My first rule is to make any rule I please. The myths I choose to elucidate the problem of learning are: (1) Adam, eating of the fruit of the Tree, is thus opposed to God's will, learns from it sexual guilt, and is expelled from the Garden (= Paradise). (2) The Sphinx stimulates curiosity; hubristic vow to be ruthless in its satisfaction at no matter what cost—suicide, incest and death are the rewards of success, and pestilence for failure. (3) A co-operation to build a tower up to Heaven is punished by God who destroys the method of verbal communication that made co-operation possible. (4) The youth who seeks a mirror in which to observe his beauty is punished by God. This last choice is made in the hope that it will serve to elucidate problems of curiosity and learning associated with the personality of the investigator himself—his need to find a mirror, that is to say a tool, which will help him to satisfy his curiosity, his *loving* curiosity, about himself. The curiosity, one might say, is not disinterested. (The lack of integrity vitiates it if one is expecting scientific curiosity.) The punishment seems peculiar.

Perhaps the way to use a myth is to associate to it; this may be the analytical counterpart of the algebraic calculus that is used for a specific task when its variables are given values. Free association to a myth is the equivalent of giving the elements a value as if they were variables in a formula. The values are those that are relevant to a particular problem, and the particular problem is the personality of the person who produces the free associations. By attributing these values to the variables of the myth we understand that those qualities are, for that person, constantly conjoined. So far, so good. But what does this mean in practice? Does one ask the patient for free associations on the Oedipus myth? Or on Narcissus? This certainly does not appeal to me. Rather, I would say that, listening to the free associations, one would think something like this: the patient is wanting me to agree with him; it is obvious from the way he is putting forward a suggestion that he has a beautiful personality. It appears to me that it is a morally beautiful personality; my personality is likewise beautiful; in fact I am to be a mirror of his excellence. But there is more of this story, the myth of Narcissus: there is a god who turns him into a flower. What is the patient saying that corresponds to this? There *must* be something because my myth tells me that these elements are constantly conjoined; or perhaps this is not the right myth. Either it is the right myth, and I have so far failed to see this aspect of it as it has appeared, or I am mistaken in thinking this is the myth to be employed. Perhaps I should seek for a more appropriate one—the Oedipus myth, for example.

I can see objections. It will be argued that no analyst could possibly have such a store of myths available in his psycho-analytic armoury as this procedure would seem to desiderate. It may further be objected that there is no reason why an analyst should store myths rather than theories; surely the analyst should be asking himself, as his patient talks, what is the appropriate psycho-analytic theory—not what or which of all the myriad myths ought to be dragged in as appropriate.

Psycho-analytic theories, as propounded by the best analysts, have served the cause of scientific development well, but Freud owed more of his discoveries to his use—the unconscious method of his use—of the Oedipus myth than to other more easily recognizable aspects of his scientific method. The real nature of psycho-analytic methodology has never been properly assessed;

there is a danger that the successes of the movement will be attributed to the ability of its students to apply conventional scientific method, and not always the best examples of it, rather than to the intuitive flair that made it possible for Freud at least to do more. One consequence is a tendency for the movement to proliferate jargon—a danger that besets even mathematics, although there it is disguised somewhat through appearing as correct axiomatic formulation that is inadequately appreciated because it is no longer seen in relationship with a more concrete background. There are times when psycho-analytic theory is so propounded that it is made to sound, as a bad teacher of his subject makes mathematics sound, as if it were 'an ingenious manipulation of symbols in accordance with certain arbitrarily prescribed rules' (Semple and Kneebone, *Algebraic Projective Geometry,* p. 1). An appreciation of the importance of the use of myth in scientific method is necessary for further progress, or to arrest a process of retreat from positions already won, because it helps to keep the concrete background of psycho-analytic theory in view. If this is the case, is it not analogous to the low-level hypotheses of empirically verifiable data, rather than to algebraic calculi? And if so, should not the concrete background be provided by psycho-analytic practice rather than myth, which seems in danger of being a *substitute* for a concrete background rather than the concrete background? This objection could be valid if indeed a study of myth is to be used in the study of the individual, not instead of it. That is to say, the analyst should have at his disposal certain myths, as the scientist has certain mathematical procedures; he should frequently produce his free associations to them so that he is familiar with them and their use; and he should then learn to detect from his patient's material which is the appropriate myth, and from that what is the appropriate interpretation. Free associating to his chosen myths would then become the analyst's form of practising his craft so as to remain in training for his work. The choice of myth that he would use for the purpose would be an indication of his scientific affiliation.

Suppose an analyst did not include in his canon the Oedipus myth: it would be an indication for considering to what extent he was able to regard other psycho-analysts and himself as embracing the same discipline and therefore able to communicate with each other profitably. But this, though important, is relatively not so important as the part that association on chosen myth, and selection of the myths on which to associate, plays in the promotion of psycho-analytic intuition and, more precisely, in the repair and reinvigoration of the analyst's α-function. Perhaps for the first time my suggestion makes it possible to give a practising analyst precise advice, and even instruction, on how to keep in training. He should not bother so much with attempts to keep notes about patients but to take, say, the Oedipus myth, and write his free associations on it, noting the date. This he can repeat as often as he likes—the free associations will never be the same for different dates. If, amongst his associations, a patient's name appears, that name can be indexed if he feels he needs notes on his patients. This procedure can be repeated, five days a week, for the same myth or for such other myths as he feels disposed to include in his canon; and he can discard and return to any given myth as often as he chooses. It would be as well to use a version, or versions, of the myth for whose historicity there is scholarly evidence, as, other things being equal, it seems that a version that has withstood the passage of centuries is probably more likely to have powerful appeal to the human mind than one that may be an ephemeral aberration and therefore of too great particularity.

This procedure promotes analytic intuition in the following way: suppose the Oedipus myth is the chosen exercise; it will not be chosen unless it has some immediate relevance for the analyst, and its relevance must be that the analyst has an emotional experience that is either repeating, or threatening to repeat, itself. Even this will not explain the choice of myth, but the analyst can draw his own conclusions on that matter at his convenience. The point is that his free associations should show him what the features are, in his present situation, which are interpreted and given a meaning by the myth on which he has chosen to associate. It will again be observed that this course of action differs from the accepted view of analysis. It is not using conscious material to interpret the unconscious; it is using the unconscious to interpret a conscious state of mind associated with facts of which the analyst is aware. The interpretation of the dream will give meaning to the known facts and feelings of the analyst's life, just as scrutiny of an ordnance survey map can give meaning to natural features clearly visible to the traveller and bring him to a realization of the point that he has reached on his journey. The myth embodies the constants and variables valid for any period of life: the free associations ascribe the immediately current values to the variables, and the scrutiny of the material reveals the problem, which is the step essential to its solution, if any.

Now let us apply the Babel myth to destruction of the α-function. One point that immediately obtrudes is the hostility of the Deity to the aspirations of men who wish to build a city and a tower to reach to Heaven, and to make a name for themselves to prevent their being scattered [*Genesis* XI 1–9]. The people are making bricks and slime, which are then to be put together to make the tower to reach Heaven. It seems like an artificial breast–penis. And what of the name to prevent scattering? The word as a hypothesis which brings the scattered objects together and keeps them so? It is the God who is opposed to the hypothesis, the word (as hypothesis), and it seems as if the people who *have* come together are to be scattered; the hypothesis or selected fact is to be destroyed, the fragments scattered upon the face of all the earth. This is an attack on an attempt to reach Heaven: it is an attack on linking—the language that makes co-operation possible.

[Undated]

The claim of psycho-analysis to be a scientific procedure has often been challenged by scientists of other disciplines. Stirred by a desire to repudiate what seems to be a denial of the analyst's aspiration to be honest and to state his findings truthfully, psycho-analysts tend either to assume that the criterion is based on a misunderstanding of their work, or else that there is such a thing as scientific method employed by physicists, chemists and others, but that it cannot be used in any valuable way in their own work. The explanation of this attitude probably lies in the nature of psycho-analytic training, which has to cover such an enormous area and is so closely associated with the cure of patients that the would-be analyst can hardly find time to concentrate on the essentials of psycho-analytic theory, let alone investigate metalogic and metatheory. It is likely that if he does so, he will rapidly conclude that they have no relevance to his work and so dismiss both as insignificant.

Yet he would be wrong, and it is one of my aims to show that metatheory and metalogic are of great importance in all scientific work, and of peculiar significance for the psycho-analyst—nowhere more than in the psycho-analysis of severely disturbed patients of the kind known to psychiatry as psychotic or borderline psychotic.

I shall approach the subject as if my aim were to see in what way the criticism that psycho-analysis is unscientific is justified. To do this it is necessary first to try to understand what constitutes scientific method and by what criteria it is possible to determine whether a given method is scientific or not. To this end I propose to consider the views of physicists and philosophers. I choose these two disciplines because it would generally be conceded today that it is in the field of physics that scientific method has achieved its greatest successes, and in the field of philosophy—particularly through the labours of the philosophers of science—that the most rigorous investigation of the methods by which these successes have been achieved has been set in train.

I must say at once that the idea that there is any generally accepted view of what constitutes scientific method, or indeed that there is *a* scientific method, is one of which one rapidly becomes disabused. The search, as I hope to show, is rewarding; the more thoroughly it is carried out, the greater and more fascinating is the complexity that is revealed. In the first place it is clear that psycho-analysis is not alone in being vulnerable to criticism of the scientific soundness of its methods and results.

[Undated]

METATHEORY

In the following pages there are grouped together a number of propositions under a few specific headings. The headings, together with the descriptive matter, are brief to a point that makes me fear they may be regarded as cryptic; even so, for the purpose they are to serve they are far more lengthy, complex and imprecise than they should be, compared with their nearest counterparts in other scientific disciplines. For the functions they are to serve approximate to those that are performed by the lemma (proposition taken for granted) in Greek geometry, the postulate, the definitory hypothesis used as a premise, the hypothesis taken from one scientific deductive system to act as a premise in another, and even the word, regarded (as I think it can be) as a hypothesis as it is understood in the light of the constant conjunction theory of Hume. It may be thought that this is a condemnation of these groups of propositions, but although I am aware of their defects I am doubtful whether these defects are not inherent in the task I have set myself, rather than in my performance of it.

The discoveries of psycho-analysis make it no longer possible to be satisfied with the methodology of scientists or philosophers of science even in the refinements of method they have produced to counter their own dissatisfaction. The psycho-analyst is in the curious position of studying a subject that illuminates the most ineradicable source of unscientific inquiry, namely the human mind, using that same mind as his scientific instrument, and having to do so without the comfort of thinking his observations are made by an inanimate machine that, by virtue of being dead, must be objective. But clearly an inability to be satisfied that the methods of scientists of other disciplines are scientific decreases rather than increases the psycho-analyst's hope to be more successful. Yet the attempt must be made to use psycho-analytic experience to improve on classical scientific method, and to use such improvements to fortify the procedures we employ. It is as a part of this attempt that I am using these groups of propositions. I consider them to be psycho-analytic definitory hypotheses that I propose to employ as premises in deductive systems that I elaborate later. I shall call them premises (from mathematical logic) for short. My desire to make them as short and precise as possible is frustrated because precision demands elaboration in a subject dependent, as in metaphysics, on the use of words that have already a penumbra of associations that render them at one and the same moment suitable for employment in the psycho-analytic context, and yet permeated by meanings that need to be discarded if their use is not to mislead. This fact has made it necessary for me to lengthen my verbal embodiment of the premise by references to the provenance, the genealogy so to speak, of the idea I wish to express, and although I have limited this severely to the psycho-analytical provenance and, as I am well aware, to only a small part of that, it yet amounts to a considerable lengthening of an already long description and still does scant justice to the ideas or to the workers who have previously employed them. It would be pleasant to think that omissions and failures were attributable to faulty selection from the material of previous workers, but I fear that the true explanation is likely to be ignorance of the work, maybe even important work, that others have done but of which I have been unable to keep informed. However, I hope that I have been able, by this device that I have included in each premise, to clarify the sense in which I am proposing to employ that premise.

Frustration

A sense of frustration engenders feelings that are hard to tolerate. Intolerance varies with the individual and may be pronounced, according to the age and character of the person who experiences it. The baby experiences frustration, does not like it and makes, or is forced to make, a decision: it must decide whether to deny frustration or to modify it.

This bald statement can hardly be said to represent a fact. As with all psycho-analytical theories, it is necessary to make statements, as Freud pointed out, which are sufficiently exaggerated accounts of the facts they represent to make the facts themselves stand out unmistakably and yet not fall into caricature, which induces an opposite error. But it is true that early frustration presents the baby with a problem that has to be solved, and one on the solution of which much depends. Suppose the child to be extremely intolerant of frustration: the danger is that it will strive to deny frustration and to continue to deny it until its appreciation of the world of reality is itself impaired. In the extreme case of such denial the foundations for psychosis are being laid, for an awareness of the real world is an essential part of contact with reality. The hatred of frustration is easily extended to embrace reality itself in a way that is typical of the psychotic; it may then be extended to that part of the mental apparatus on which the awareness of reality and frustration depends.

There are degrees of intolerance of frustration, and there are degrees of intensity with which it is denied, until we reach that moderate degree of denial that passes over into the state of mind, typical of the development of the domination of what Freud called the reality principle, in which frustration and its associated feelings, painful though they are, are tolerated sufficiently to enable the personality to entertain the possibility of modification of frustration rather than denial.

Denial of frustration

Let us consider denial of frustration, taking as our example an extreme degree serious enough to produce psychotic reactions, but not so extreme that the patient is inaccessible to an analytic approach. As I have said, the intolerance of frustration extends to an intolerance of reality; since modification of reality is precluded by the state of mind itself, the hate is directed against the mental apparatus on which awareness of reality depends. Provisionally we may accept the view, put forward by Freud, that this apparatus has the following components: a capacity for thought that is available as a substitute for immediate action of the kind designed, under the dominance of the pleasure principle, to relieve the psyche of accretions of stimuli; a system of notation associated with the development of a capacity for attention on which memory depends; an awareness of sense data. The denial of frustration therefore involves denial or destruction of these functions. Again, it is a matter of degree, and some functions—notably those concerned with awareness of sense data—may suffer relatively less damage than others.

Modification of frustration

Suppose the intolerance of frustration to be less extreme: the functions I have listed as marked for destruction when the intention is to deny frustration are cherished because they are essential to the task of modifying frustration by modifying its source. This may be the environment, including special though temporary features of it, or, as in psycho-analysis itself, features in the personality that might be supposed to intensify the painful aspects of the frustration experienced. These same features of the functions peculiar to domination by the reality principle are therefore subject to quite different treatment according to the degree of intolerance of frustration: if it is great, then denial and destruction; if moderate, then growth and development. Later, these functions of the reality principle will be examined more rigorously. For the present I wish to leave the discussion of frustration at this point: the psyche copes with frustration by methods that can be seen to fall into one of two classes of reaction: denial, or appreciation with a view to modification.

Concern for truth and life

I must make clear my choice not only of these terms, but also of the realities they represent for the second of my fundamental postulates (hypotheses or premises). No single word can adequately express the ideas to which I want to draw attention. By 'concern' I mean something that has in it feelings of consideration for the object, of sympathy with it, of value for it. The person who has concern for truth or for life is impelled to a positive, not merely passive, relationship with both.

A concern for truth may seem to be so closely related to impulses that operate under the dominance of the reality principle as to make it scarcely worth while to distinguish it from them by singling it out for special mention. The reasons for linking it with a concern for life may seem equally to be obscure, but I hope to justify both procedures.

The concern for truth must be distinguished from a capacity for establishing contact with reality. A man may have little capacity for that through lack of intelligence, training or even physical endowment—he might be defective in one or more of his senses, to take an obvious example. Yet this same man can have an active yearning for, and respect for, truth. Conversely, a highly gifted and well-equipped person may have little concern for truth about the realities with which his endowment permits an easy contact. Such unconcern will clearly be a matter for attention by the analyst for whom the psycho-analysis of the patient has truth as its criterion.

Concern for life does not mean only a wish not to kill, though it does mean that. It means concern for an object precisely because that object has the quality of being alive. It means distinguishing between objects because one is alive and the other is not. It means considering that the difference is an important one. It means being curious about the qualities that go to make up what we know as life, and to have a desire to understand them. Conversely, a lack of concern for life means regarding a living object as indistinguishable from, or as being unworthy of being distinguished from, a machine, a thing or a place.

Finally, concern for life means that a person must have respect for himself in his qualities as a living object. Lack of concern means a lack of respect for himself and, *a fortiori,* of others, which is fundamental and of proportionately grave import for analysis. It is clear that lack of such respect means lack also of a safeguard against murderous or suicidal impulses. But there are other implications scarcely less serious, though less obvious. I shall consider them as I discuss concern for truth and life conjoined.

The patient who has no regard for truth, for himself, or for his analyst achieves a kind of freedom arising from the fact that so much destructive activity is open to him for so long. He can behave in a way that destroys his respect for himself and his analyst, provided he always retains enough contact with reality to feel that there is some respect to destroy; and this he can always assume if his analyst continues to see him. If his analyst does not continue, then he has destroyed the analysis. But destruction of the analysis is to be avoided, for it entails loss of freedom—at least till a new object is found—thus introducing a need for moderation that is apparent at other points in the closed system that the patient strives to produce. An obvious instance of this is the need to avoid successful suicide or murder. In brief, it is necessary for the patient to avoid any step calculated to effect change, and yet to change enough to ensure more analysis either for the reason that he has temporarily become a greater liability and needs more care, or because he shows such promise that it would be wrong to stop just when affairs have reached so happy a posture. But it is clear that the limitations on freedom, and the sequent frustration, are associated with the patient's sensitiveness to reality. He must therefore lose some of this freedom in keeping analysis going.

But I am exceeding the boundaries of the discussion as I wish to preserve them for the present. I conclude by repeating that my wish is to direct attention, as a matter of psycho-analytic significance, to the degree to which any analysand displays concern for truth, life, and truth and life together.

Violent emotions

Violence, attributed to the emotions by me here, is not intended to imply only quantity of feeling. I shall consider only love and hate because I regard them as comprising all others; I do not separate love and life instincts, or hate and death instincts, nor shall I consider whether the violence implies an origin in the instinctual endowment or is secondary to an external environment stimulus. It may on occasion be due to a deficiency in a capacity for thought, or some other function proper to the onset of the reality principle which tends to produce arrest at a stage where action is a method of unburdening the psyche of accretions of stimuli, and so contributes to the physical expression of love or hate which can be characteristic of violence. Violence, then, though related to quantity or degree, contributes to a qualitative change in the emotion. The qualitative changes make love and hate possess appreciably cruel strains together with diminishing concern for the object. Both love and hate thus become more easily associated with a lack of concern for truth and life.

The breast

The term, 'breast' is here used and discussed as a definitory hypothesis. 'Breast' is the name of a hypothesis breast, and the hypothesis breast is to be understood to imply that certain mental phenomena and their corresponding actualities, if any, are constantly conjoined. It will be seen that I treat the name given to an object, the word 'breast', as a hypothesis, and follow Hume's view that a hypothesis is the expression of a subjective sense that certain associations are constantly conjoined, and is not a representation corresponding to an actuality. In psychoanalysis the hypothesis is also the actuality that it represents: breast is a hypothesis that certain phenomena are constantly conjoined, and the hypothesis states that it is itself that constant conjunction.

Breast, like all other hypotheses, is a condensation. It is a condensation into the verbal counterpart of a visual image, which is itself a condensation. I proceed now with the expansion of the condensation, but only to that limited extent sufficient to indicate by the nature of the constantly conjoined associations something of the nature of the hypothesis breast.

I am treating breast as an α-element, not as a thing-in-itself, a β-element, or as a symbol. By virtue of its function as a hypothesis, it is also capable of the functions of the selected fact that has qualified as a hypothesis through public-ation, and therefore differs from the selected fact that has a private function. It also has affinities with a fundamental postulate in a scientific deductive system. It has similarities, by virtue of its character as an α-element, to 'the elements'—as that term was originally understood when it was used by Euclid for the elements of geometry. Finally, I am displaying a facet that is extremely close to that attributed by Freud to the condensation in a dream-element, which condensation can be expanded by free association 'to six, eight or a dozen times as much space' (Freud, *Interpretation of Dreams* [1900a, *SE 4*], p. 279).

So much for the metatheory: now to consider the theory. There are a number of hypotheses relating to the breast. Some are: the breast is a link between two objects; the breast is a source of good things to its possessors; the breast can be maltreated, gouged out, cut, split. To what do these theories relate? The first refers to happenings observed in an analysis; these are believed to be related to each other and are given a meaning if they are considered by the observer—be it analyst or analysand—to be a breast. They are seen, by virtue of the hypothesis that they are a breast, to share certain characteristics, and together and individually to share in linking two objects together. Characteristics and function are believed to be made evident by the application of the term to the appropriate happenings. Put in another way: in an analysis occasions will be found to arise when the series of statements (emotional expressions and other attributes of the meeting between analyst and analysand whose connection with each other and with the known objects of the meeting is either undiscerned, or seems to be of a kind that offers no clues that are relevant to analysis) may be seen to be so related and to have such relevance if they are recognized as the breast. The breast, then, is a definitory hypothesis that can be used by the analyst to provide the patient with the selected fact that he cannot find for himself.

Two points require comment. First, I have spoken of certain events or happenings as being given coherence, without saying what these events are to which breast gives coherence. This is deliberate and is due to the fact that they must be regarded as constants to which a value has not been assigned. Even this is not quite accurate, for amongst them are variables whose function—in the sense in which that term is used by the mathematician—is not given and may not be discoverable. Second, I have used as the name for a definitory hypothesis the word, 'breast', which has a historical meaning that is simple and direct. It may therefore be said already to be a definitory hypothesis—in my terminology—which indicates the constant conjunction presumably for a number of simple phenomena such as woman, warmth, love, sensuality, and so forth.

Why is such a word used? In what sense is it illuminating to employ a term with such a penumbra of associations (many of which are physical, concrete, primitive and sensuous) to provide a definitory hypothesis, functioning as a selected fact, for the situation in analysis which, on the face of it, bears no resemblance to the historical meaning of breast? The situation in the analysis that requires the use of the term, 'breast', requires it precisely because it has become so divorced from the penumbra of associations adhering to breast that it bears superficially no resemblance to them. It requires it because breast, if the interpretation is correct, is a hypothesis in the Humean sense which fixes a constellation of associations that are constantly conjoined but have lost their connection with the material expressed by the free associations of the analysis, these last having become conjoined with material now alienated from, or never in contact with, the penumbra of associations of breast. The juxtaposition, by interpretation of breast, to the events of the analysis can be seen to resemble, as I have already said, a provision by the analyst of a selected fact that the patient cannot find for himself, but there are also important differences. The selected fact is a discovery made by the patient or individual and is the tool by which he ensures the constant progression, the very essence of learning and therefore of growing. This is represented by the sequence: paranoid–schizoid position, selected fact (precipitating coherence of the elements of the paranoid–schizoid position) ushering in the depressive position, which then instantaneously reveals yet vaster areas of hitherto unrelated elements belonging to domains of the paranoid–schizoid position which were previously unrevealed and unsuspected—a revelation that contributes to the depression peculiar to the depressive position. The *selected fact* then is an essential element in a process of discovery. The *interpretation*—employing definitory hypotheses, such as breast, which have many resemblances to, and in some respects are identical with, the selected fact—is concerned not with *discovery* so much as with *repair*. This difference, important as it is, must not obscure the fact that the definitory hypothesis employed in interpretation, and the selected fact, are in one respect identical: they must be α-elements. We shall see later the disastrous consequences that follow from an absence of α-elements.

The penis

Most of what I have said about the breast may be said about the penis in its function in the theory I am propounding. The metatheory is identical, but now that I have discussed the use of the name, 'breast', and the breast, it is possible to add something to what I have said about the metatheory.

The first point is that an attempt to clarify metatheory is embarrassed by the lack of philosophical and scientific equipment appropriate to the needs of psycho-analysis. I have been reduced to educing the qualities associated with (a) scientific hypothesis, (b) psycho-analytic theory of dreams, (c) Humean theory of the hypothesis, (d) the selected fact of Poincaré, to produce a hybrid to describe the scientific nature of the usage, breast. Probably the best plan is to name the class to which breast belongs, 'the class of interpretations'. I propose accordingly to call all the objects I choose for discussion in this chapter, 'interpretations'. The interpretation then is a word or phrase that must be an α-element, must be interchangeable with a visual image, and must be capable of the functions of the selected fact. To this must now be added that it has, when it comes to any attempt to produce in psycho-analysis the counterpart of reduction of a high-level hypothesis to formulation in terms of empirically verifiable data, the resistant qualities of a scientific deductive system in which the lowest members in the hierarchy are statistical hypotheses. The psycho-analytical interpretation, by virtue of its having the characteristics of a statistical hypothesis, cannot be verified empirically in the sense in which empirical verification has hitherto been understood. This does not mean that psycho-analysis is unscientific—

psycho-analysts may be; so may chemists, physicists, philosophers, logicians and others—but it does mean that the philosophy of science, together with mathematics, lags too far behind the development of psycho-analysis for the necessary concepts to be available. In the meanwhile, I propose to improvise temporary solutions of our problems by these short interjections of metatheory between the discussions of successive elements of theory.

We have discussed shortly what I now call, 'the interpretation breast'; there follows a similar discussion of 'the interpretation penis'.

This interpretation, in its visual aspects, is more elongated than the breast. The verbalization of the visual image, which is inescapable, imposes rigidity on the interpretation that, if it could be recorded for public-ation (as I am trying to do at this moment by translation into words) in a manner that preserved its qualities as they are preserved in private by the method of recording that is available to the mind through the operation of dream-work-α, would retain one of its most important qualities, namely plasticity. These two interpretations, breast and penis, are plastic; that is to say that in the mind their visual image can alter enormously and yet retain its identifiability without loss or diminution.

Splitting

'Splitting' is the name of an interpretation: the interpretation has affinities with a constant conjunction hypothesis, a statistical hypothesis, an α-element. The visual image is fleeting, as in a dream: it seems to be there, and then not there. For example, it is a mass of Y's associations of person after person, all of them on a flat plane; it flickers, and they have gone. But surely this is 'splits', or rather some thing for which 'splits' is the right name. Perhaps splits are a way of indicating splitting, a way of producing a visual image of splitting, or an image, an ideogram. I am not convinced by this. I am struck more by the fact that these splits appear and then they are gone. In this respect there is much in the consulting room that has this dreamlike quality. That is to say that there is some aspect of the sessions that fades and then reappears quite clearly in the way that a well-remembered dream appears and then fades. There is plenty that is not like this: Y, who talks as if it were all rational and straightforward, man-to-man stuff, has a way of denying psychosis. It may be true that what needs watching is this dreamlike stuff. But if so, what has happened to the α-theory? I am lost and see no connection. Perhaps it is that under the rational, which is being used as denial, are only α-elements.

I think 'splitting' calls up the wrong visual image. What does it look like, or feel like, or sound like? What does Y do? Not splitting. X is much more like it, and comes as near as he can to applying a gridiron of splits like a chip-potato machine, so that one is left like a series of pieces ready to be fried. Splitting is done by a single wedge-like object (the penis) or by the gridlike object. This welling up of a field, or sea, or mosaic of splits presents an appearance not unlike what one would expect to see representing the paranoid–schizoid position. It may be that the patient's trouble is that the paranoid–schizoid position is indistinguishable in his mind from a terribly split object. This means that Melanie Klein is right in saying that the depressive-position depression is about all the destruction the patient has wrought. But has she regarded the splits as being parts of the whole object that has been destroyed? One aspect of this must be the problem it produces for learning when every synthesis reveals more of the unsynthesized, particularly in analysis, when every gain in self-knowledge appears to reveal how little is known. This depression is quite common, but it may be that the rational depression at discovering how little you know about yourself is deepened by the feeling that the devastation of personality is even greater than expected. The devastation is seen to be the *consequence* of curiosity, and the synthesizing aspect of the experience is lost to sight. The greedier the curiosity, the greater the amount of destruction revealed. Yet there remains the problem: why does the fragmented, uncoordinated mass of elements loom so large and thus overshadow all else? It only seems to beg the question to say it is a depressed personality: it may be nearer to say it is one that is immensely greedy to be creative.

[Undated]

It would be useful to take a leaf out of the mathematical logician's book and consider concepts such as, 'breast', 'penis', etc., as conjunctions, or the emotions as connectives, or whatever it was that was thought to be most accurate. But in fact these terms are not very suitable for psychoses because I am concerned here with something that approximates to psychoanalysis of the state of mind that in one person becomes a psychosis and in another an invention of mathematical logic. The failed mathematical logician might develop a psychosis, and the aborted psychosis might determine its experiencer to turn to mathematical logic. We may have to invent, with such assistance from the mathematical logician as we can get, a mode of abstraction for terms such as, 'penis'.

The first need is to consider what it is that we want to abstract from such a term: if it is its function, for which of its functions do we need to find an abstraction? At the same time the question obtrudes: how is the meaning of the original object, from which the abstraction is to be effected, to be retained? The answer is, by preservation of the visual image and hence the importance of the term, 'penis', for example, for this term has the merit of being able to evoke a visual image. So we must never attempt abstraction without concretization.

What is to be abstracted? Its quality as a link. Very well; call it, '*a*'. What of its meaning as a sexual symbol? Call it, '*b*'. But some people think it dirty and disgusting, and that it should not be mentioned because it is dirty and disgusting. Call it, '*c*'. But anatomists consider the term to connote a physical structure. Call it, '*d*'. The physiologists, on the other hand, consider it . . . Call it, '*e*'. And so on—almost for ever, one might think.

In these examples I have not been able to produce an abstraction without particularization. For example, '*c*' has been chosen to represent that which stands for something very particular—a person or persons being disgusted by the term, 'penis'. It is clear that something has gone wrong with this approach. Suppose we start again, and say that '*a*' is the abstraction of 'penis'. Can we then regard '*a*' as a variable that may be given one of many values, e.g. a link, or an object of disgust, or an anatomical structure? Or we may say that the term, 'penis', is the name we give a visual image, and that the visual image is an abstraction, a variable that can be given many different values. Here we differ from the mathematical logician who makes a mark on paper that, one supposes, is not able to call up any visual image but itself; nor do we attempt a painting, sketch or photograph. We employ a word on the understanding that it is an abstract visual image. Do we differ from non-scientists in this? The statement, 'Dogs are animals', would seem to use the term, 'dog', as evocative of a visual image that, if not abstract, is at least a variable that is probably given a value by speaker and listener alike. But it is understood that though it is a variable, the degree of abstraction is limited. It is not supposed that 'dog' can be given the value of a cat or a pebble. We must assume that it is evocative of a visual image that will permit the requisite amount of freedom and yet also impose a limit. Yet both 'dog' and '*a*' call up visual images in that both are seen, and both are marks on paper. But if I *say,* '*a*' or 'dog', then '*a*' simply calls up a visual image of the letter of the alphabet, whereas 'dog' calls up a visual image of an animal.

Let us now consider this situation in which the patient says, "Blood everywhere"—he calls up a visual image in my mind, but I do not see any blood that appears to correspond in reality to the visual image he calls up. But by his behaviour I am given to understand that he expects me to do just that. On the face of it, I suppose that the evidence that is presenting itself to his senses is the same as that which presents itself to mine; if that is so, then his interpretation and mine are obviously different. (I am using the term, 'interpretation', in the way I have already explained, that is to say, as the name in metatheory for those words, or collections of words, which indicate constant conjunction of elements.) In this situation I am confronted by elements for which I can find no selected fact. I cannot, therefore, draw together certain elements in a manner that appears to give them coherence. I can direct my attention to one of two groups of phenomena: I can attempt to illuminate the facts that he, so I gather, sees and feels blood everywhere, and I don't—I may try to find a selected fact that will give coherence to the elements of this situation; or I may give attention to a quite different set of elements, namely those associated with what seems to me to be the patient's state of mind. The two sets of elements need not be separated. For example, I may decide that the patient is mad; this selected fact will make elements in both sets cohere. But in either event I must exercise the wide-ranging activity of which Freud says, 'A special function was instituted which had periodically to search the outer world in order that its data might be already familiar if an urgent inner need should arise; this function was attention', and which I have replaced by α-function. To this I now add, since I am engaged on the specialized task of psycho-analysis, my theory of the use of myth. I therefore exercise α-function on the facts, my interpretations of the facts, and my knowledge—such as it is—of mythology. By this means I hope to arrive at a psycho-analytic interpretation. But at this moment I do not wish to pursue the search for a psycho-analytic interpretation; I wish to scrutinize the nature of the method I am pursuing, and to do so with a particular aspect in mind of the problem I am investigating, namely the fact that the patient has produced what I call an interpretation—blood everywhere—of some experience. I, in this very sentence, am expressing my interpretation of what I think are facts, namely the facts covered by the phrase, 'what he is doing'. Further, I am seeking an interpretation (based on the idea that what he is doing is expressing an interpretation of some experience he is having) of what this experience can be which is expressed for him by the words, 'blood everywhere', but which I do not think can possibly be expressed for me by those words. To do this I shall use my theory of α- and β-elements, and assume that the difference in view lies in the fact that I am using α-elements, and he is using β-elements.

[Undated]

Theories for use in the psycho-analysis of disorders of thought

The scientific principles on which this book [a preliminary outline of *Learning from Experience*] is planned I have explained elsewhere. But it may not be out of place to summarize the main points for the benefit of those to whom this form of presentation is unusual. First, a warning: the reader may feel that what is said is obscure and difficult. Allowing for the intrinsic difficulties of the subject, I believe that much of what is felt to be obscure on a first reading will appear less so if the reader will not allow himself to dwell too long on his first encounter with an obscurity, but will press on till the end, when I think he will have a fair idea of the whole and will thus be in a position to return to the earlier obscurity to find it much more comprehensible. But of course I realize that ultimately the difficulties of the subject, and my limitations in exposition, will make the value of the book depend very much on the skill and patience of the reader, and the goodwill with which he repairs the deficiencies of my work. I can at least promise that he is not being called on to waste his time because I have grudged mine.

The first part of the book consists of theories. Each theory is set out on the same plan, which is essentially that of a scientific deductive system. That is to say, first there are a number of hypotheses so arranged that they follow logically from the premises and from the preceding hypotheses. Consequently each hypothesis has a preceding premise, and is itself the premise of a succeeding hypothesis.

This system is in accord with that pursued by those sciences, particularly physics and mathematics, whose success both in results and in the pursuit of those results has been one of the outstanding features of our era. At the same time, this may not at first be apparent because psycho-analysis, in common with other biological sciences, does not as yet lend itself to the degree of abstraction that makes it possible for the physicist and the mathematician to set out their scientific deductive systems in a manner that is at once exact and brief. The employment of verbal descriptions, often lengthy, contrasts with mathematical formulation and the formulations of the mathematical logician in a way that tends to obscure the structure of these theories and, consequently, their similarity to those of the physicist and mathematician from which their form is derived.

I have followed each scientific deductive system with a discussion of the premises and an acknowledgement of the source, usually the work of a practising psycho-analyst, from which they are derived. I have added comments of my own when it has seemed to me that they would be helpful.

The second part of the book is devoted to the use of these theories in the practice of psycho-analysis. First, I discuss the problem inherent in bridging the gap between hypothesis and empirical data. This is not exhaustive, but its disadvantages are compensated for because the solutions of the problem I adumbrate are implicit in later sections of the book. It will be evident that the suggestions I make can only be provisional approaches to this problem.

An intrinsic part of this disquisition will be a detailed investigation of what is meant by, or is comprised in, the meaning of free-floating attention and counter-resistance. This is of importance not only in itself, but for the light it throws by contrast on what it is that the patient is unable to do.

From this I shall pass to that aspect of practice that consists in theory construction, which is preliminary to interpretation. This will involve the use of already existing theories, including those I put forward for consideration here. I shall make it clear that this involves, on the part of the analyst, not only a knowledge, a working knowledge, of existing theories, but the analyst's capacity for freedom of mental movement from the paranoid–schizoid to the depressive position, and the reverse. This also will assist in comprehension by contrast of one of the major difficulties of the patient.

In the third part of the book I shall attempt a description of a few clinical episodes, which I shall then use to illustrate the process of matching theory with data. I hope to make these sufficiently illuminating to enable the reader to grasp the importance of attention in determining what kinds of material are presenting in an invariably complex situation which, as invariably, is disguised by a superficial appearance of monotonous similarity to previous experiences, and a monotonous similarity of one part of the session to all other parts of the same session.

In the fourth part of the book I shall consider some of the effects of the establishment of a capacity for verbal thought, including the obtrusion of neurotic symptoms familiar in the analysis of the non-psychotic personality

In the fifth and final part of the book I shall consider some of the implications of the analytic experience for the patient, for the patient's environment, and for the analyst.

I have advised the reader to read straight through this book, not to dwell too long on difficulties, and in this way to gain a working knowledge of the book itself. But the book will have failed for the reader if it does not become an object of study, and the reading of it an emotional experience itself. My hope is that it will be an experience leading to an increased ability on the part of the analyst to mobilize his own resources of knowledge, clinical observation, theory construction (in the sense of propaedeutic to interpretation), and so to render this work out of date and hasten the day when what is perhaps the most distressing malady a patient and family have to endure will be classed as 'curable'.

A secondary but important aim is that the form in which I have presented the material will lead to a more rational, and therefore more certainly communicable, method of expression of psycho-analytic theory than obtains at present.

[Undated]

Dispositions

A man may be disposed to envy, or to violence of emotion, or to regard truth or life highly, or to be intolerant of frustration. Whatever it is that causes him to be so disposed, I shall call his state of mind at the time he is so disposed, his 'disposition'. The propositions I use as premises are all in this sense dispositions. But, as I write this, it is brought home to me how difficult it is to verbalize with accuracy without losing meaning, or to write meaningfully without losing accuracy.

'A disposition.' Does this mean something in the psyche? Are there such things as dispositions? At once a problem is, what does one mean by 'thing'? He is disposed to be envious; he has an envious disposition; his disposition is to be envious. All these sentences mean something. It does not seem unreasonable to claim that there is such a thing as an envious disposition. Very well: then there are envious dispositions, truthful dispositions, narcissistic dispositions, violent dispositions, loving dispositions—to take instances from the premises I have chosen. Since I want to say that there *are* such things, that is to say, things in actuality, in reality, which are represented by the word, 'disposition', it is essential always to use the word in such a way that the reader will be correct in assuming that I mean what I meant on the previous occasion, that there is in reality something that is represented by the word, 'disposition'.

If this were a difficulty peculiar only to this immediate context, the point would not be worth labouring, but it is inherent in psycho-analytic work and confronts the analyst at every turn. The problem is not new to the philosopher, but the analyst's position is more difficult because he is concerned with the practice of psycho-analysis, that is to say, he has to apply his theories in an empirical setting. Even so, this might amount to no more than the difficulties confronting the scientist who has to express his theories in terms of empirically verifiable data before subjecting them to experimental test, were it not for the fact that the experimental test of psycho-analysis and its theories differs in important respects from the experiments of the physicist whose procedures were marked for their rigour and commended on that account even by Kant. The physicist has, or used to have, his laboratory: the analytic situation that the analyst seeks to preserve is only similar because, I suspect, we attempt to establish an identity with the known which in fact is inadmissible in any but the most superficial way. The tribulations of the physicist since the quantum mechanical physicists have shown that their lowest-level hypotheses, their empirically verifiable data, are statistical hypotheses, may help the analyst to feel that the gap dividing him from the most rigorous scientific discipline of all has become less wide, but it does nothing to bring his subject nearer to being scientifically impeccable. Still less does it contribute to the elaboration of a method or, failing that, an understanding of the need for a method that will place all science, his own included, on a firmer basis. Furthermore, Heisenberg's exposition of the philosophy of quantum mechanics shows that the dependence of the physicist's observed facts on a relationship with facts that are not and can never be known has abolished the limiting walls of his laboratory, and therefore the laboratory itself, so that the physicist has difficulties with his laboratory analogous to the analyst's difficulty with his consulting room and analytic situation. But it does not help psychoanalysts to help themselves, or the physicists to know this, unless through knowing it we can make a breakthrough on the psycho-analytic front. Hence the need for investigating the nature of our own abstractions to a scientific view.

Our scientific theories and systems of hypotheses need to be expressed with great exactitude through an instrument of verbal expressions which has inherent in it defects due to its origin and the penumbra of associations carried by its verbal units, and then has to be applied to a situation—clinical psycho-analysis itself—in which conversational English (or French or German, or whatever other is the native tongue of the participants) plays a dominant part. At first sight this looks as if the attempt to produce a rigorously scientific body of theory is a labour in vain; the errors and inexactitudes that the scientist in the analyst has striven to exclude are reintroduced in the act of translation into conversational usage. The danger is real, but it can be seen in better proportion if it is realized that the working formulations of rigorous analytic theory are being applied to just those situations and emotional perturbations from which both the perfections and imperfections of language as a means of communication originally sprang.

Looked at in this light, the problem, though severe, assumes more manageable proportions. The exactitude that is essential to the theoretical formulation is essential because the function and context of the theoretical formulation requires it, whereas the context of a psycho-analysis itself does not. The exactitude demanded in the context of the psycho-analysis relates to a different problem and needs to be a characteristic of a number of converging features, some of which are time, emotional stress as it is experienced by both participants, and an unknown emotional experience that is only known to be unknown and must be recognized as such. The richness and variety of the respects in which both parties are ignorant must, as I hope to show later, not be allowed to be ignored.

There is no question of exactitude of time in the scientific formulation which must be true independently of time. Exactitude is not related to emotional situations, but must be characteristic of an entirely unemotional statement, though the statement itself purports to represent emotion. The exactitude of the theory also relates to a standard that is neither narcissistic nor socialistic, whereas the interpretation relates to a standard that is both.

To state the matter in yet other words: I may say that the psycho-analysis displays an emotional situation, a crisis in the relationship between the patient and analyst, and the patient and himself. Furthermore, it is a crisis similar to, and perhaps identical with, the crisis in the child's life that has to be dealt with by the development of a capacity for thought on the part of the mother and infant, and a capacity for the transmission of that thought by means capable of ultimate development into methods suitable for public, i.e. social, communication. These methods of public communication are language, music, arts and mathematics. The psycho-analyst employs language in his work; it is possible that this might account for a certain prominence of verbal thought in psycho-analytic discussion. Even so, I consider it to be so important that nothing is lost by stating the problem as if it were exclusively associated with verbal thought and verbal communication, which is what I propose to do, though it will be seen that I cannot regard it as unconnected with other forms of public communication. This same language has to be employed in private communication, i.e. in that relationship with himself that is known as the patient's thought. Looked at in this way, disorders of thought can be regarded as an expression of an elaboration of a defective method of internal and external, private and public, communication which has obstructed the development of verbal thought and has thereby left the patient with a defective tool with which to correct mistaken solutions of the emotional crisis, and mistaken solutions of the problem in toolmaking that were posed by the emotional crisis for which the tools were needed. It may be as well here to see that neurosis and psychosis in individual and group are not only problems in themselves but set further problems in the necessity to produce tools adequate for their solution. To this extent the original problem repeats itself phylogenetically and individually. This paper, as part of psycho-analysis, is itself a minor attempt at the solution of the problem of elaboration of the tool.

The tool of psycho-analytic theoretical language is:

1. A means of establishing a relationship,
2. A means by which collaboration in a common task is assisted, and
3. A means by which a man establishes a relationship with himself.
4. It expresses the relationship.
5. A man's character, like the properties of a chemical substance, can only be expressed in terms that refer to the

nature of the relationship that he establishes with people and things, including himself.

6. A man's senses only give information about the relatedness of one object to another. The information given by the senses is worthless except as material suitable for the formation of judgements about relatedness.
7. There is a vocabulary suitable for, and adapted to, the description of sensual information, mostly adjectival.
8. There is a vocabulary similarly adapted to defining by naming sets of sense impressions that appear to be constantly conjoined: these are nouns, e.g. table, chair. Such terms may be regarded as having the characteristics of hypotheses: 'table' is the name given to a number of phenomena constantly conjoined with a thing-in-itself, or thing in actuality, or a realization of what, without it, would be hypothesis only. In this respect the noun must be regarded as a succinct method of stating a hypothesis that certain no longer explicitly stated qualities and a realization are related.
9. The fact that the entire vocabulary in any language is formed to serve man's preoccupation with relatedness is not observed because the relationship with which man is preoccupied is possession—to possess or to be possessed. This tends to colour the belief in, and attitude to, things in themselves—realizations.

This is seen in

10. the words used to express relatedness of the self with itself and other things or people. Terms such as, 'love', 'hate', 'know', are hypotheses expressing a constant conjunction between feelings not related to the senses, and two classes of things: (a) those expressible in, or represented by, terms that are succinct hypotheses of constant conjunction of certain sense impressions, and (b) those represented by terms that are succinct hypotheses of the constant conjunction of impressions not related to the senses.

    An example of (a) would be, 'I hate the sea'. 'Hate' is a name representing the hypothesis: I have an impression that a number of feelings that are constantly conjoined and are as constantly incompatible with certain other feelings, the constant conjunction of which I usually name, 'love', are related to a thing that is constantly conjoined with certain impressions of sight, smell, etc., and the constant conjunction of those things and smells I usually state succinctly by the word, 'sea'.

An example of (b) would be, 'I hate depression'. The first part of this statement is as before, but 'depression' is the name of a series of feelings that are constantly conjoined but are related to no senses that I am aware of. The bias towards possession as being the essential quality of all relatedness tends to the supposition that the person hates a feeling that he has, and obscures the fact that he is hating—that is to say, he has a particular kind of relationship to a feeling (depression) that is itself the expression of a particular kind of relatedness.

What is the tool of psycho-analytic theoretical knowledge for?

The answer would seem to be that it is for precisely the same purpose as all other language, and that the only difference between psycho-analysts and others is that analysts consciously use language for the purpose for which it was intended, and others use it for precisely the same purpose but without realizing what started them off on having a language at all, or what they are employing it for. It is as if a man picked up a book but forgot, as he studied it, why he had picked it up.

One of the consequences of not knowing what the activity is—namely the exploration of relatedness—for which language is being elaborated is a preoccupation with whether it is possible ever to know anything. The difficulty arises because it is not appreciated that 'X knows Y' is the expression of a special kind of relatedness, and the answer to the question depends on whether a link can be forged which serves the purpose of relating X and Y in actuality in such a way that the factual experience is correctly represented by the statement, 'X knows Y', when that statement is freed from the possessive connotation. If 'X knows Y' is not freed, and is accordingly allowed to retain an element of 'X possesses a piece of knowledge called Y', or that 'X contains a piece of knowledge called Y', then 'X knows Y' is a statement valid in itself and meaningful, but it cannot represent anything in the world of reality, for in the world of reality there is nothing for it to represent. It is a statement suitable for expressing a theory of knowledge appropriate to a stage of development in which knowledge is felt to exist, as a concrete object is felt to exist, but it must be stripped of such primitive components before it is capable of representing an actuality, or supposed actuality, without being incompatible with other statements representing other facets of the same actuality. I maintain that if the statement is stripped of all meanings that prevent it from expressing a relationship between X and Y in a manner strictly parallel to the expression of relatedness embedded in 'X loves Y', and 'X hates Y', then not only do contradictions that make it incompatible with other hypotheses of relatedness disappear, but there is an actual situation that it represents suitably. There is one further respect in which 'knows' can be made to approximate to reality; that is by making it express an activity continuously pursued so that X is conceived of as being actively engaged in a relationship of knowing Y, in the sense in which the phrase, 'getting to know', is sometimes employed. The point will receive full treatment later, so I shall not dwell on it more than is necessary to make the statement, 'X knows Y', capable of representing the actuality represented by the statement, 'X psycho-analyses Y'.

Before proceeding further I want to make it clear that when I say of the statement, 'X knows Y', that in so far as it carries a meaning of 'possessing a piece of knowledge' there is nothing in the world of reality for it to represent, I do not mean that it is an untrue statement; it can be perfectly true, just as a mathematical calculus can be true and yet have no known corresponding realization. Although a statement represents an empirically verifiable fact—the statement has a corresponding realization—that statement is not therefore true, and consequently not capable of protecting the personality from the mental deterioration attendant on starvation of truth. Whatever 'truth' may mean, it does not mean a quality whose existence or non-existence is established by the correspondence of a statement with a realization. Truth and absolute truth are statements of a judgement of a statement. Thus the statement that 'the sun rises' is a true statement. If I were asked whether it was absolutely true that the sun rises, I should say, "No". As a hypothesis, there is no corresponding realization that it represents. But though I know this, I also know that there is a set of phenomena that can be made to appear related, are given a relatedness, if I produce a hypothesis that the sun rises. What are related to each other by my statement are appearances; and the appearances are characteristics of my relationship with stimuli. Furthermore, they are characteristics of a particular form of relationship with the stimuli—an 'I know' relationship. But I have already said that I know that the statement, 'The sun rises', has no corresponding realization. How then can the statement, 'The sun rises', be said to be true and part of an 'I know' relationship? The answer is that the 'I know . . .' relationship is between me and a set of phenomena some of which might be, to take an example, that my friend wants to see a particular view at sunrise, that he wants my company, that he thinks I can be relied on to wake at a time suitable to fulfil his aim, and so on. With all these I have an 'I know . . .' relationship. What I am concerned with is a set of phenomena with which I have an 'I know . . .' relationship as contrasted with an 'I love . . .' or 'I hate . . .' relationship. For my purposes I need a theory that will relate these phenomena to each other. The phenomena are already selected from out of many millions that are discarded as irrelevant (e.g. that no rain has fallen in the Gobi desert), and a further selection could be made by putting in one class all those that have been related by my theory that 'the sun rises'. As I have said, this statement is true because within a circumscribed area it has the effect of relating appearances, phenomena, with which I have an 'I know . . .' relationship. But if I am asked whether it is absolutely true, I assume that I am expected to remove the limits circumscribing my area in order to make it limitless; I assume I am to state whether this theory that 'the sun rises' will demonstrate a relatedness between all kinds of phenomena, and also a realization to which the hypothesis that 'the sun rises' corresponds. For this set of elements, facts and phenomena, the statement is not true.

Thus, 'truth' is the name I give to the quality that I attribute to any statement that is a hypothesis relating to phenomena with which I have an 'I know . . .' relationship. The function of the hypothesis itself, as I have already said, is to state a relatedness between elements that, without it, would remain discrete and therefore unable to yield the feeling of meaningfulness that is the inseparable emotional accompaniment of an observation of relatedness embodied in a hypothesis. Consistent with this usage it is correct to say that the statement, 'The sun does not rise', is untrue when it is the hypothesis which is employed in the same set of phenomena as I have used in my example, even though it can be shown to correspond with a realization and to be an accurate representation of the realization. One reason for this is that the theory is to be used for a limited number of phenomena in a context that shows clearly that the theory is to serve a purpose that is social and not, say, to illuminate an astronomical problem. It may serve as a useful introduction to later elaborations of these points to consider why anyone would resort to hypothesis perversely in the trivial social context; as it is an imaginary example, we may suppose the statement to be made as an expression of feeling, either as part of some joke, or perhaps to mislead. In either event, the relationship between phenomena and the observer is not that of 'I know . . .', but of 'I love . . .', or 'I hate . . .'. A hypothesis employed as part of an 'X knows Y' relationship is to fill a quite different function from that which is [breaks off here]

[Undated]

I know X = relationship

'Knowledge' has no meaning unless it means that someone knows something, and this, as I hope to show, is an assertion of relationship, or of some part of a relationship.

The term, 'knowledge', I propose provisionally to employ to describe a state of mind indissolubly associated with a relationship between communicable awareness on the one hand, and the object of which the person feels thus aware of the other.

I must give some explanation of my choice of the term, 'communicable awareness': the term, 'communicable', is not synonymous with 'conscious', for a person may be conscious of something yet unable to communicate his awareness. Or he may be unconsciously aware of it and yet able to communicate his awareness to another who can interpret his communication though he himself cannot. I may be unconscious of my fear of something of which I am aware (and indeed of my awareness of it) and yet communicate my fear to another who has no difficulty in understanding from my communication that I am afraid, and of what it is that I am afraid. Obviously such communication depends for its efficacy on the capacity for receptiveness of the receiver, and therefore there can be no hard and fast way of determining the point at which awareness may be said to be communicable. But this is a difficulty that will be discussed when we come to the problem of restatement of a hypothesis in terms of empirically verifiable data. For the present I wish simply to establish my contention that the awareness must be communicable.

The instance I have given (that I might communicate my awareness of something that I fear) may serve as an introduction to the kind of relationship with an object which I claim when I say that I know it. I may say that I fear an object, but this statement does not include the statement that I know it. Indeed it may be an essential feature of my fear that I do *not* know it. But the statement that I know it may include the fact, stated or not, that I fear it. In some respects, then, to say, 'I know X', is an inclusive statement; it implies an inclusive relationship wider than one implied by 'I love X', or 'I hate X'.

My aim is to define a common usage, which definition would obtain a large measure of support. This aim becomes more practicable if we attempt to describe that limited use of 'to know' which is implied when the speaker means that in saying, 'I know X', he is really meaning a kind of relationship with X which is to be specifically discriminated from all the other kinds of relationship signified by 'I hate X' or 'I love X', 'I see X', and so on.

In an analysis, the action of the analyst in being an analyst means two things: in so far as it is an investigation, it means 'I want to know you', but in so far as it is interpretation it means 'I know you'. This is an example of the kind of relationship I wish to use the expression, 'I know X', to describe. It is between communicable awareness and the patient.

The meaning of the word, 'know', is determined by its context. In attempting to define my use of it, I am wishing to control the context so that the word has a more rigid meaning, and thereby a meaning less liable to fluctuation. The same purpose informs the attempt to address my comments to a selected audience. I hope that if the audience is literate, the penumbra of associations it possesses will reinforce the meaning I wish to convey. Clearly this limitation is again imposed by selecting a philosophical or psycho-analytical audience.

Nevertheless the word, 'know', in the statement, 'I know X', has constantly changing meaning, and these changes in meaning remain out of the control of the person making the statement, no matter how carefully he may strive to make it exact by definition, by control of the context in which he uses it, or by selection of those to whom he addresses his observations. My point may be clarified by the exaggeration of an extreme view, namely that we cannot know the meaning at any moment of the word, 'know', unless we know all the meanings of the word at that time—and that means never. Such a view is ordinarily of no practical consequence, yet it may serve sometimes to point the way to an understanding of some of the difficulties that are of practical importance. Amongst these are those that arise because it is a problem even to achieve the relatively modest aim that the writer may and should have: to know all the meanings with which he is at any moment investing the word.

[Undated]

Kinds of relatedness

'Caused by'. But also the mathematical symbols for addition, subtraction, multiplication and division. Are these expressions of relatedness? And if so, what is their history in the development of the individual?

This and this and this and this = a table. (*addition*)

A table without legs or a top or hardness or softness = a hallucination. (*subtraction*)

A table *multiplied* by today and tomorrow and the next day and the next day = lots of tables.

But if it is the same table? And if two people have to share it, is the table *divided* by two?

[Undated]

The cause and the selected fact

The cause and the selected fact are alike in that they are both ideas that have the power of being associated with an emotional experience that at one moment gives rise to a sense of creative synthesis *and* awareness of still unsynthesized discrete objects. Every emotional experience of knowledge gained is at the same time an emotional experience of ignorance unilluminated. The sense of creative success with its accompanying elation is therefore inseparable from a sense of failure to synthesize the discrete objects, the elementary particles, which are revealed by the success.

Dominance of the life instincts carries with it the continued repetition of this experience. In extreme form, fear of this experience can lead to repudiation of the life instincts, and the reinforcement of the death instincts that are idealized and libidinized.

The fear and intolerance of the cause or selected fact ultimately contribute to increasing attacks on the individual's equipment for feeling and satisfying curiosity, and therefore contribute to the forces operating in producing senility. Senility is a process analogous to destruction of the ego and of α. It thus contributes to the shortening of physical life, just as destruction of α and the associated loss of contact with reality in infancy endanger life.

The selected fact relates to synthesis of objects felt to be contemporaneous or without any time component. The selected fact thus differs from the cause that relates to the synthesis of objects scattered in time and therefore with a time component.

The suicide of the Sphinx, and the Oedipus myth, are both verbal accounts of pictorial solutions (visual images) of the same problem: one solves it by death; the other by re-entry into the mother's womb. Both solutions are intended to evade the emotional experience of cause or selected fact, i.e. the interplay between paranoid–schizoid and depressive positions. This interplay cannot be carried out without visual imagery of the Sphinx, or of an internal parental intercourse.

If cause is transferred to epistemology, as I think it should be, what is the link between hypotheses in a scientific deductive system?

If I say destructive attacks lead to fragmentation of α, it cannot mean (according to my theory) that they 'cause' fragmentation: it must mean that the individual cannot make destructive attacks on α without thinking that α has been fragmented. If the patient makes destructive attacks on α, or what he feels to be α, then he thinks I had no umbrella in London, he took a taxi, I had pneumonia [*see* p. 186] and so on, in disjointed bits that seem to him to be objects, i.e. bits of his personality indistinguishable from things in themselves. Though cause has no realization corresponding to the concept, the patient regards cause as having an existence as a thing in itself, not independent of thought but as a part of his personality possessing independence in the sense that he cannot control it.

Such a patient, having only objects at his disposal—which, as we have seen are unserviceable for anything but projective identification—cannot feel he is able to discern a link between discrete phenomena or their counterpart in reality; such an idea is not appropriate to a state of mind in which only bizarre objects exist and can only be projected, evacuated, or internalized by a mind that is a bowel. There is therefore no possibility of his feeling that he has discerned the link that brings phenomena together, and therefore cannot have the emotional experience that the non-psychotic personality recognizes under the name of 'cause'. His experience is quite otherwise: he feels that various objects have cohered; they are felt to have done so voluntarily, and independently of his volition; yet since the objects are part of his personality, he is responsible for their voluntary and independent concatenation.

But I have said that 'cause' should be, and is, the name of the emotional experience inseparable from the interaction between paranoid–schizoid and depressive positions. The solution of this contradiction lies in the difference between the emotional experience known to the psychotic, and the emotional experience known to the non-psychotic personality, both of which experiences have the name, 'cause'.

I have already adumbrated the nature of the emotional experience called 'cause', as it is experienced by the psychotic: we must now consider the nature of this experience as known to the non-psychotic part of the personality.

Disregarding for present purposes the fact that the non-psychotic believes that cause is a phenomenon with a corresponding realization and belongs to the domain of ontology, and considering only that part of his beliefs which relates cause to the domain of epistemology—that is, as an emotional experience—we can see that he feels he has discerned a link between phenomena. For the psychotic the objects have come together in a cruel juxtaposition: for the non-psychotic the previously discrete phenomena are felt to be unchanged but related, and the emphasis is not on the objects (phenomena) but on the relatedness. The relationship is variously described, but usually as 'logical', and the effect of discerning this relatedness is felt as subjectively therapeutic. What, then, is logical relatedness as contrasted with, say, cruel juxtaposition? The psychotic view impels towards splitting and dispersal, whether under dominance of life instincts (L), or death instincts (D); under L, the objects are scattered to prevent destruction, and under D, they are the explosive result of it. The non-psychotic view impels towards further discovery and synthesis.

Differentiation of cause and selected fact

So far I have spoken of 'cause' and 'selected fact' as virtually interchangeable terms used as names for an identical emotional experience. I shall now use 'cause' exclusively for those emotional experiences in which *time* is intrinsic, whether this is explicit or implicit in the material. Time is a component in all emotional experiences; therefore the emotional experience I call 'cause' will be intrinsic to the experience described or discussed, and to any scientific deductive system which is constructed to represent it; it follows that it will be implicit in any calculus corresponding to the scientific deductive system.

The term, 'selected fact', I reserve for use in emotional experiences of thought about phenomena in which time is excluded, and in all scientific deductive systems and the corresponding calculi which are constructed to represent such phenomena.

In so far as an exercise of the logical faculty is an emotional experience, time is intrinsic; this fact will be reflected in any scientific deductive system and its associated calculus, which is constructed to represent the experience of exercising the logical faculties. But logic is not impregnated with time, although it may be concerned with it as an object of thought for which it supplies the laws. A logical formulation, therefore, cannot be described as a cause: it will be called a selected fact. A mathematical formula is, for the same reason, also a selected fact. A logical formulation or a mathematical formula may nevertheless be called a cause, but only in so far as it has been an element in an emotional experience and is therefore represented in the appropriate scientific deductive system and its associated calculus. In the system of logic or mathematics to which it belongs it remains a selected fact and is timeless.

Mathematics and logic are unaffected by the passage of time, though time is intrinsic to the discovery of logical formulations or mathematical formulas. They 'are', independently of whether they are known, i.e. independently of whether there is an observer to observe them or not. They are therefore no part of experience or knowledge since there need be no one to experience or to know them. [Marginal comment: 'This is running counter to my statement that maths is only a way of thinking.'] This fact contributes to the comparative absence of awareness of time as a component in the problems associated with disturbances of thought, whether the disturbance is of the kind observable in an attempt to solve problems of acceleration of freely-falling bodies without the discovery of the differential calculus, or of the kind observable in a psychotic patient who is incapable of articulated thought.

The elements of logic or mathematics are contemporaneous: the elements of experience are dispersed in time.

[Undated]

Suppose I want to go to Oxford Street but do not know how to find it. I may have to ask someone, or consult a map, or try to remember something that I believe would give me a clue, or . . . But it is obvious that if I stick to concrete examples of what I may have to do I shall not succeed in my immediate aim, which has nothing to do with Oxford Street. So instead of thinking of all the different things I might have to do before starting to go to Oxford Street, I shall see if I can find a short way of saying what I want you to know when I start writing of concrete examples of learning, such as consulting maps, policemen, and so forth. I have to make these concrete examples abstract; I have to abstract from the concrete the essence of my communication. But now that I have written this last sentence I am wondering whether abstract, concrete, essence, communication, are good words for stringing together in a sentence that has now perhaps become too abstract to teach the reader what I mean. My first attempt threatens to become so burdened with verbal descriptions of concrete images that the reader may feel overwhelmed by them to the detriment of his ability to learn what I mean.

Yet those visual images that I began to verbalize are only a small fraction of the many that were in my mind: the Radclife Camera; being lost in Turkestan with no policeman to ask and no knowledge of the language to help me frame a question about Oxford or Oxford Street; chain stores and uniformity; everyone talking the same language; a Brahminy bull helping himself to goods on a stall that I was not allowed to touch . . . I am not sure that I remember what I set out to say. But I think I know one thing that my visual images or free associations are saying, and that is something I did not mean to discuss. I was thinking of the sweets the Brahminy bull could have, but I—I was quite small at the time—could not. With an effort I can get back to the point; it is to do with learning and teaching.

If I want to go to Oxford Street and do not know how to do so, I must learn. If I want to teach something about learning, I must know how to learn and how to teach. I shall start again.

Suppose I want to go to Oxford Street but do not know . . . . There is much I need to know before I can ask the question. I begin as an individual with a place in time and space, and in the history of others. Closely related to the problem of locating Oxford Street is a vast amount of remembered experience. Some of this is mine; the rest is located in the society of my time, and I need to find it and to know *how* to find it. With regard to myself, I need to consult my store of experience; in some respects I can see how I do this. I need to know what I mean by 'Oxford Street' if I propose to get there. I have no difficulty in knowing that 'Oxford Street' is not just a noise in my head because I am able to have an image of the Radcliffe Camera, and so the noise, 'Oxford Street', becomes a sound, and the sound is now felt by me to have a meaning. The visual image of the Radcliffe Camera has therefore proved, with other associations, to be a repository of emotional experiences on which I automatically draw in order to understand a current problem with a view to solving it.

But my current problem is not how to go to Oxford Street; it is how to make public certain ideas of mine about learning and teaching. And while attempting to solve the problem of how it is to be done, I found myself wondering what I would say. It then occurred to me to answer my question by an illustrative example. That is how it seemed to me consciously, and that is how I would explain my behaviour consciously.

The other explanation that occurs to me is that the supposed illustrative examples are really α-elements filling their function as a repository of my experience, and being called upon to yield that experience so that I may the better be able to solve the problem of this communication here. In this the elements recall problems associated with solving problems by non-verbal means—the non-existent Turkestan policeman—but not only pre-verbal.

Now I can proceed with these free associations—or rather I can treat these images as free associations and attempt an analytic approach. This would depend on my regarding my immediate problem as one arising predominantly from an internal obstruction, i.e. an obstruction in my psyche, and on my believing that the method of solution was psycho-analysis. But may there not be some other way in which these images can be utilized? In fact I have gone to sleep. Does this mean that the natural *modus operandi* is to have these images and then 'sleep on them'? Or to allow them to work as elements in unconscious waking thought when, my mental apparatus being in good order, a solution will emerge without my ever being aware of the unconscious waking thoughts that have effected it? *The Old Wives' Tale* [Arnold Bennett] certainly credits 'sleeping on' a problem with efficacy.

[Undated]

It has just come to me that the mathematician is one who is capable of α and that it has this consequence: he can see the essential characters in, say, the paranoid–schizoid and depressive positions, or the Oedipal situation, or primal scene, or any other. These situations, or complexes, are seen concretely and, at some point, in visual images. For example, Euclid's geometrical patterns can easily be visual images that are made abstract. But the mathematician is able to produce abstractions, and signs for these abstractions, and can then replace the abstraction or its sign (reversing the direction of α) with a *particular* concretization.

If my idea is right, then Euclid could say good-bye to the 'elements' (I.5, Elefuga). That is to say, the 'elements' could be worked—transformed, in his case—into an abstract visual image (the theorem) and then still further abstracted by Descartes (or rather the use of the system of co-ordinates he worked out) so as to form the whole system of projective geometry, and then abstracted still further to form the system of algebraic geometry. Now the calculus thus elaborated lies ready to use.

Leaving aside the question, for the time being, of how this process of abstraction is to take place and how α affects it, we can see that the calculus that has been produced is available for the solution of all kinds of problems which, on the face of it, are far removed from the basic facts ('elements', in this case) from which the original abstraction was effected. But it is probable that it will only serve effectually for the solution of problems in which the concrete facts, which are to be substituted for the variables of the calculus, have a value relative to each other which is similar to the values the original basic facts had relative to each of the other basic original facts. Put in other terms, a Newton explores astronomical space, elaborating his laws of motion in doing so by virtue of an already existing calculus, or calculi, which derived originally by a process of abstraction from the facts of the first space of all—the infant's space of breast, the Positions (paranoid–schizoid and depressive), Oedipal situation, primal scene. There is, then: a basic pattern, an abstraction, calculi and reapplication of calculi.

A Newton then owes his freedom to investigate to a series of derivations from a basic pattern; but that same pattern also imposes a limitation on his freedom in that only such data tend to be regarded by him as will lend themselves to a scheme fitting in with the original basic pattern. In an extreme form this can lead to such a limitation of selectivity of observed facts that the 'discovery', e.g. of the origin of the solar system, is really not much more than a projection onto astronomical facts of a crude and very easily detected emotional problem centring, say, on the primal scene. But in another observer of the stature of Newton, the facts now drawn together by aid of the calculi already in existence can be seen not to be adequately represented by the laws of motion and their representative calculi.

Thus there is produced anew the situation, described by Poincaré, of disparate elements lacking any coherence. Confronted by this repetition of the Positions, again all depends on the individual's capacity for α. The new Positions can again be negotiated, depending on α-capacity, new visual images, new abstractions, and further calculi, and so on.

In this lies the possibility of belief in the value for scientific enquiry of the original basic patterns, and at the same time an indication of the nature of the limitations from which human intellectual exploration and enquiry is bound to suffer. We can ultimately only see in the universe that which lies within the compass of our mental equipment, and that in turn means that we can only see that which lies within the compass of our ability to solve through α-capacity certain basic elemental positions and patterns, such as the paranoid–schizoid and depressive positions, primal scene and Oedipal situation. All that lies outside those few elementary patterns can only be grasped by virtue of α-capacity which can be brought to bear on a derivation from a derivation from a derivation . . . to the nth.

March 1967

Reverence and awe

[Synopsis and notes of a paper given at a joint meeting of the Los Angeles Psycho-Analytic Society and Institute and the Southern California Psycho-Analytic Society, on 20 April 1967, in the Mount Sinai Hospital Auditorium. There is no record of the actual presentation.]

The Kleinian theory of the paranoid–schizoid position and its dynamic relationship with the depressive position can be seen to indicate a configuration that is constantly encountered in the realm of thought. I have drawn attention to the recurrence of this pattern in *Learning from Experience*. I shall indicate what I mean by two quotations, neither from psycho-analysts, which display it. The first is from a mathematician, Henri Poincaré, in *Science and Method*; the second from Eric Temple Bell in a chapter on Cause from his book, *Men of Mathematics*.

1.

> If a new result is to have any value, it must unite elements long since known, but till then scattered and seemingly foreign to each other, and suddenly introduce order where the appearance of disorder reigned. Then it enables us to see at a glance each of these elements in the place it occupies in the whole. Not only is the new fact valuable on its own account, but it alone gives a value to the old facts it unites. Our mind is frail as our senses are; it would lose itself in the complexity of the world if that complexity were not harmonious; like the short-sighted, it would only see the details, and would be obliged to forget each of these details before examining the next, because it would be incapable of taking in the whole.

2.

> . . . the theory of numbers, which in the seventeenth and eighteenth centuries had been a miscellaneous aggregation of disconnected special results, assumed coherence and rose to the dignity of a mathematical science on a par with algebra, analysis and geometry.

I suggest that this constantly recurring phenomenon can at the present time be very clearly seen in the development of psycho-analysis. I do not propose to go into this and the oscillations of the group from persecution to depression and back again, beyond drawing your attention to its existence; my object is to give an account of a relatively short clinical episode, which is merely a particular instance of well-known psycho-analytical theories. It may seem unfamiliar but I hope you will agree that it is a perfectly fair account of a general theory well known to psycho-analysts.

If psycho-analysts can abandon themselves to analysis in the psycho-analytical sessions, they are in a position when recollecting the experience in tranquillity to discern their experience as part of a greater whole. Once that is achieved, the way is open for the discovery of configurations revealing yet other and deeper groups of theory. But the discoverer must be prepared to find that he has started another round of group oscillations. Persecution ↔ Depression.

My example, which I have called 'Reverence and Awe', is taken from the analysis of a patient who came to me after an experience of many years of analysis. He had no doubt at all that he had benefited greatly from his experience, and yet he was dissatisfied. I expected to find that greed played a large part in his make-up, but from what I knew of his analyst I thought it very unlikely that this point had not been adequately dealt with. It seemed probable that the explanation would have to be found elsewhere. My reason for taking the very restricted sample from his analysis with me is to draw your attention to material, the pathology of which is familiar to you already, but which I interpret in a way that may be less familiar. I hope you will satisfy yourselves that despite apparent strangeness the reality that I am representing by my interpretations is in no way novel. I draw your attention to this point because I am convinced that this happens more frequently than psycho-analysts realize and gives rise to unnecessary confusion and controversy. In my opinion it does not indicate differences in the theoretical outlook of psycho-analysts but is symptomatic of the stage of development that the psycho-analytic group has achieved. That stage is described by my quotation from Eric Temple Bell.

For reasons of discretion I have had to discuss this patient in such a way that he cannot recognize the material. I believe, however, that in essentials the account does not give a misleading impression of the actual case.

I deliberately made no enquiries about this patient's previous psycho-analytic history, working on the principle that either the difficulties had been adequately dealt with and were therefore no longer relevant, or that they still remained to be dealt with, in which case they would present themselves in an entirely novel manner in accordance with the changes that had occurred within the patient. I regard this point as of great importance: information given about such incompletely dealt-with difficulties is bound to arouse expectations in the psycho-analyst, making it very difficult for him to keep an open mind. While he is waiting for the appearance of material that he has been led to expect, he fails to observe correctly the material that is actually presenting itself. The repetition of such failures must be guarded against because it undermines his observations and therefore the soundness of his interpretations.

The patient was a man of medium height, fifty-three years old, with greying hair and an alert and lively manner. He at once embarked on a torrent of free associations plentifully sprinkled with information about various psycho-analysts whom he had known. The information was mostly trivial, but I was given to understand by his manner that he had plenty more. For example, he would mention some analyst known to him and show me that he knew certain matters about his private life and difficulties. I soon gathered that he believed I knew the man and that the details he mentioned were well known to me. I regarded this communication as fiction. At the same time he was making it clear that he was not going to be fooled by me or any other analyst. After he had gone on pouring out material of this kind for some five or ten minutes, I stopped him and said he was showing me that there was very little about being an analysand that he did not know. I said that his statements bore the unmistakable stamp of being free associations and had very little resemblance to the kind of thing that might be said by any ordinary person engaging in a conversation. I said that I thought he was very anxious to prove to himself that nothing was happening, or was likely to happen, with which he was not familiar. He complimented me on the brilliance of my interpretation and indicated what a relief it was to find that I was not wedded to any rigid psycho-analytic theories. There was no apparent awareness on his part of any irony or sarcasm in what he was saying. I did not feel called upon at this stage to make any observation on what he was saying or the manner in which he said it.

I should explain that I regard the psycho-analyst's capacity to observe and absorb as much of the analysand's material as possible as important for the following reasons:

1. It will enable him to combine what he hears with what he has already experienced from the patient to give an immediate interpretation in the circumstances of the actual session.
2. At the same time he will observe features that are not comprehensible to him but will contribute at a later stage to the comprehension of material yet to come.
3. There are still other elements of which the analyst will not even be conscious but which will build up an experiential reserve that in due course will influence his conscious views about the patient's material on a specific occasion.

Reason 1, although apparently leading to the operative interpretation, is of less consequence than 2 and 3 because the interpretation is merely setting a formal seal on work that has already been done and is therefore no longer of much consequence.

Reason 2 is of great importance because it is part of the dynamic and continuing process on which the whole viability of the analysis depends. The more the psycho-analyst is open to these impressions, the more he is prepared to participate in the evolution of the analysis.

Reason 3, although more remote, ensures the long-term vitality of the whole psycho-analytic process. In short, the nearer the psycho-analyst can come to observation of the kind I am desiderating here, the less likely he is to fall into the wastes of jargon, and the more the analysis will approximate to being a unique emotional experience recognizably related to an actual human being, and not a conglomerate of psychopathological mechanisms.

The patient, for the time being, relinquished his flow of 'free associations' and began to talk as if he was having an ordinary conversation. I gave some more interpretations, that he appeared to accept but without any comment on their 'brilliance'—which as far as I was concerned remained undimmed. But now there came into the picture a series of reactions that showed that he thought the interpretations were correct, and I was helped to make them so by his intelligent co-operation.

I hope to make clear some of the bewildering aspects of the patient's statements. It is virtually impossible in print to give any idea of the confused outpouring of statements in sessions when he was expressing envy and admiration. It is also impossible at the time to keep track of his statements, and therefore a reproduction is only an artificial representation. Provided this is understood the following will give an idea:

"She does it on purpose to upset me. The alignment of the tea-caddy was wrong again. She has set her mind on Geoffrey going to school at X which is very expensive. Laura is very good with Clementine but Clementine was extremely upset by Margery" (his wife). "She mentioned food again and she knows very well it would upset me. The pasty that I get from my usual shop is always very good. I do not think there is any chance that Geoffrey will get into Y. The headmaster told me that if he were border-line, then they might try to push him in, but his mark is frightfully low—only about sixty. I think Z has a lower standard, but again, it is very expensive and I do not think Geoffrey would have a chance. Margery again mentioned food when she knows it is very upsetting to me."

It would be wearisome if I were to continue this description, but it will give a fair idea if I say that three or four sessions a week would be taken up with this kind of outpouring. Such sessions were in marked contrast with others in which the patient spoke with the coherence usual in ordinary conversation with someone with whom one is on confidential terms.

The problem for the analyst is what to do with material of this kind. It is necessary to draw the patient's attention to it and, if possible, to get him to compare it with the way he talks on the other occasions. I do this in order to get the patient to see that there is a problem, without necessarily suggesting what the problem is. I find it necessary to have some basis for agreement on what the material is that requires interpretation. This, however, is not easy to do because the nature of the material, its characteristics and content, are not clear for some time. For example, if the analysand is expecting the analyst to interpret it, it means that he thinks the analyst must be well-nigh omniscient to understand such a flood of material and what it is supposed to convey. The interpretation that the patient expects the analyst to be omniscient is one that I want to stress. There were, however, many others drawing attention to the fact that he spoke as if every item he mentioned was equal in importance with every other item. I had, in fact, to spend some time on this, basing my interpretations on the theory that his conversation to me had been subjected to splitting attacks that left the conversational link in a state of fragmentation. Interpretations of this kind did something to slow down the flow but did not noticeably decrease the number of sessions in which I had to cope with it. I spent several months drawing attention to the extent to which splitting was taking place. I pointed out that sometimes I was fragmented as if I were a woman or a breast, the fragments represented by the names of various women. Sometimes I showed him that he was not tolerating the problem of his boy's education which he had to solve, and was reacting by splitting that up into bits. Very often each bit represented a problem that could be solved, but the problem as a whole was not solved.

On occasions when I could make this clear he sometimes reacted by going into a state of depression, blaming me for making things difficult; on other occasions he reverted to my 'brilliance', that is, my god-like qualities or, alternatively, my devilish 'dazzling' of him so that he could not see the point.

Many sessions passed carrying their individual characteristics so that on the face of it one could easily stress the unique quality of each session. Indeed I believe that it is very important that the analyst should retain his freshness of outlook so that he never falls into the mistake of treating any session as if it were the repetition of a previous session. Even in instances where it appears to be almost indistinguishable, the problem for the analyst is how to retain an over-all knowledge of the human being and his psychopathology so that he would be able to deal with the greatest diversity of human beings while at the same time not losing sight of the fact that the personality with whom he is dealing is unique. This is so easily said that one feels it is almost a banality when put forward to a psycho-analytic society—as I am doing—but in the reality of a psycho-analytic session it is very easy to lose sight of this simple basic principle and begin to give interpretations in terms so near to being statements of basic psycho-analytic theory that they lose meaning for the patient. Conversely, it is possible for the analyst to react against the feeling of being confronted with a unique and therefore unknown situation. Throughout these many sessions to which I have been referring, despite all their diversity to which I hope I was able to give due weight, it was possible to see the resemblance that they bore to each other as approximating to the Kleinian theory of progress from paranoid–schizoid position to depressive position.

I have found it important to regard every session, no matter how familiar the material may seem to be, as if one were scrutinizing the elements in a kaleidoscope before they shake into a definable pattern. The temptation is always to terminate prematurely the stage of uncertainty and doubt about what the patient is saying.

The most likely way for an analyst to do this is by giving an interpretation before the moment is ripe for the pattern to emerge; the analyst's armoury of psycho-analytic theory and experience is easily sufficient to supply him with plausible interpretations for this purpose. This is familiar to us all as a manifestation of counter-transference, but I want to stress the closeness with which the course I am advocating approximates to the feelings of persecution proper to the paranoid–schizoid position. It may be argued that an analyst should be so well analysed that he does not suffer from feelings of persecution, but I am not concerned with what *should be* the case but rather with what *is* the case. I certainly cannot claim for myself—who have been analysed by Melanie Klein—that I am incapable of experiencing feelings of persecution; in our present state of progress I think any analyst would be rash to think that he was. Since these feelings are very painful, naturally the analyst is anxious to terminate them prematurely in the way I have indicated. I suggest that for a correct interpretation it is necessary for the analyst to go through the phase of 'persecution' even if, as we hope, it is in a modified form, without giving an interpretation. Similarly, he must pass through the depression before he is ready to give an interpretation. Again, he should not give an interpretation while experiencing depression; the change from paranoid–schizoid to depressive position must be complete before he gives his interpretation.

Conversely, while listening to the patient the analyst should dwell on those aspects of the patient's communication which come nearest to arousing feelings corresponding to persecution and depression. In my experience this gives as good a check on the soundness of one's interpretative validity as anything I know. On the whole I am more satisfied with my work if I feel that I have been through these emotional experiences than I do if the session has been more agreeable. I am fortified in this belief by the conviction that has been borne in on me by the analysis of psychotic or borderline patients. I do not think such a patient will ever accept an interpretation, however correct, unless he feels that the analyst has passed through this emotional crisis as a part of the act of giving the interpretation.

There were many fascinating aspects of this analysis including problems associated with the mention of number, as in the instance of his boy's obtaining sixty marks. It was not, I think, central to his psychopathology but was nevertheless very important.

He constantly reverted to feelings of admiration, which were not only clear in the transference but cropped up again and again in situations outside analysis altogether. Many times I had to give interpretations showing him that he was virtually worshipping 'God', although he had repeatedly said that he was not religious and had no belief in God. I pointed out that his reactions to the 'God' in whom he appeared emotionally to believe were hostile because He could not stand up to intellectual scrutiny. His reactions reminded me very much of the savage who is supposed to beat his gods if they do not grant his wishes. He seemed finally to accept that he felt an intense need for someone or something for which he could entertain feelings of reverance and awe. His resentment was related to his inability to feel this in any particular instance.

The problem of the patient's continuing dissatisfaction may be a function of his age. This would, however, apply to him at whatever age he was being analysed. This brings me to my point that at this stage of the history of psycho-analysis emphasis requires to be placed not so much on psycho-analytic discovery, but on the correct observation and interpretation of clinical material while it is unfolding in the analysis. There is a great difference between idealization of a parent because the child is in despair, and idealization because the child is in search of an outlet for feelings of reverence and awe. In the latter instance the problem centres on frustration and the inability to tolerate frustration of a fundamental part of a particular patient's make-up. This is likely to happen if the patient is capable of love and admiration to an outstanding degree; in the former instance the patient may have no particular capacity for affection but a great greed to be its recipient. The answer to the question—which is it?—will not be found in any textbook but only in the process of psycho-analysis itself. I do not in any way decry the need for a thorough grasp of the major analytic theories, but I think that anyone who has experienced an analysis as part of his or her own training and development is likely to have no difficulty in achieving that. I would sound a note of caution by reminding you of Freud's words: 'Once again I owe the chance of making a discovery to my not being well read.' ('On the History of the Psycho-Analytic Movement' [1914d] *SE 14*.)

[Undated]

['Notes on Memory and Desire' was published in *The Psychoanalytic Forum, 2,* Number 3 (Autumn 1967). These notes were probably written somewhat later.]

Introduction

Not a scientific paper but a super-scientific paper, i.e. a psycho-analytic paper dependent on advanced, psycho-analytic methodology. It is *not* sub-scientific.

The practising analyst, seeing patients tomorrow or the day after, is an essential, intrinsic part of the understanding of this address, though not in the least bit necessary for understanding the words and syntax.

Memory

Includes:

a. Remembering and forgetting.
b. Freud's notation (['Remembering, Repeating and Working-Through', 1914g], *SE 12,* p. 147 et seq.), 'A Note upon the Mystic Writing Pad' ([1925a] *SE 19,* p. 227) and *Civilization and Its Discontents* ([1930a], *SE 21],* p. 71).
c. Elements that can be categorized in accordance with the Grid—all of which are transformations.
d. Possessiveness, ♀, Past, Desirability.

Desire

Not mentioned specifically by Freud but other terms, such as 'wish', obviously describe facets of the constant conjunction I bind by the term, 'desire'. Examples: holiday, cure of patient, end of day's work—all have the same configuration.

Aspects of Memory and Desire

1. Background of sensuous experience: pleasure ↔ pain.
2. The dominance of the visual image. This is related to *inaccessibility*—peculiar to objects of memory and desire. Freud's remark, 'It has only one justification. It shows us how far we are from mastering the characteristics of mental life by representing them in pictorial terms'. ([*Leonardo da Vinci and a Memory of His Childhood,* 1910c], *SE 21*, p. 71). The sense of sight seems to bring objects into reach when not within scope of other senses.

   Memory—the object is past, internal and possessed.

   Desire—the object is future, external and coveted.

Scope of discussion

Not psycho-pathological, not primarily as features of the patient, but as functions of the analyst.

Certain commonly accepted views

1. Need for a 'record' (Notation, Grid Cat. 3 [*see* opposite]).
2. Object of analysis.

Neither has relevance to the practice of psycho-analysis.

Both obstruct participation in the analytic experience.

As aspects of the analyst's work

Memory and Desire should be banished because:

1. The mind becomes saturated by sensuous and pleasure–pain elements; both are misleading (false, Cat. 2)

THE GRID

	Definitory Hypo theses 1	ψ 2	Notation 3	Attention 4	Inquiry 5	Action 6	. . . n
A β-elements	**A1**	**A2**				**A6**	
B α-elements	**B1**	**B2**	**B3**	**B4**	**B5**	**B6**	**. . . Bn**
C Dream Thoughts Dreams, Myths	**C1**	**C2**	**C3**	**C4**	**C5**	**C6**	**. . . Cn**
D Pre-conception	**D1**	**D2**	**D3**	**D4**	**D5**	**D6**	**. . . Dn**
E Conception	**E1**	**E2**	**E3**	**E4**	**E5**	**E6**	**. . . En**
F Concept	**F1**	**F2**	**F3**	**F4**	**F5**	**F6**	**. . . Fn**
G Scientific Deductive system		**G2**					
H Algebraic Calculus							

2. Analytic objects cannot be appreciated by the senses—no shape, smell, touch, sight etc.

Therefore appreciation of O is hindered and K → O inhibited.

Consequences for the analyst

1. Increase of anxiety because there is no barrier against fears of acknowledged dangers.
2. No barrier against guilt because of no known substitute for acknowledged and conventional therapeutic aims.
3. Isolation from group basic assumptions.

Consequences for the work

1. Increased reality of phenomena, and therefore of objects that are to be interpreted.
2. Changed order of appearance of analytic phenomena in the analysis.
3. Increased awareness of the unique nature of every psycho-analytic experience and of psycho-analysis itself.
4. Clear emergence of O.
5. An experience common to all practising analysts becomes evident because of invariants; their *accidental* disagreement is diminished, and therefore communication is increased.

Consequences for the analysand

Inefficiency of his sensuous (including pictorial) representations of his mind is made clear by the less obstructed view of what he displays.

Psychotic's attacks on linking

1. He stimulates Memory.
2. He stimulates Desire.

[Undated—1968]

Notes on ritual and magic

I define 'magic' as a resort to control the physical environment. I reserve 'ritual' to define that aspect of magic which is concerned to control the spiritual world.

I shall be concerned mostly with the discussion of ritual, but while I wish to preserve scientific rigour in discussion, I do not wish to give the impression that the rigidity imparted by the limitations of rigorous discussion has any counterpart in the nebulous domain that is the object of this discussion.

I can indicate the difficulty by reminding you that what a scientist today might regard as the physical environment at some period in history appears quite consciously to have included spirits, good and bad, and to the observation of a psycho-analyst may still—at least unconsciously—include good and bad spirits. Indeed, we assume, without usually recognizing that it is an assumption, that there is such a thing as a psyche that can be scientifically studied, that is studied with no allegiance to anything other than the truth. As psycho-analysts we are aware that such a claim for our investigations would be rash indeed, except as an assumption to be investigated.

Investigation was founded on the belief in one underlying principle of magic: astrology and alchemy. Astrology is applied astronomy based on observation and mathematical calculations. Alchemy is experimental chemistry. Investigation suffered from inaccurate observation, erroneous assumptions and false conclusions.

The belief in a universal spirit or principle animating the world has been and is powerful—a psycho-analytic fact.

Ritual and psycho-analysis

Ritual or ceremonial magic is aimed at the control of the spirit world by various means, from short spells and charms to lengthy and highly elaborate ceremonies including prayers and invocations.

The gap between theories of psycho-analysis on one side and invocation and prayer on the other is narrow. Sometimes it becomes narrower; sometimes it widens. Similarly, the gap between inaccurate observation, erroneous assumptions and false conclusions on the one hand, and scientific method on the other, cannot at present be determined through inability to discriminate.

The subject matter of psycho-analysis and ritual is reified; it then becomes subject to magic; ritual becomes scientific method; scientific method reciprocally becomes ritual.

Objects transformed and transferred to the objective domain come under the Rules of

Magic	→	Astrology Alchemy	→	Astronomy Chemistry	→	Island Universe Nuclear Physics

and then, transferred back to the domain of the psyche, they again come under the sway of ritual, the ritual being thinly reminiscent of scientific method, and scientific method often betraying a curious and disquieting resemblance to ritual.

[Undated—1968]

Drugs are substitutes employed by those who cannot wait.

The substitute is that which cannot satisfy without destroying the capacity for discrimination of the real from the false.

Whatever is falsely employed as a substitute for the real, is transformed thereby into a poison for the mind.

The substitution of that which is peripheral to action instead of that which is central must cause imbalance.

Imbalance is betrayed by the resort of the helpless to an assumption of omnipotence.

Immaturity, confusion, helplessness and impotence are replaced, in those who are intolerant of frustration, by prematurity, order, omnipotence and power.

That which should be a prelude to action is replaced by action; action is replaced by what should have preceded it.

Hubris is the sin of Oedipus, the planners of the Tower of Babel, Adam and Eve, the animal that uses action as a substitute for thought, and thought as a substitute for action (not a prelude to it).

Craving for fulfilment, unlike pursuit of fulfilment, announces the existence of a vacancy (minus).

Areas of turbulence centre on a messianic idea.

The 'knot' resembles a 'vacancy', and both resemble the turbulence of the 'messianic idea'.

The knot excites curiosity.

The vacancy excites greed, substitutes, prematurity, memory and desire.

The messianic idea excites fear of disruption of ♀ and attracts destructive, restrictive forces.

The messianic idea stimulates growth and maturation.

Turbulence may signify maturation.

'Vacancy' consists of greed, envy, hate, destruction, paranoia.

* * *

'Fears' are as opaque as 'hopes'. Is 'hope' different from desire? Yes; like knots; it is desire + time.
Or,

Desire + Frustration = Hopes ↔ Fears.

[Undated—1969]

The positive and negative therapeutic reactions are in essence the same; they are therapeutic reactions intended to take attention away from psycho-analysis. Like the insistence on 'cure' as an objective for taking up analysis, they are objectives for continuing or stopping; they are 'covers', rationalizations, 'reasons' operating in a role as slave to . . . what? The passions? Or some unknown such as hatred of doubt?

When a small attendance at a meeting is deplored, it is explained that had the complainant been in charge, how much better the result would have been; when he is one of the absentees, how good his reason for absence was. These are 'therapeutic' explanations; they heal the traumata of decision. But decision is an essential of 'achievement' or the transformation of thought into action—be it thought as a substitute for, or a prelude to, action.

* * *

Murderous, sadistic, 'malign' hate seems to be devoid of insight and to provoke a corresponding lack of insight—or unwillingness to use it—in myself; a 'damned-if-I'll-give-an-interpretation' feeling. Why should I give him an interpretation without being given what I call 'evidence'?

* * *

I feel a deep lethargy. I cannot see my way, and when I cannot see my way I feel no disposition to act as if I could, or in a way that would give substance to a reassuring phantasy that I could. *I do not know*. Nor does anyone else. It is absurdly simple really—unless one wants to complicate it. When there is nothing to do—don't do it!

* * *

There is one luxury that should be sacrificed: that of talking about, or even thinking about—except in the strictest privacy—one's anxieties, sacrifices, austerities, or what it may cost one to lead the life one has chosen.

> 'Shape nothing lips; be lovely dumb:
> It is the shut, the curfew sent
> From there were all surrenders come
> Which only make you eloquent.'

Gerard Manley Hopkins,
'The Habit of Perfection'

[Undated—1969]

Much psycho-analytic 'controversy' is not controversy at all. If listened to for any prolonged period, say a year, but preferably two or three, a pattern begins to emerge, so much so that I can write a chairman's address suitable, with the alteration of a phrase or two, for practically any paper by anyone at any time. Thus:

"Ladies and Gentlemen, we have been listening to a very interesting and stimulating paper. I have had the great advantage of being able to read it in advance, and though I cannot say I agree with everything Dr X says" (chiefly because I haven't the faintest idea what he thinks he is talking about, and I am damned sure he hasn't either), "I found his presentation extremely—er—stimulating. There are many points that I would like to discuss with him if we had time" (thank God we haven't), "but I know there are many here who are anxious to speak" (in particular our resident ex-officio permanent bores whom no one has succeeded in silencing yet), "so I must not take up too much of our time. There is, however, just one point on which I would like to hear Dr X's views if he can spare the time." (At this point I prepare to give one of the favourite bees which reside in my own bonnet its periodical airing. It does not matter in the least how irrelevant it may be, or how unlikely Dr X is to have any views whatever on the subject, or how improbable that I would want to hear them if he had—the time has come and out it goes.) "It has often occurred to me" (and only the poor devils in my Society know how often that is) "that . . . etc. . . . etc."

[Undated—1969]

The failure of a function should excite suspicion. It may be due to a natural lack; or it may be a Category 2 element [*see* The Grid, p. 295]. What is that? The maintenance of a theory known to be false in order either to keep another out, or because there is no better. Is this a field on which a pattern can be traced?

The capacity of the mind depends on the capacity of the unconscious—negative capability. Inability to tolerate empty space limits the amount of space available. Curiosity should be part of the dependent group, but it can share fight–flight qualities [*see* Bion, *Experiences in Groups*] when the wish is to avoid impending discovery (Category 2). Is any impulse one way only? No. What then are the poles? Are there poles, or is there some better scheme?

* * *

The paranoid–schizoid and depressive positions are related to a part of the domain of thought, that part of it in which there exist thinkers corresponding to the thoughts awaiting someone or something to think them. The thinkers might be likened to objects sensitive to certain wave-lengths of thought, as the eye or radio telescope is sensitive to a particular range of electromagnetic waves. Such thinkers can be impinged upon by thoughts that are too powerful in relation to the sensitivity of the receiving apparatus. Or they may be unmatched by a reciprocating thinker.

The human being, despite similarities to other human beings, may not, through over- or under-sensitivity, have an apparatus adequate to thinking the thoughts. He becomes aware of these thoughts usually through the medium of what is ordinarily known to him as religious awe, and is variously expressed as incarnation, evolution of godhead, platonic forms, Krishna, mystic experience, inspiration, and the like. Thus the source of emission of the received or evolved thoughts is felt as external, God-given, derived from a particular person or occasion, phrase, book, painting, awareness of a constant conjunction. The fate of the thought and the thinker is to follow one of the paths I have indicated as peculiar to ♂♀, or some variation. In some circumstances the impact is incandescent, growth-producing, and then the individual thinker becomes an emitter or intermittant. A chain reaction is set up, as I have already described it in terms of the messianic thought, mystic, etc. The problem is whether one is to regard this model, ♂♀ [*see* Bion, *Attention and Interpretation,* pp. 122, 123] as a model for a configuration that underlies certain groups of particular instances, or is it simply a way of regarding meaningless, incoherent, unrelated phenomena, and making them appear to have coherence and a meaningful pattern? Does it in fact matter which it is? Do facts arrange themselves in this pattern, or is it a peculiarity in the individual that he finds it necessary to discern this or similar patterns in the facts he observes? The craving for validation may then be a wish to localize the emitter in God, universe, person, conscious and unconscious, by instruments that are micro- or macro-scopic and appear to confer authoritatively the guerdon of truth.

2 March 1969

Reading notes again, I feel exasperated by their futility, but I am at least 'exasperated' by them. They must therefore have something to them, or they could not exasperate. 'Exasperated'—feeling of anxiety of 'theft' analysis while leaving me open to accusations of plagiarism, etc. This is persecution by the feeling that one's reward in analysis is not success or money or admiration; in short, that there are no rewards corresponding to one's preconceptions. The exasperation is at the 'note'; consciously, at what it contains. Interpretations occur to me, but for all I know I gave them at the time and I feel no more certain either way. Perhaps the point is that the note has a value, but I have no idea what. Or is it the paranoid–schizoid reaction that I have already described? Ps $\leftrightarrow$ D.

21 March 1969

There are certain 'uses' of things in themselves that could be analogous to 'uses' of modes of expression; they might form the basis of, or one axis of, a new Grid. Thus: money may be used to measure the status of a man or a woman, as in wergild, bride-purchase, religion. It can then be transferred to measure exchange values (commerce). It can then be debased in the sense of both change of base and change of value, i.e. to give substance to a fiction. For example:

A. Analyst fee: low ↔ high; to correspond to psycho-analytic value of the psycho-analyst, i.e. a measure of value.

B. Analyst fee: low ↔ high; to cloak and hide the value of the man or woman 'psycho-analyst'. The monetary value is de-based as the communicative value of speech, the 'currency of words', becomes debased.

In A, the money derives its value from the person to whom it is assigned, accredited, paid. In B, the person derives his 'value' from the possession of money that, already having value from its origin, is used to cloak his worth.

[Undated—1969]

Determination of direction in a group

Suppose the group consists of twelve people, 1–12. No.1 and No.4 appear to be in disagreement. No.1 appears to be 'reactionary'; No.4 appears to be 'progressive'.

Question: to whom or what is No.1 reacting? No.4 denies that it is a reaction against him. But it appears that No.1 is reacting against No.4's personality. Is this another plane? On what plane is the study taking place? All planes? If not, which?

Definitions wanted

1. Void, Infinite: formless.
2. Drift: movement that is incoherent, patternless, unregulated.
3. Streaming: movement that appears coherent or regulated. Both Drift and Streaming require a point from which observation is made.

Since a moment's thought shows a point to be inadequate, we are led to the definition,

4. Base: the distance between two observers separated in
5. Space: for example, one at No.1's position in the room; the other at No.4's.
6. Time: for example, one in the present; one in time past; and one in time to come (= future).

   Streaming requires direction, and therefore a method of notation or signification of apparent origin and apparent destination. Thus,

7. Radiant: may serve as the direction from which movement seems to radiate. Its association with light or heat may also be useful. The study is of what I call, provisionally, the mental phenomena of the group as observed by me. It will therefore be coloured by my point of view. Impressions received or radiated by me may themselves be regarded as radiants in so far as their origin appears to lie in me or my direction. These I regard as having a common vertex. I propose to regard the twelve members of the group as each representing or marking a vertex. These vertices, for reasons that will appear later, are not to be regarded as necessarily identical with the group individual members. The next terms, therefore, are
8. Vertex, and
9. Obscurity: can be regarded as analogous to a low-pressure area (Radiant being analogous to a high-pressure area).

Finally, I shall use the terms,

10. Thought: for which a thinker is not epistemologically necessary, and
11. Lie: for which a thinker is logically and epistemologically necessary.

It may at first appear strange to postulate thought without a thinker, but the convenience of doing so is considerable and will become more apparent later.

With these few terms as a preliminary and provisional equipment, we may commence the investigation.

No.1, who is a man of capacity, has made himself well known to the group through his constant attendance and the frequency of his intervention in discussion. From what he has said, it is clear to all that he holds a position of responsibility in his firm, is accustomed to being listened to with respect, and does not like—though he tolerates—a subordinate position. He now speaks: "I feel that it does not really matter what Dr Bion says; everybody listens to him and behaves as if his authority precludes discussion. When I speak, I am made to feel I don't know what I am talking about."

No.4 "Oh, I don't agree at all. On the contrary, I think we pay a great deal of attention to what you say. After all, Dr Bion is the doctor . . ."

No.1 "There you go again. 'Dr Bion is the doctor.' We all know that, but what about it? I know other doctors. My doctor, whom I may say I like very much and who is a very good man, often tells me things I don't agree with."

No.4 "But you listen to what he says about medicine?"

No.1 "Not always. As a matter of fact, I have poured his medicine down the sink before now."

[Breaks off here. No continuation.]

August 1969

What I do, or think I do, is to draw attention to certain patterns that I observe in the behaviour of my patients while they are with me in the consulting room. These patterns appear to me to be discernible and, sooner or later, describable in language which I can formulate and which, sooner or later, the analysand can understand. For this they must be able to learn my mode of communication—however defective. And I must be able to make a formulation which the analysand, granted that the evidence available in the analytic room can also be used to contribute to his comprehension, can understand if he will permit my formulation and his experience to reinforce each other.

To sum up: I must interpret while the evidence that I am interpreting is available to the analysand's and my scrutiny, and at no other time. These aims appear to be within the capacity of certain kinds of patient. It is supposed by me that the successful achievement of this aim is worth the patient's while. Why?

* * *

Anxiety arises because one knows that analysands come with an idea of cure, and one knows it is almost certain that they will not get, and cannot get, what they call 'cure'. Almost—but not quite. But even supposing one can lead them to something better—a very large supposition—even that is far from certain. What then? Is it possible simply to say, "Try it"? Much analysis, and even more psychotherapy, is ludicrously omnipotent and optimistic.

March 1970

Today I saw very clearly the absolute un-necessity for a session to be anything but a session in its own right. 'Progress' could then mean that instead of presenting one fact in six months, the patient comes to present six facts in one session. In short, he becomes a multi-dimensional personality—a three-dimensional physical identity, and a multi-dimensional psychical identity.

May 1970

As electromagnetic waves can be employed conceptually as a part of a theory embracing an enormous range of physical phenomena, so I wish to employ the concept of α-elements to embrace an enormous range of mental phenomena.

β-space

I shall suppose a mental multi-dimensional space of unthought and unthinkable extent and characteristics. Within this I shall suppose there to be a domain of thoughts that have no thinker. Separated from each other in time, space and style, in a manner that I can formulate only by using analogies taken from astronomy, is the domain of thoughts that have a thinker. This domain is characterized by constellations of α-elements. These constellations compose universes of discourse that are characterized by containing and being contained by terms such as, 'void', 'formless infinite', 'god', 'infinity'. This sphere I shall name by borrowing the term, 'noösphere' from Teilhard de Chardin [*The Phenomenon of Man*], but as I wish to avoid too great a penumbra of associations, particularly those activated by the term, 'sphere', I shall employ a sign that is as devoid of meaning as I can make it (compatible with retention of its capacity for communicability), Σ (sigma).

α-space

The objects of α-space I shall suppose to be real, with their own reality, both infra-real and ultra-real. Perceptible to ordinary thought are objects usually confused with and regarded as indistinguishable from objects of sense, namely certain active constellations of thought that are associated with the discipline of biology and spoken of in those terms.

The classic psycho-analytic view supposed the mind or personality to be identical with the physical identity of a person. The object of my proposal is to do away with such a limitation and to regard the relationship between body and mind (or personality, or psyche) as one that is subject to investigation.

Thus, a nation is said to have a 'character', but the Σ associated with a nation is *not* identical with the σ (soma), though as a psychological aid in communication it may be convenient to speak of the nation's 'mood' as such-and-such. I should hope to approach a more rigorous formulation by saying, Σ (national: Persian), or Σ (individual: John Smith), or Σ (war: Ruritania/Rumtiphoo/Titipu). Similarly with various relationships somatically considered between individuals; and then extra-psychic and endo-psychic, still somatically described as an aid to comprehension of Σ constellations.

In mathematical terms one may provisionally suggest a linear formulation, a scale, which can be supposed to represent the 'mind' (psyche) as an instrument of investigation.

$$10^1\ 10^2\ 10^3 \ldots 10^{n-1}\ 10^n$$

$$10\ 10^{-1}\ 10^{-2} \ldots 10^{-(n-1)}\ 10^{-n}$$

In the domain of physics a similar linear representation can be offered for the province of electromagnetic waves ranging, say, from angstrom units to metres. Between 10^{-3} and 10^{-5} would lie the visible region. Similarly, somewhere on the Σ scale would lie the sense-able (think-able?) range. That is to say, there would be Σ phenomena which by definition are matched by corresponding receptor organs.

The aspects of Σ I wish to discuss present special difficulties because there is no apparatus available for their formulations, so I have to employ the inadequate written word. What follows will therefore have to be couched in terms that are adapted for use in a more primitive mode of communication. The formulations I employ must be regarded as Grid category C [*see* p.

295], no matter how much they may appear to be elements of a sophisticated formulation.

I am supposing that there is a psycho-analytic domain with its own reality—unquestionable, constant, subject to change only in accordance with its own rules even if those rules are not known. These realities are 'intuitable' if the proper apparatus is available in the condition proper to its functioning. Equally, there are certain minimum conditions necessary for its exercise. Approximately, in C-category terms, this activity depends on the presence of a personality, an operating intuition, a minimum degree of intuitive capacity and intuitive health. The conditions in which the intuition operates (intuits) are pellucid and opaque. I have already indicated that from the intuitor's vertex opacities can be distinguished sufficiently to be given names, however primitive and defective the ascriptions may be. These are: memory, desire, understanding. All are opacities obstructing 'intuition'. I have therefore stated that the psycho-analyst should exercise his intuition in such a way that it is not damaged by the intrusion of memory, desire and understanding.

Such freedom from opacity cannot be achieved during the psycho-analysis if the intuition has already been damaged by indiscipline at any time. The more nearly the psycho-analyst can approximate to freedom from these—and no doubt other 'opacities' as yet unidentifiable—the more confidently can he discount the origin of his observations as due to the 'personal equation'. This is well known and has been recognized as one of the motives for undergoing a psycho-analysis. What has not been recognized is the ephemeral nature of such psycho-analytic achievements and the need for the establishment of freedom from memory, desire and understanding as a permanent, durable and continuous discipline.

Suppose the psycho-analyst has been able to achieve a state in which he is the kind of 'person' capable of (psycho-analytic) intuition; suppose further that he is capable of maintaining such a state. Then, and only then, is he in a position to have certain experiences that I shall attempt to formulate.

The uniformity of Σ can be intuited as displaying areas of disturbance, 'turbulence', 'opaque' areas contrasting with areas of 'pellucidity'. The visible spectrum with its Fraunhofer lines can itself be used as a model (though a very crude one) for purposes of exposition, provided that its crudity is recognized and that the damaging effect of understanding on intuition is borne in mind.

These areas of turbulence indicate a constellation that may be ephemeral or may display a certain durability. The durability is significant and calls for appreciation of its domain: it may be significant of Σ, or of Σ (nation: Ruritania), or Σ (era: Christian), or Σ (individual: John Smith). There are certain Σ areas that are relatively stable to a point where the fact that one is in contact with an individual (sense-able, and therefore denoted by me as σ, indicating somatic) becomes peculiarly seductive and therefore conducive to the misleading conclusion that Σ (individual: John Smith) is identical with σ (John Smith). But psycho-analytic scrutiny convinces one that Σ is the significant fact, and σ important only in so far as it is receptive or emittive of Σ. To put it another way: Σ is covering a range of 'wave lengths' belonging to the psychotic range. This area is characterized by extremely 'short waves', lack of range, and therefore lack of discrimination—what a musician could describe as inability to 'hear', or adjust to what is said in such a way that the statement made cannot be 'heard' unless it is exactly and precisely attuned to the receptor. The same can be said of what is seen: there is something in the range of colour perception analogous to perfect pitch in music. There is no response to a statement unless it is precisely and exactly addressed to the receptor; there appears to be no way in which emitter and receptor can be adjusted to each other if some degree of correction is required—a 'miss' is absolute, 'as good as a mile'.

In the domain of 'perfect pitch', the patient may be glad to be told indignantly, "You know perfectly well what I mean!" as a cover for his own suspicion that he knows nothing of the kind. He may even welcome the inherent implication that he is like everyone else in order to escape from an 'inescapable' sense of isolation and loneliness. Such a patient will welcome the attention of the psycho-analyst as an assurance that he is believed by someone to be comprehensible. Entire languages are learned to give substance to a belief that he is like everyone else, and to foster that belief in himself or others. He will welcome the idea that he hears what others hear when an orchestra is playing. He resists 'millions of interpretations' of phrases, music or colours. He can see 'millions of colours' where the psycho-analyst can only see 'white light'. He conceals as best he can that to others he appears, or would appear, 'tone deaf' or 'colour blind'. The analyst is predominantly important because the patient cherishes the belief that the analyst 'understands' him.

February 1971

The psychotic personality needs to have his *awareness* of sensuous experience brought home. The trouble may be the obtrusive and non-verbal nature of the experience; say, the buzzing of a fly. This is to be brought home together with the post-verbal awareness of the experience of the buzzing of the fly; for example, "You are feeling I am annoyed by the noise you can hear". If I said, ". . . by the buzzing of the fly", it would not be accurate because the patient does not know what I am annoyed at. 'Unconscious' and 'conscious' do not meet the problem. 'Unconscious' could sometimes be replaced by 'obvious but unobserved'.

* * *

Fear and hatred = powerfully obtrusive feelings; they are therefore liable to draw attention to the 'unknown self' → premature and precocious 'solution' to obviate feelings of hatred and fear of the hatred and fear. Abolition of feelings → hatred of sense of unreality.

The messianic idea is an unknown idea; it is hated and feared. It is dealt with by projection, materialization. It is, as a result, not an idea but something less frightening, a person or thing. Persons, physically, can be put a stop to, either by idealization (and proved to be real) or by realization (and proved not to be ideal).

Thus a series of events begins to cohere. For example, Aristarchus conceives of the possibility that the earth goes round the sun. There are no instruments by which the idea can be further elaborated. In the course of centuries the idea again begins to form, and this time instruments can be fashioned—for example, by Galileo.

The established order is disturbed, including the established web of thought—the racial web of thought, including profound 'religious' beliefs such as that associated with sun worship. The belief in the sun as God is quite rational; if you must have a god, it is not a bad god to have. Therefore Galileo tends to menace the existing web of thought, both scientific and religious—in so far as scientific thought can be regarded as relatively conscious, superficial, rational; and religious thought as relatively unconscious, profound, irrational, but still operative. The more it is in fact *not* extinct, the more it is capable of instigating emotional reactions in the noösphere [*see* p. 251]. Curiosity, which might stimulate discovery of the unknown, stimulates the need for a defensive termination of the unknown messianic idea, or person, or movement. It may be overwhelmed; if so, no problem. Or it may destroy the establishment, including the established work of the noösphere—which I now prefer to regard more as 'noamorph'. But in some respects it is convenient to regard it as possessing limits and therefore approximating to a sphere—the noösphere. The two names must not therefore be regarded as two conflicting theories to which there correspond two conflicting realities, but two conflicting representations of the same reality. In the realm of physics a similar conflict appears in wave and quantum mechanics of light.

For the most part, discoveries do not have great resonating force. For example, the advances in the physical sciences, quantum mechanics, astronomy, relativity, have so far not had much percussive force on the domain of thought—in which I include thoughts for which there is as yet no thinker. The landing on the moon, however, may be one of these percussive events: it is significant that one reaction—in the USA at least—has been that the nation cannot 'afford' the space programme, though it has partially broken out again, probably because international rivalry—a very powerful emotional force—has not been so far controlled by the emotional force hitherto more disguised than displayed or illuminated by the term, 'economics'.

It seems reasonable to suppose that our somewhat insignificant speciality, psycho-analysis, has already exhausted its impetus and is ready to disappear into limbo, either because it is a burden too great for us, as we are, to carry, or because it is one more exploration destined to display a blind alley, or because it arouses or will arouse fear of the unknown to a point where the protective mechanisms of the noösphere compel it to destroy the invading ideas for fear that they will cause a catastrophe in which the noösphere disintegrates into the no-amorph. This catastrophic change could be brought about by advances in astronomy, physics, religion, or indeed any domain for which there may as yet be no name. The principles of psychical growth are not known. It is significant that even Newton, Leibnitz, Descartes were not able to formulate such principles in the sphere of mathematics, though the differential calculus was such an attempt.

[1971]

"We had sex." A curious expression that is not known to me. I suppose I 'had sex' from an early stage of my life. The earliest and most primitive meaning is a sensuous one; the primitive is, by my definition, based on a background of experience gained through the senses of smell, sight, hearing, touch and taste.

According to E. D. Adrian (*The Physical Background of Perception*), the earliest senses are light rays and sound vibrations, 'for these show what is happening at a distance', and 'intelligent behaviour is guided by them far more than by what is touching our skin' (also hair, particularly vibrissae around the snout when the eyes are defective).

Other senses, according to him, are not concerned with general policy, but 'with what we are going to do next'. This involves information about 'the body surface' and also tensions in muscles, temperature gradients, movements of viscera and concentrations of various substances in blood. There are 'many varieties of receptor apparatus—each sensitive to particular factors in the environment.'

The developmental scale would suggest that the earlier epistemological experiences are concerned with the sense of touch. Sensuous pleasure and pain would be external contact between skin and womb; internal, between ectoderm and mesoderm and entoderm. Chemical substances in blood—poisons—would also be in contact and might contribute to a sense of being peripatetic. The contact would be extended by the sense of smell (located in the vibrissae?) and the sense of sight.

Broadly, the sense of touch would be related to 'what to do', the realm of transformation into action. Most of this operates autonomously without the intervention of the mind, or is transferred through education to the autonomic; for example, from desire for mobility to 'walking'.

The distant receptors—sight, smell, vibrissae, intuition—are associated with 'distant' perceptors—wisdom, intelligence.

The short-range receptors—skin, genitalia—are associated with action (bowel sense, bladder sense).

The distant transmitters: eyes, smell (primitive?), phonation.

The two parallel lines of a railway track are seen to meet at a point, *P*. In sensuous visual reality this is the case; in tactile experimental reality they do not meet; in olfactory reality they do not meet. The olfactory sense, though a distant receptor (according to Adrian) seems ineffective if called upon to contribute information on this particular problem. The tactile senses have to augment their short range by some other source—like sight? And sight has to augment its contribution by—touch?

* * *

Thoughts do not have to be 'used'. Their sexual value is enhanced, if not transformed, because there is no impairment of their ideal 'reality'. Conversely, their reality transformation is impaired if transformation is not effected.

The thoughts can be 'formulated' and then used either as a prelude to, or a substitute for, action. In this respect thoughts resemble money—they can be stored or exchanged.

The crux lies in the fact that certain *decisions* appear to effect *irreversible* changes. Decisions are a kind of thought: their value is effected by their real or apparent irreversibility.

10 July 1971

'My subject is poetry, not language. Yet the roots of poetry are in language' (Ernest Fenollosa, *The Chinese Written Character as a Medium for Poetry*, p. 10).

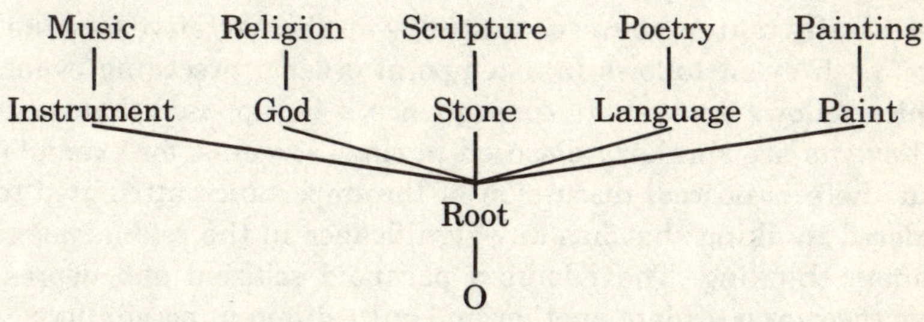

What is important? The root? The flower? The germ? The conflict? The durability?

14 July 1971

The English grammatical formulation of psycho-analytic theories is one that employs a form in which succession plays the important role. 'Dog bites man' does not mean the same as 'man bites dog', and this gives a strong prejudicial colouration to all formulations in favour of the idea of events necessarily taking place successively—in the narrative formulation each event follows in a temporal order a preceding event, which follows another. In consequence it is supposed that mental events are similarly disposed in time—dreams, for example. But there is no real discussion of the importance attributed to ordered thinking that has any significance in the realms *not* of human thinking. The Kleinian paranoid–schizoid and depressive theories postulate another and quite different possibility.

15 July 1971

'Man bites dog' does not mean the same as 'dog bites man'. The introduction of succession—temporal and spatial order—is an essential quality which alters the meaning of the unaltered words: bite/dog/man. The ideogram for 'horse', 馬, and the alphabetic, 'horse', have a historic similarity because both assume, 'understand', and therefore leave out a precedent phrase or phrases between 'horse and ideogram' and the 'visual image'. There is similarly something between 'visual image' and 'thing-in-itself'—what I have called by the meaningless term, 'α-element'.

A pictorial schematic formulation:

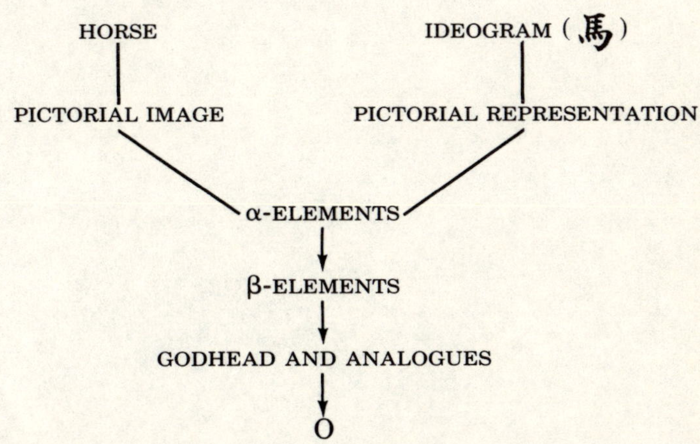

The scheme can now be considered as providing an analogue for similar schemes in which the sense of sight is replaced by taste, touch, smell, sound, etc., from infra-sensual to ultra-sensual. Psycho-analytically it means postulating a psycho-analytical domain. I would borrow for my own purposes the term invented by Teilhard de Chardin, the 'noösphere', supposing it to be included in a 'psychosphere'. Analogous to the supposition of a definitory hypothesis of 'thoughts without a thinker', the psychosphere would be without a noösphere [*see also* p. 251].

To recapitulate: returning to the discussion of dreams related to visual images, I consider that dreams would need to be thought of as belonging to a far more widely extended C category [*see* p. 295], much more extended than one enclosing only visual or any other sensuous images, though in 'practical' psycho-analysis only elements within the sensuous range would, by definition, be experienced. Sooner or later, the investigation would have to be extended to infra- and ultra-sensuous areas first, then from noösphere to psycho-sphere.

July 1971

Predictive psycho-analysis and predictive psychopathology

A Fable for Our Time

In the year 30070 a revolutionary discovery took place. It is from that event, and in honour of it, that our present time-scale originates. It is difficult at this time—300 n-years later—to be sure of the events; even something as simple as the fabular meaning of n.y. tends to be obscured in the minds of the vulgar by still older fables and associated locutions. The present writer has met with lower orders who believe the letters to stand for 'new years' or 'nuclear years', under the impression that our time-scale derives from a supposed atomic disaster occurring in year 1 of our era. In so far as it is possible to reconstitute the past from the scanty remains, something resembling the following account took place.

A man, whose name is lost but who must have been a genius of outstanding proportions for that age, made a discovery of an exceedingly simple kind. In those days there still existed a rudimentary science called, 'psycho-analysis'. The term was made up of two parts: 'psyche', which referred to an undeveloped mind or personality, which was believed to have given rise to the so-called 'psyche'; and 'anal', derived from an anatomical structure, notably that part of it concerned with the evacuation of the waste products from 'eating'—a habit very similar to that which can be observed in the 'domesticated' forms that we have derived from them. As far as we can now tell—or even conjecture from certain archaic vestigial survivals of our domestic forms—the psycho-analysts, for so I shall call them for short, connected their excretions—quite correctly—with what they 'ate', and developed elaborate rituals as part of the religion of cleanliness, which were supposed to placate, or render harmless, the remains of what they had devoured. If the destructive rituals failed, as was supposed to have happened on those occasions when disease wiped out a few thousands of them, redoubled efforts were made to increase the efficiency of the cleansing rituals by sometimes using various difficult-to-obtain metals in the form of representations of the excretions. This ritualistic manufacture completed, the product was called Money and was set up for worship.

For a time the new religion flourished—reinforced and improved by the psycho-analysts—but greed led some elements to substitute inferior substances like paper for the hard-to-obtain metals such as gold. This development—associated in mythology with names such as Lord Jesus (nicknamed, The Christ), Lord Keynes, and even some dissident psycho-analysts such as Lenin and his associated 'Communists'—led to the undermining of the religion of Money, which was finally devalued. This anti-religious attitude did great harm to the hierarchy and certain areas like Russia, America, China and Africa. Groups found themselves virtually without authority which had formerly been provided by the hierarchy whose skilful manipulation of a mental characteristic of these creatures, called 'idealization', had led to their being regarded with reverence; it was an attribute of their personalities which approximated them to the deities in whom they could see and admire themselves.

These creatures, remote ancestors of the animals we use as new material for certain parts of our machinery, used this 'science' as a means for investigating the past of each single individual and, later, the past of the groups or hordes in which these creatures moved. This whole 'science' was believed to be superior to the earlier activity known as 'religion'.

About religion we have been able to discover little, partly because the study excites scant interest amongst us, partly because the remoteness of the past is such that it is doubtful whether the investigation could be carried out without an enormous and unrewarding expenditure of even our resources. It is known, however, that the practice of religion was regulated by a special hierarchy. This organization was taken over, elaborated, but otherwise hardly changed, by the new religion, which was called a science. Ritual, an essential feature of the religious observances, was likewise taken over, and even now evidence is being discovered showing how elaborate these rituals were, and how much time and money were devoted to their proliferation. The new religion had to establish its superiority to the old, and exhaustive steps were taken to stamp out all evidence of the past. Even the rituals had to be disguised; the word, 'ritual', was replaced by the term, 'scientific'. In those times it was the habit of the hierarchy to hunt out and destroy all evidence of potential growth. In this it must not be supposed that they were without ingenuity and even a kind of rudimentary foresight. 'Brainwashing' was, for example, immensely improved and brought to a very considerable and meritorious degree of efficiency. The expression derived from the same sources from which Money had sprung—namely, the anus.

Up to this point all seemed to be going well; the new religion had triumphed and was established as the 'science of psychoanalysis', with its hierarchy firmly in control and its ritual 'scientific method' codified and recognized as the hallmark of the New Era.

Again we are hampered by a period of obscurity and ambiguous evidence. As far as the remains that have come down to us can be pieced together, the rules of psycho-analytic investigation—which were rigidly enforced so that there could be no breach in the solid foundation of what was already known and described as 'history'—began to be assailed by ominous and inexplicable attacks. One trouble-maker, called Smith, seems to have caused the authorities much difficulty. (Smith was a common name, usually associated with welding.) The evidence is scanty but enough for us to assume with plausibility the existence of an Ur Smith.

By legendary repute at about the time now known as 1 NY, one of the priesthood, of eccentric manner and history, was interrogating an individual supposedly even more eccentric than himself. The records, such as they are, indicate that at this period one of the obligatory rituals was supposed to separate the psychotic from the non-psychotic personalities, the whites from the blacks, the candidates for the Establishment from the candidates for the Loony Bin. This ritual, known as Selection, was attended by much anxiety, and it was obligatory for representatives of the various factions to be present to force their candidates onto the Establishment and so save them from being placed in the Loony Bin, or Not Yet category. As the officials and candidates were virtually indistinguishable from each other, almost everything depended on the numbers that could be mobilized in support of, or against, the course to be prescribed for the given candidate.

Apparently, in the instance that has now become the pictorial symbol for the year 1 of our era, NY, Ur Smith's candidate had not reached the day for selection and would, in the ordinary course, have been destined almost certainly for the Bin.

To understand what follows, it is necessary to explain the incredible barbarity of the customs of those times. See-ers, in common with all others, were subjected to a period of what was known as 'prolonged and deep analysis' by one or more of the priesthood employing one or more of the 'methods of scientific investigation' (rituals). These investigations were confined to elucidating 'the facts'. This was a device introduced by the priesthood to exclude any possible risk of controversy, doubt, or exercise of judgement, by limiting the material on which the pronouncement of fitness was to be made to those facts that were deemed to be known for certain. Since, by definition, the material consisted of facts that were known to have happened already, it was an article of dogma that, the foundations being solid and the brains of the judges as undisturbed by doubt or anxiety as they were solid, the outcome would of necessity be scientifically unassailable. To the great admiration and comfort of the hierarchy, a professor of statistics who had previously become one of their number pointed out, at a meeting called to discuss selection, that the method of counting the numbers supporting or opposing the candidate was by a happy chance both democratic and scientific because the introduction of numbers at last introduced 'mathematics', and therefore 'science', into the constitution of the Society. We need dwell no longer on these reconstructions of legend, but move on to firmer—though still legendary—foundations by considering 'Smith'.

He claimed to keep an open mind, meaning that he was open to entertain ideas that were new to him. He seems to have been unaware that such a claim was tantamount to an admission of instability and a lack of rigid frame so necessary for disciplined thinking. It is indeed extraordinary how he had escaped from being 'treated' by the more sturdy and reliable members of the establishment.

His candidate, a woman, thought she was 'the Virgin and the Duke of Wellington'. It was some time before he realized that she was not referring to the titular heads of one of the many groups of the period, but that she was describing certain voices or people that were interfering with her mind. He continued to listen—his one great weakness—and for a long time sheltered her from the authorities to whom he knew he was legally bound to deliver her. Indeed he was in great danger both for harbouring a person who, in the quaint terminology of the time, was a menace to herself and others, and because he himself had begun to investigate her behaviour on the supposition that the present, future, and unknown were what required scrutiny rather than the past, the known. He also believed that there were thoughts that had no thinker. Had this come out, there is no doubt that he and his woman candidate would have been classed together, and would have had their brains scientifically and humanely destroyed.

Through years of danger Smith managed to carry on his investigation to a point where it was clear that his candidate was really a new type of immature animal and was not suffering from some malformation of character.

There was known to him an ancient legend of a dictator earlier in world history who had decreed the massacre of what were known as 'The Innocents'. He suddenly suspected that this was an earlier instance of what he was now witnessing —the early embryonic stages of a personality rightly and instinctively, though clumsily, recognized as a menace to the existing order. He realized that he would be a victim of his curiosity either through being disposed of by the group hierarchy for disregarding the rules and well-tried procedures of science, or by being executed by the woman as soon as she had developed sufficiently to know how to rid herself of him. She was developing fast, and had already reached a stage where she openly declared her intention to strangle him at the first opportunity. She often expressed her contempt for ancient legend and all the characters in it, professing her determination to dispose of Smith and all other such mentally ill-formed and monstrous personalities, reserving her scorn particularly for such characteristics as the passionate feelings of love or hate that she considered to be peculiar to the human animal. Her attitude to her genital parents was one of ruthless and icy scorn. They feared her as if aware that she regarded them simply as a matter for calculating assessment.

Smith appears to have been able to tolerate these threats, though fully aware of the conventional view that he risked being murdered or held responsible for murder committed by her. He ignored the warnings that poured in on him both from his own perceptions of danger, and from the lessons of his training. . . .

[Undated]

In arithmetic the statement, $2 + 3 = 5$, expresses a relationship between specific numbers.

The statement, 'Two apples and three plums = five fruit', expresses a relationship between specific objects in a specific emotional field—a 'cultural' field in which it is agreed that apples and plums are accepted as possessing sufficient 'fruitiness' to qualify as 'fruit'.

In algebra the statement that $a + b = b + a$, will apply to any numbers. Any number, 'a', and any number, 'b', will together make the same result as '$b + a$'.

In this way the number may be seen to proceed from:

$$.. + xxx = sssss \longrightarrow 2 + 3 = 5 \text{ (any objects)} \longrightarrow (a + b) = (b + a).$$

But is this reversible?

Father + Mother + Infant = Oedipus complex (any F + M + I)

* * *

Which is the idée mère? Idée mère ⟷ Messianic idea ⟷ Any idea. Who owns it? Judgement of Solomon: whoever is to preserve the survival and development ⟶ growth (non-cancerous) of idea = the Owner.

September 1971

It is often said that faults are more easily seen in others than in one's self. Indeed, this would seem to be the main justification for employing someone other than one's self to be the analyst to whom one goes. The disadvantages of the arrangement become clear when the observer, psycho-analyst, sees faults that are his own in place of the defects of the analysand who supposedly has come to have *his* defects exposed, demonstrated (and dealt with?).

* * *

The relationship between myself and my colleagues here in Los Angeles could be accurately described as almost entirely unsuccessful. They are puzzled by, and cannot understand me—but have some respect for what they cannot understand. There is, if I am not mistaken, more fear than understanding or sympathy for my thoughts, personality or ideas. There is no question of the situation—the emotional situation—being any better anywhere else. I could say much the same for England. 'The old order changeth, yielding place to new. . . .'

* * *

"Is this a dagger that I see before me, the handle towards my hand?" Suppose that on further examination it appears not to be, then the system of verbal expression, even the system of sensible experience, needs extension. It cannot deal with the domain of non-existent reality, of thoughts without realization (like Euclidean geometry with spatial realization), of sight available or accessible only to the blind, of thought without content. It took time for Balaam to achieve the standards of thought of his ass.

Who saw the dagger before him, the handle towards his hand? Shakespeare? Where was it? Where is it now? The words in print bear no visual resemblance to a dagger. Nor do the sounds, if the words are transformed into spoken speech. Suppose a very good musician reads a musical score: does he become hallucinated? Does he suffer from auditory hallucinations?

1971

Psychiatry at a time of crisis, II

Part I was delivered to the British Psychological Society in 1947. I do not remember what I said, and I do not suppose that anyone has even heard of it; so everyone, including myself, can be said to start more or less fair. Even with regard to language there are similar advantages and disadvantages because I propose to use English—my English—which you do not know, and you use your English, which I don't know. There are similarities however; so there is liable to be a prejudice on both sides that when you use, or I use, what appears to be the same word, our different memories will lead both parties to think they understand each other. In this respect both parties suffer from memory; and since you probably want to understand, and I want to make myself understood, both parties also suffer from desire. I propose, therefore, to make the best of a bad job by illustrating what I want to communicate, and to do this by using your presence and mine as a source of illustrations of what I wish to communicate.

What has been called, 'a scientific meeting', I propose to call, 'a group'. I consider that the group is composed of an aggregation of 'individuals'. These two statements are what I shall call 'definitory hypotheses'. About these two definitory hypotheses there can be no argument; they are merely definitions. Anyone is free to use other terms.

The title I have chosen has undertones and overtones. I was there when I gave the first paper, but others who were not there are now participating in an experience that goes back to something of which they cannot be aware because they were not there; they are entering into an experience that is, so to speak, the 'second chapter'.

To illustrate this in group terms, I am going to use a verbal formulation of a visual imagination. For this I use archaeology, about which I know virtually nothing. The visual image, in contrast to the definitory hypothesis, may be regarded as a preconception or prejudice, and *is*—again unlike the definitory hypothesis—open to argument. Here are the two 'visual images' . . .

[Breaks off here]

Psychiatry at a time of crisis

[An Address from the Chair to the Medical Section of the British Psychological Society on 22 January 1947, and published in *The British Journal of Medical Psychology, 21,* Part 2 (1948): 81–89. It is reprinted here by kind permission of the Society.]

A visit to the occupational therapy department of a military psychiatric hospital during the early part of the war convinced me that, in the methods employed to deal with neurosis, some sort of equilibrium of insincerity had been achieved by patients, doctors and community alike. The nature of this equilibrium was not understood or even observed; I concluded that the only occupation that could be therapeutic was the study by the group of the nature of the affliction from which they individually and collectively suffered.

When I had the opportunity some years later of putting this idea into practice the result was a powerful release of emotion which showed itself chiefly in heightened morale amongst the patients, acts of indiscipline by two warrant officers of the staff—*ex officio* stable personalities—and minor but persistent obstruction of obscure origin. The experiment was brought to a close by the authorities, and since it has not proved possible to investigate their state of mind I cannot suggest a cause of failure.

Subsequent developments, in particular the Civilian Resettlement Units set up by the War Office, have persuaded me that this experiment had the characteristics of a chain reaction and so had the requisites for growth. But it showed, too, that something in the dynamics of unconscious tendencies in a group made the group peculiarly sensitive to any investigation of its emotional tensions. This sensitiveness manifested itself particularly in the class that Arnold Toynbee calls 'the dominant minority' (*A Study of History*, p. 77). 'The ailing civilization', he says, 'pays the penalty for its failing vitality by being disintegrated into a dominant minority, which rules with increasing oppressiveness but no longer leads, and a proletariat (internal and external) which responds to this challenge by becoming conscious that it has a soul of its own and by making up its mind to save its soul alive.' I shall have more to say of the dominant minority later.

From what I have said so far you may think that in speaking of crisis I had in mind the last war; this is not so. Let us consider for a moment some of the events that men and women of my generation have witnessed in the past forty years. In this period Russia and the United States have risen to supremacy. The British Empire has ceased to exist, and its place has been taken by a loose federation, the exact nature of which will probably not be determined for many a year. Germany, having achieved immense power, appears now to be annihilated. During the same period mankind has achieved depths of barbarism that will ensure that our era will go down in history as one in which all the bestialities of recorded time have been easily surpassed. Indeed, our only claim to fame and our brightest hope for the future is that it never will be surpassed.

Forty years ago civilization bore an aspect almost benign from the purely personal point of view. Yet even we who live in a land that was never invaded can give an account of personal catastrophe and suffering that could not have been foreseen in 1907.

In technical advance the changes during this time have been immense. Forty years ago the Channel had not been flown; twenty years ago broadcasting was in its infancy. It is probably true to say that man is more skilled in the mechanics of handling anything from an aeroplane to a mass of his fellow-men than he was forty years ago. It might be instructive if members of our section were to attempt to record their own experiences during this period, first recording the development of material comforts—refrigerators, cars, wireless sets and so forth—then recording their personal losses in terms of domestic happiness. If the psychologists in our section could make a survey of material which the section as a whole could supply it might provide surprising and valuable information. If I were to say that in the past forty years great technical advances had been accompanied by a great increase in human unhappiness, many would agree. But I could equally well say the technical advances and catastrophes alike had had no effect whatever in depressing the survivors, and it is characteristic that either opinion can be held and action based upon it without one shred of evidence that the opinion was justified in fact. And this is precisely how political, economic and international affairs are habitually conducted. A machinery for fact-finding is required, and unless it is provided by people with our training and outlook, no one else is likely to do so.

However problematical the effect on the individual of the events of our time, we may be quite certain that the state of mind of the individuals making up national groups has had a profound effect upon the events of our time. Our belief that this is so would have been strengthened during the past forty years by a series of technical developments that I have not mentioned—namely, the developments in treatment of the neuroses; before this audience I can describe the advance quite briefly as being from sal volatile to psycho-analysis.

There is no corpus of knowledge that does for the study of the group what psycho-analysis does for the study of the individual. The material that is relevant for our study is embedded in the information amassed by several at present widely separated disciplines. All I wish to show is that many thinkers have been more or less closely preoccupied with a subject which to them remained ill-defined but which to-day has begun to assume clearer outlines. I consider only Western Civilization.

In *The Nature and Destiny of Man,* Reinhold Niebuhr makes a distinction between what he describes as the Classical and Romantic approaches to the subject. He is referring to the Platonic and Aristotelian views of the organization of the state as contrasted with the approach made by thinkers such as St Augustine, Marx and Engels, and Nietzsche. Accepting this subdivision, I would say that the Classical writers were wedded to a belief in the supremacy and integrity of reason while the Romantics were more aware of the emotional component in human relationships. To me it appears that, as far as they go, it would be mistaken to ignore the importance of the Classical contributions. Even to-day the Platonic view of the importance of the function of the individual is implicit in vocational guidance and such derivatives as the Annexure Schemes of the army (a scheme by which men could, on psychiatric recommendation, be placed in an arm of the Service or a locality where they could render service within the limitations imposed by their psychiatric condition). My criticism of the thinkers here labelled as Romantic is that they had a genius for the manipulation rather than the comprehension of unconscious emotional impulses. It is perhaps this fact that gives Christianity the appearance, described by Flügel in *Man, Morals and Society,* of not having 'an adequate and positive goal for social and political endeavour' and an 'attitude of indifference to the larger social problems'. For the most part, references to external events seem to be made not with a view to expressing the desirability for external change, but rather to indicate a framework within which the individual had to carry out his internal readjustments.

Flügel's criticism that not enough has been said to assist the aggressive or dominating individual seems to be borne out by the history of our time. On the other hand, Niebuhr criticizing Nietzsche doubts the value of a feeling of vitality that is achieved by the release of aggressive impulses. This appears to be a reaction from the optimistic liberal outlook that assumes that emotion and reason are easily harmonized, but on further reflection Niebuhr leaves an uneasy feeling that in a liberal world there is only room for a desiccated intellectualism.

To me it seems that in so far as man has set about the regulation of external relationships by law, he has been tolerably successful; the failure arises when it comes to producing any method for dealing with the underlying emotional tensions in human relationships. And yet it is precisely these primitive unconscious tensions that present the fundamental problem in all human relationships. Whenever they obtrude themselves as an intrinsic element in the problem that is being studied, men retreat into further exploration of the possibilities of external regulation. These repeated preoccupations with machinery, being themselves nothing more than a by-product of the failure to grapple with the main problem, never achieve any higher level than the technicalities of police operations, no matter how magnificent the language in which they are clothed.

Now this is doubly unfortunate; not only is the main problem shirked, but the leaders of communities have, by the nature of the refuge they have found in their failure, ceased to be the creative leaders that Toynbee describes as essential for the healthy growth of civilization, and become instead the dominant oppressive minority.

Though it may appear that a failure to grapple with the main problem—if this is a just estimate of the situation—is all that is required to explain our present distresses, it is relevant to my purpose to draw attention to another component in the success or failure of attempts at the solution of problems of human relationships. I refer, of course, to the training of those whose lot it has been to interpret and apply the theories and doctrines of the original thinkers. Part of the difficulty in assessing the value of a leader, e.g. Jesus, is that we have to go by the results that his *followers* produce—not the leader himself. We have to bear in mind that it is not enough for the leader to be creative if his followers, through ill-training or unfitness, bear all the characteristics of the dominant minority. I would remind you again of Flügel's criticism of Christianity after it had achieved a dominant position.

What I have said about the political scientist and the religious leader seems to me to be equally true of the philosopher—he falls back defeated when the factor of emotional impulses obtrudes. This will, I am sure, be very ably denied. That is my point: it is the function of philosophy to deny it.

The position of the historian appears to be too often little more than that of the national bard translating into modern terminology, sometimes in the guise of science, sometimes literature, rarely both, the primitive war-songs of the tribe. Had he been more, he would have been more prominent in the investigation of guilt of the parties to the last war. When he is not being manipulated by the emotions of the group, he, too, is falling back from the hard task of grappling with and elucidating them.

It occurs to me that my criticisms may seem censorious; if so, I repent, for it is hardly just to renounce other disciplines for not having a technique with which we psychiatrists have not yet equipped them. My object has been merely to insist that there is a central core of material that is of vital concern to investigators in these fields and that until its existence, and indeed its very nature, has been understood, no further progress is possible.

At this point I must bring forward some speculations—I cannot call them more than that—on the interplay between technical advance and emotional development. It seems that man in his growth cannot solve any problem without immediately opening up more problems that present themselves for his solution. Thus, having achieved his adjustment to one member of the family, he has to learn to adjust to two. Having learned to walk, he is immediately presented with a vastly greater field than the one he has hitherto known, and this new and more complex world demands investigation and further development. Having achieved speech, his horizons are again expanded, with similar consequences. And so on through his life. On the success with which he meets the successive demands created by his own progress depends his mental health, and on his mental health depends the success with which he meets the new demands—I will not attempt to disentangle the interplay. At the risk of being accused of Aristotelian dichotomy, I propose to treat as separate entities a kind of simian capacity for acquiring technical skills on the one hand, and a capacity for full emotional and intellectual development on the other. One of the peculiarities of technical skills of the mechanical type is that these skills are easily communicated; this we must contrast with emotional development, which is not. As a result a man who is peculiarly gifted in scientific invention can almost immediately put fresh power into the hands of thousands of his fellow-men; mimesis in that sphere is both easy and satisfactory. In the field of emotional and intellectual development the situation is very different; mimesis is of no value and, indeed, is a great danger, for it produces a spurious appearance of growth; no method of communication of emotional development has yet been found which is not hopelessly limited in its field of influence. The result is that in the social group the fate of technical advance lies, on the whole, in the hands of the more technically gifted. But the fate of emotional development lies, on the whole, in the hands of the emotionally under-developed but mimetically well-equipped. Hope must therefore depend on the development of a technique of emotional development, and, one would imagine, that is precisely what we in this Society are concerned to provide. But there are still some aspects of the acquirement of technical skills that I want to discuss. They are these: technical developments have a way of repeating early situations; thus modern methods of travel repeat the problems and stimuli presented by first attempts to walk; modern methods of communication repeat, on a more complex level, the problems of infant speech; modern weapons of destruction have produced a repetition of problems of infantile destructiveness; modern facilities for leisure have repeated the early problems of curiosity and play. And I would remind you that in social group situations the problems are created for the individual not by his own technical advances but by the technical advances of people vastly more skilled than himself.

The kind of technical advance that produces these problems is not always obvious. I remember talking to a friend who lived in the Fen country, and I remarked that the advent of the motor-bus must have made an enormous difference to the isolated life of villagers. He replied that it had made very little; the real revolution had occurred on the introduction of the bicycle. Before that a villager scarcely knew of the existence of a village three miles away. With the arrival of the bicycle new realms of social contact were opened up, and this brought with it fresh problems for the villagers. The more gifted made use of their opportunities; the others stayed where they were. This example is interesting simply because it indicates that what is a stimulus to one community is not necessarily a stimulus to another. Clearly, motor transport would be more important than the bicycle in a mountainous district once roads were established. Of course it is not merely technical progress that produces problems for emotional development; we have also to bear in mind those organizations of society which in themselves produce problems for the majority of those living in that organization. It is possible for society to be organized in such a way that the majority of its members are psychiatrically disinherited.

I should not like to be called upon to define what I mean by psychiatric disinheritance; nevertheless, I hope my meaning will be clear enough for all practical purposes. It seems to me that, within wide limits, for his full development man requires scope for the development of his political appetite. To-day I suppose we should describe this as scope for personal relationships, but I mean personal relationships over a wide range. It has been claimed for the Greek city-state that its members were able in person to exercise their capacities for human companionship in many different functions. This view, which I associate largely with Lowes Dickenson, and more recently with Gilbert Murray, obviously may contain more of wishful thinking than historicity, but nevertheless it seems to me to contain the germ of an idea that should be retained as a criterion in our consideration of the psychologically hygienic community. The point that is made is that in the small community it is possible for men to exercise their special talents without being condemned to the frustration and atrophy of their other desires. A citizen of Athens was not represented in parliament—he was a member. He took part, if he wished to do so, in legal decisions. He was called upon to defend his country, and he had to produce food. Obviously it is no easy matter to decide at what point a desire for specialization from within the individual becomes transformed into an externally imposed denial of all but one or two special skills. This should not, however, prevent us from keeping a critical eye on the kind of spiritual drift which leads communities into the elaboration of forms of association that are as destructive of the psychological health of the individual as a community without a public health service would be of its physical health.

The few remarks that I make now are by way of defining the scope of the field of inquiry which seems to me to be necessary. The suspicion that an inquiry was needed was brought to my mind most powerfully in the war when it appeared to me that the majority of patients that one saw belonged to the psychologically disinherited class. Obviously they may have disinherited themselves, but it did not appear to me to be so, and in any event this is one of the problems that require investigation. Even if we admit that the individual is a more than willing participator in depriving himself of the full range of personal relationships, we still have to bear in mind the educational system of home and school which has allowed him to progress along a path of progressive limitation without any awareness that he was, in fact, doing so. No doubt, once frustration occurs, renunciation of the frustrated impulses produces some degree of comfort, and the renunciation is made easier by the piling up of external difficulties against the satisfaction of those impulses. As psychiatrists, we are well aware that such a renunciation is in fact never wholly efficient. Stimuli are removed but return as provocations on another level. We are bombarded with stimuli to which no direct reaction is possible. The newspapers inform us of political problems and decisions that move us emotionally, but to which we can make no direct response. The machinery of the press does little more for us than to insure that we start and end the day with our daily dose of a sense of frustration and impotence. We contemplate an aeroplane crash in Newfoundland but can do nothing for the victims. We follow the fortunes of our favourite football team but cannot even help by giving up smoking. The vast apparatus of films and cheap fiction feeds phantasies of a world in which moral problems present no intellectual difficulties, and personal relationships assume an irreducible minimum of complexity. Such a state of affairs is worse than escapism because, by being a substitute for reality, it denies the pleasures and pains of reality.

The value of a group decision in an industrial concern may derive from a restoration to the individuals of the group of a part of their inheritance. As a prelude to scientific investigation it is worth speculating on the possibility that, first, the Trade Union movements, and now unofficial strikes represent a reaction against psychological disinheritance far more than profound dissatisfaction with wages or lack of material comforts.

Part of the inheritance of all living things is pain and adversity. It is at least as easy to be cruel by a denial of this as a component of a man's life, as it is to be cruel by the denial of mutual help.

Donne said that 'affliction is a treasure and scarce any man hath enough of it. No man hath affliction enough that is not matured and ripened by it.' No one to-day is likely to complain that there is any shortage in this commodity, but is it possible that our elaborate machinery, social as well as individual, for the denial of the existence of everyday troubles and difficulties has led to a revolt that has taken the form of an artificial production of calamity on a vast scale? Some such feeling may beat the bottom out of the quite commonly expressed idea that war and its attendant hardships are good for the race.

It is, of course, extremely improbable that any single component of this kind will provide more than a starting-point for investigation, but I propose to discuss group relationships from a fresh angle.

The growth and decline of civilizations has always excited the curiosity of mankind and has recently been studied in great detail by Arnold Toynbee. In all investigations there is a preoccupation with the part played by adversity in compelling the emergence of culture and a reciprocal interest in the part played by ease in producing inertia or, alternatively, in the case of a civilization that has already developed, decline and disintegration. Race and environment have both been cited as fundamental causes, but neither has been accepted as really explaining more than a modicum of the facts. It seems obvious that a gifted race might naturally be expected to produce those characteristic features of society that make us classify that society as civilized, and history certainly seems to support the view that difficult conditions, though they might prove too difficult and so lead to extinction of a community, have, in fact, time and again been associated with growth of a high level of civilization. Means, quoted by Toynbee (see *Ancient Civilizations of the Andes,* pp. 25–26) states, 'Environment . . . is not the total causation in culture-shaping . . . [it] is beyond doubt, the most conspicuous single factor. . . . But there is still an indefinable factor that may best be designated quite frankly as *x,* the unknown quantity, apparently psychological in kind. . . . If *x* be not the most conspicuous matter in the factor, it certainly is the most important, the most fate-laden.' Toynbee himself elaborates in detail theories based on the relationship of the groups within and without a given society. In particular, he stresses the part played by the interplay between a dominant creative group and the internal proletarian mimetic group on the one hand, and a similar out-group on the other. He appears to attribute change to the effect on society of a loss of creativeness in the dominant group, which becomes at the same time oppressive and disinclined to lead. Here I will observe that in groups if the psychiatrist becomes disinclined to lead, he certainly becomes oppressive. I merely quote them as indications of an awareness that psychological factors are playing some unknown part in the growth and development of groups. I may be pardoned for mentioning that in 1943 I drew attention to the need for the community to gain insight into the psychological origin of at least some part, and in my opinion a major part, of its distresses. I propose now to make some tentative suggestions that I hope will be recognized as claiming to be no more than hypotheses worthy of investigation.

First, I will say that I have no difficulty in accepting the importance of environment or of racial characteristics as playing very important roles in the growth or development of civilization, just as I have no difficulty in recognizing the importance of an individual's inherited characteristics when he comes for treatment, or the importance of the circumstances of his life. But I need no persuasion to agree with Toynbee that explanations based on race or environment or senescence are quite unsatisfactory. I will explain in a moment why I consider environment, particularly as it gives rise to adversity on the one hand or ease on the other, to be important. Before doing this, however, I will say at once that I suspect the unknown psychological factor that Means speaks of to be the capacity that is shown by individuals in a community for a personal relationship and the quality of that relationship.

To return now to the part played by environment: it will be remembered that observers such as Bagehot and many others have been struck by the fact that environment is such a conspicuous factor. We need not be detained by instances where the environment has been too difficult for the society. If we consider the difficult but productive environment, the main feature of such an environment is that it compels co-operation through the driving force of the impulse to survive. Those members of the community in whom the impulse was not sufficiently strong to compel co-operation would not survive. The society as a whole, however, gradually masters its objective difficulties, the individual members co-operating with the sort of ease and the sort of difficulty that we have all of us witnessed in air raids and similar types of dangerous situations. The history of civilizations that have arisen in this way seems, if the historians are reasonably correct, to have followed much the same pattern in that they achieve a life of ease and then disintegrate. The society that has been in easy circumstances from the first appears to develop no culture but to remain in a state of sottishness, often made hideous by anxiety. H. Drummond (in *Tropical Africa*) says that the African 'does not need to work; with so bountiful a nature round him it would be gratuitous to work'. They live, he says, 'without clothes, without civilization, without learning, without religion'. Though he describes them as thoughtless, careless and contented, he states that the village communities live in terror of one another and of their common foe, the slave trader.

The point that strikes me as most important for the community that finds itself in a bountiful environment, whether that environment existed in the first place or was produced by the efforts of the society itself, is that in both instances a very important element has come into the life of the society: that element is leisure.

I am fully aware that in using the word, 'leisure', I shall give rise to a very mistaken impression if you think that by it I simply mean a rather pleasant absence of work. On the contrary; I mean to convey by this word a dynamic state of personal relationships which, properly induced and properly used, is one of the most potent forces in psychiatric investigation. To explain this statement I shall illustrate my point by telling you of the one leaderless group technique that I never succeeded in establishing. The machinery of it was quite simple: I suggested that in every series of War Office Selection Board leaderless group tests there should come a point at which the testing officer would have collected his group of candidates about him and then, as it were, subjected them to a quarter of an hour or twenty minutes' delay, as if waiting while some administrative hitch or other was straightened out. During this time he would casually watch what the men did. A similar technique, if such it can be called, is employed by myself in my therapeutic groups. The whole point is that the group has nothing in particular to do. It will of course be obvious that there is a similar quality about an analytic session. What happens is that the personal relationships between members of the group immediately obtrude themselves on the attention of each member of the group and on the conscious attention of the observer, if he will permit it.

I suggest that the unknown psychological factor in the growth and decay of civilizations need not really be unknown. It is of course always present, even in the society facing adversity, but its obtrusion into consciousness can be more easily resisted when there are real tasks, vital to the survival of the community, to be done. Its obtrusion can still be resisted when a state of leisure develops, but distractions have a way of drawing attention to the thing from which distraction is sought. In the absence of any leadership towards resolution of the problems of personal relationships, disintegration of the group takes place. It may be argued against this that civilizations in the past have succumbed to conquest by foreign invaders. This, I suggest, is only one manifestation of the same thing. I will repeat as my justification for this statement a phrase I have used to describe the rationale of the leaderless group techniques when explaining the relevance of personal relationships to tasks that an officer is called upon to fulfil in war: 'If a man cannot be friends with his friends, he cannot be an enemy to his enemy.' A group composed of such persons will succumb to an internal hostile group.

I shall now attempt to demonstrate four themes that appear to me to emerge from my speculations.

The first theme is the concern of widely separated disciplines with the problems of individual and group relationships. The priest, the philosopher, the political scientist, the law-giver and the statesman have all been concerned with this problem, but all have failed to produce anything but pontifical, and often ephemeral, solutions. This failure has been due to the fact that since the existence and operation of unconscious emotional impulses in the community had not been recognized, leaders in these activities were flung back onto superficial and therefore sterile reconsiderations of the *machinery* of personal relationships. The suggestion is made that knowledge of the nature and operation of the unknown factor has, during the last fifty years, begun to be provided in varying degrees by the followers of Freud, Jung and Adler.

The second theme is concerned with the interplay of advance in technical skills and the development of emotional growth. The production of techniques for dealing with emotional growth appears to be leading to a resolution of this dichotomy.

The third theme, concerned with the growth and decay of civilization, seems to lead to the conclusion that the growth of civilization is a product of the response of the community to a challenge presented to the community. The advances in psychiatry that I have mentioned indicate that the challenge that confronts civilization to-day is not environment but the operation of unconscious emotional impulses. The growth of civilization depends upon a successful response to this challenge.

The fourth theme indicates that technical advance helps to produce leisure and that leisure is the state that is most conducive to the obtrusion of unconscious emotional impulses in human relationships. The work of the atomic scientists presents mankind with a dilemma: on the one hand lies the destruction of mankind; on the other the production, by virtue of increased power and the need for restricting bellicosity, of leisure. The history of technical advance therefore also indicates that the problems of personal relationships will shortly obtrude themselves as demanding a solution.

These four widely separated themes therefore converge, not only on the same problem, but at the same time, and that time is the present.

In the early part of this address I referred in passing to the disappearance of the British Empire. The spectacle of a great power divesting itself of material possessions has, in the light of our past history, something of the characteristics of an introspective withdrawal. I will not put forward my reasons now for thinking that this may be an event of great significance in the development of civilization. It does, however, resemble in some important particulars the picture presented by Toynbee of the Hellenic society when it was, according to Thucydides, 'repressed from all sides over a long period of time' (p. 190). Toynbee points out that during this time the expansion of the Hellenic society was transmuted, thanks to Athens, 'from an extensive into an intensive process', and that this was 'the age which in the sight of posterity stands out as the acme of Hellenic civilization'. If there is anything in this comparison, then my four themes seem to converge not only on this subject and in this epoch, but also in this place.

It would be pleasant to think that psychiatrists were now destined to lead in the development of civilization still further. If I have given the impression that this is my view, my address has failed in its purpose. It is one thing for a community to be placed in a position where it has a challenge to meet, but quite another, as our survey has shown, for it to accept the challenge and overcome it.

In the first place, the nature of the challenge and the challenge itself must be perceived. Just how difficult that is can be illustrated by the obvious point that we cannot be sure that we all mean the same by the words, 'unconscious emotional impulses'. I am only too conscious that I am speaking of certain phenomena that are demonstrated in the course of the psychoanalytic relationship, but I have no reason to suppose that these phenomena are the phenomena described in the same words by other investigators using different methods.

Then, from what has been seen of the communication of intuitions of earlier leaders in the field of personal relationships, it is obvious that an enormous amount depends on the selection and training of the followers. They must be, and yet seldom are, capable of leadership and capable of something more than imitation of the original thinker.

Further, a means must be found whereby the peculiar kind of facts in which we deal can be properly investigated and recorded—you will remember my remarks on the lack of material on which to base any judgement about the relationships between technical and emotional progress in our own lifetimes.

Finally, the group that aspires to lead has to steer between the Scylla of arousing so much anxiety that it is suppressed, and the Charybdis of inspiring a widespread but mimetic discipline whose mechanicalness, as Toynbee calls it, infects the quality of the leaders and forces them by loss of creativity to degenerate into a dominant oppressive minority. Whether our country, of all countries, and our group, of all other groups in the country, are capable of meeting the challenge of our time will only be determined by what we ourselves do. Psychiatrists may leave the challenge to be taken up by other groups in the nation, or the nation may leave it to other nations. Or mankind may simply postpone once more, through lack of creative leaders or through imcompetence, the solution of the problem to future generations. If that is so, the outlook is black indeed. And that, Ladies and Gentlemen, is what I mean by Psychiatry at a Time of Crisis.

1971

The supreme importance of transference lies in its use in the practice of psycho-analysis. It is available for observation by analysands and analysts. In this respect it is unique—that is its strength and its weakness; its strength, because the two people have a 'fact' available to both and therefore open for discussion by both; its weakness, because it is ineffable and cannot be discussed by anyone else. The failure to recognize this simple fact has led to confusion.

* * *

The ideogram evokes free association; the alphabet does not. What of the Miltonic spelling? Its emphatic intonation? And ideogrammatic impulsiveness in geometry? Is it related to the visual image as algebra is not? But arabic numerals are not more related to the ideogram than algebraic. The first few Roman numerals are nearer to ideogrammatic, visual tallies than are arabic numerals.

* * *

'Unconscioused' = *unbewusst*. Oh, for a similar word for 'projective identification'; 'identijected', as contrasted with 'unconscioused'.

* * *

The matter of ownership crops up with territory; it certainly causes trouble in the realm of ideas. Why? Does anyone claim ownership of a lie? Of course not, because as the question is formulated the lie is worthless—it represents worthless property. [*Added as a footnote*: 'But what about Judith and Holofernes? That lie, deception, was valuable.'] [*see* The Book of Judith from *The Apocrypha.*] Worth is that which enhances the value of the person to his community; it must be distinguished from apparent or reputed worth. In the domain of thought, values are contingent. An attempt is made to differentiate contingent values from absolute values by assuming that absolute values are those that are deemed to be so 'in the eyes of God'. What does that mean?

[November/December 1973]

[Transcribed from a tape recording.]

The murderous stranglehold—transformation into many varieties including the schizophrenic patient who covers himself completely with blankets and just peers at the analyst through one small hole with one eye only. One feels that there is a method by which the port of entry is felt to be so tiny that whatever can come into it gets tremendously compressed to a point where virtually it has had all the life squeezed out of it. It sounds like a vagina that might be a kind of penis, but a penis that has a very small opening and a very small point of egress, with these compressing and concentrating effects which finally compress and squeeze the life out of the thing itself.

There might equally be expansion in the opposite direction. But the real thing is this entry and egress, with this very narrow sort of port-like entering into a penis, or a vagina that is far too small to be able to take anything in and far too small to be able to let anything out. I am sure this theme needs to be followed up in its many applications.

I might write a book that could be drawn up in terms of the Grid, either by a special index arranged in the Grid order of the primitive nature of the thing—not to do with thought at all, the elements—through to the things that are various transformations of visual imagery, and so on. I must consider this more deeply according to the two axes, co-ordinates—the vertical and horizontal components.

* * *

It seems to me that it isn't simply a question of the concentration that is produced by the very strangling vagina or mouth, and the very explosive penis or breast or object that is put in. In other words, the conflict is between the container and the contained thing in which they both seem to be on very destructive terms, where either the container gets split apart, or the object that is put into the container gets destroyed. This seems to be a theme that occurs over and over again; whether it is a question of my coming to the United States, or my coming to the Society, or my being excluded from the Society, there seems to be this question of the relationship of the Kleinian person, or the Kleinian theory, or the Kleinian analyst, with the existing Society or the container into which the thought or idea is put. Then there is this destructive relationship into which one or the other—the container or the contained object—is sure to be destroyed; there appears to be no way in which the relationship between the two is creative or constructive, or leads to any good outcome.

Even in this note itself one could say that the thing is repeated in the same form: I am trying to put into terms of a verbal communication some idea that is felt to be too vast. Either the speech, formulation, grammar is destroyed, or the vocabulary and grammar get the upper hand—in which case the idea is destroyed.

There must be something primitive and fundamental about this, something very difficult to describe without the destructive consequences that follow from the nature of the relationship between these two objects. Even if the container and the contained object are destroyed, these fragments are felt likely to come together in a very destructive and hostile manner. This would seem both to link up the idea of the part objects, the extreme fragmentation, and to be a continuation of a theme of the relationship between the two. If the theme is expanded in the way it is in analysis (as done by me) into a prolonged sort of interpretation, then it is felt to be something that destroys the patient's capacity to take in the idea. On the other hand, if one tries to concentrate it down, one gets to the state of simply describing the two pictorially, hieroglyphically, in a C-category way, which is then so concentrated that it becomes virtually incomprehensible. It is like a mathematical formula that is absurdly simple, but at the same time is so concentrated that it requires the whole of mathematics to understand it—like the theories in which Einstein enshrines his theory of relativity. Indeed, I think that the significance of it may lie in the fact that it is the theory of *relativity*; it is the *relationships* that are felt to be so difficult to concentrate, or even to expand.

* * *

I am inclined to think that I would have to use the Grid itself at some point in this book [*The Dream,* Book I of *A Memoir of the Future*] as a method of formulating or re-forming or showing the relationships of one aspect of it to another, with a kind of arrangement by which all these relationships were shown in a form that was different from that of the narrative of the book itself. It would display the way in which the logical or rational connections of one part with another could be formulated—although, of course, rational formulation is not necessarily an adequate formulation for something that is not really rational at all.

* * *

I can see that this is compatible with a culture in which it is assumed as a matter of course that you do not believe what you are told by anybody. It is difficult to see how they ever manage to get anything done in which you would have to know the truth. It does seem to me to be almost a cultural matter; you simply assume that the person who is speaking is speaking an untruth, or at any rate is being dishonest in the sense of making a communication that is primarily for its own purposes, not for the communication of a true statement to some other person. It throws an entirely new light on the problems of psycho-analysis and the fact that nobody is likely to believe that one is trying to tell them something that it is worth their while to hear.

[August 1975]

[Transcribed from a tape recording]

Suppose I want to have a method of measuring or of mathematical manipulation that would be appropriate to the world of emotion to which I am accustomed: I hear a baby crying; I am filled with sorrow for the poor little thing, and possibly for the parent who is concerned to look after it. Supposing, then, that I hear two babies crying—then I might be even more upset. Supposing, however, that I hear, say, fifty of them crying and wailing in the same way; instead of being fifty times as compassionate, I find that I am becoming amused at the racket that is going on. Why is it that such a thing should take place? And how should I express this mathematically? I could say that I ought to be—as far as any mathematical system known to me is concerned—fifty times as upset or depressed. But in this instance the quantity has effected an emotional change, so the emotions that I am wanting to deal with, to measure, to speak about, to cope with, have altered in quality when I would expect them to alter in quantity.

Is there some form of mathematics that would give me the appropriate answer or solution of a problem to which I want to apply it in emotional terms? I am not simply talking about the number of babies, or the number of people, but a situation in which I require a kind of mathematics that not only shows or expresses a change in quantity, but also a change in quantity inseparable from a change in quality.

In the instance I am giving I could pose the problem like this: there is myself, one of me; and there is one baby. Is it $1 \times 1 =$ depression? Or $1 \times 2 =$ depression $\times\ 2$? Or is it 1 baby + depressed person = 2 depressed people? Or is it $1 + 2 = 3$ depressed people? What happens when it ought to be $1 + 50$, or

1×50? What should the appropriate manipulation be? What should one do with the mathematical symbols in the nature of bringing them together, or perhaps, for that matter, of bringing them apart? 1 separated from 1? Or 1 separated from 50? In other words, could there be a form of intuitionist mathematics that would come much nearer to giving me answers representing the state of affairs with which I might be dealing? Would the mathematical answer seem to bear a resemblance to the emotional experience with which I am familiar?

[August 1975]

You said an earful.

How could you say with your ear? I thought it was with your mouth.

No—'You said a mouthful' means saying something important. It is a common term not intended to be formal or precise.

Ah—so you would not use it if you wanted to hit the eye-bull?

I wouldn't hit a bull of any kind.

No, no! The eye-bull.

Oh, you mean the eye-ball. I should not . . . You mean the 'Power of the human eye'.

No, no! You haven't hit the eye-bull.

No, I haven't, because I don't want to be rammed up the arse by an irate bull.

Ah, yes—Arse and Craft. In my country everyone say how beautiful the craft and arse of England are.

Ah!

Ah? Ah? What means that? Please?

[August 1975]

Psycho-analysis tells you nothing; it is an instrument, like the blind man's stick, that extends the power to gather information. The analyst uses it to gather a *selected* kind of information: the analysand uses it to gather material that he can use (1) for purposes of imitation, (2) to learn the analyst's philosophy, (3) to learn how to conduct his life in a socially acceptable manner, and (4) to become acquainted with his Self.

Although it is true that it is not his intention to satisfy (1), (2) and (3), or any desire other than (4), it is impossible to make any statement that gratifies only (4) because of the lack of precision of spontaneous English speech. The analyst can try not to pollute his interpretation on the one hand, or to speak as if he were a living computer, stranger to human heartedness, or the life that the rest of our human companions are familiar with as members of our universe.

Certain words and phrases appear to be necessary for the communication of 'happenings' recurring in that part of human experience with which I am most familiar, and which happens also to be that part of my life that is my profession—what, for lack of power to describe adequately, I call 'mental suffering'. This touches on happenings about which the analyst can do nothing, and the thoughts and feelings that the patient has about them. The distinction is important, but it is one that cannot easily be delimited and isolated for examination without the inclusion of thoughts that are properly subject to discussion in their own right.

We have to use words and phrases, combinations of words, for the purpose of communication between the Origin and the Receptor (observer, psycho-analyst). We may assume that what the psycho-analyst says about the analysand is likely to be true of the psycho-analyst himself. But for purposes of psycho-analysis it is simpler to write this as an exposition from the point of view (vertex) of the observer.

August 1975

There is a scarcity of time; a scarcity of knowledge; scarcity of ability. Therefore choice becomes of fundamental importance—choice of time, theories, and facts observed.

* * *

Memoirs of the future

Wisdom borrowed—future wisdom after the event. Prophecy wise after the event.

Prophecy without foresight. Prophetic hindsight.

Prophetic backsight. Regrets to come by Forthright Forethought.
Insight by Backsight.

* * *

Freud, in 'Inhibitions, Symptoms and Anxiety' ([1926d/1925], *SE 20,* p. 138), is curiously one-sided. Surely emotional experience is common to fetus, mother and father, but emotions *and* ideas may be compatible or incompatible. [*see* opposite page for Bion's annotations in the 1949 edition, The International Psycho-Analytical Library, No. 28, p. 108.]

end to the dangerous situation which is reminiscent of birth, the nature of the danger it fears is displaced from the economic situation on to the condition which determined that situation, viz. the loss of object. It is the absence of the mother that is now the danger; and as soon as that danger arises the small child gives the signal of anxiety, before the dreaded economic situation has set in. This change constitutes a first important step forward in the provision made by the child for its self-preservation, and at the same time represents a transition from the automatic and involuntary new-creation of anxiety to the intentional reproduction of anxiety as a signal of danger.

yet I have known M's fear "absence" of infant; why not both?

In these two aspects, as an automatic phenomenon and as a rescue-signal, anxiety is seen to be a product of the infant's mental helplessness which is a natural counterpart of its biological helplessness. The striking co-incidence by which the anxiety of the new-born baby and the anxiety of the infant in arms both depend upon a separation from the mother does not need to be explained on psychological lines. It can be accounted for simply enough from a biological point of view; for, just as

Whom does it strike? Mother or infant?

does anything? →

cf Buber I and Thou.

But a psychological ground is biological

[August 1976]

"What can I do for you?"

"That", he said, "is what I came to find out".

"Yes, but how do you think I can help?"

"But, doctor, how should I know? That is what I came to you to find out."

"Yes, but what is troubling you? Presumably you wanted to see me for something of which you are complaining."

"No, not at all. I have nothing to complain of. We are very lucky."

"You must have wanted to come for some reason . . ."

"Oh, I see—my wife sent me."

"Ah, I see."

(But do I? So far the only thing that is clear is that I am no wiser than I was when a brief note from his doctor asked me to see this patient—the husband of a woman whom he had originally treated for pneumonia. "More your line than mine", he said.)

"Your doctor must have thought you needed my help. Why was that?"

"How should I know? Didn't he tell you in his note?"

"I think he expected you to tell me yourself. So far, you know, you have told me nothing."

(A blunder—I knew it before I had completed my sentence. I sat back and waited. He returned my gaze with untroubled expression and waited to hear more. In the meantime I thought we could not simply continue to sit in silence, but I could think of no alternative. As time passed I felt a change was taking place and that the meeting was deteriorating into a contest of wills. What is a 'will'? Does Freud say? Or Melanie Klein? Abraham? Ferenczi perhaps?)

"Would you rather I went away, doctor?"

"By all means, if you do not wish to stay, or . . ."

(I left the sentence unfinished.)

"Or what, doctor?"

(I was aware of growing anger. I knew that the overt expression of feelings of any kind stimulates—'irritates', in the sense that the physiologist would use the term in describing an experiment with a nerve-muscle preparation—a personality, whether one's own or that of another self. Since strong emotions undermine the capacity to think clearly, it would seem logical to suppose that a doctor, a psychiatrist, a psychoanalyst, should achieve and retain a capacity for clear thinking, and help the analysand to achieve and maintain a similar atmosphere of calm deliberation.)

How? My ability to do so is tested every moment of my life, not only in the course of professional duty but in the day-to-day frustrations and happenings. I am still as far away from achieving success in this endeavour as I ever was. I do not think I and my analysands are exceptional in this. What *is* exceptional is that the attempt is now being made to develop such a capacity through psycho-analysis.

[August 1978]

When the patient said he dreamed he was being swept down the river to the weir—"I tell you, I never woke up so fast in my life."—what, according to me, was he talking about? In so far as I know, I was in the state of mind in which I am wide awake. Is that 'wide' enough? Or is it a state of mind that is too narrow—like 'to-fro tender trambeams' truckling 'at the eye'? [Gerard Manley Hopkins, 'The Candle Indoors'.] Or too 'wide' awake, too conscious, too rational?

'By that window' [*idem*] what sights did the patient see that made him 'wake up' so fast that he could not be swept down the stream? Was it the danger of becoming, like me, too wide awake? Or, like me, too fast asleep—in fact, the sleep of death? Or in the state of mind or 'sleep' of psycho-analysis?

'There plant eyes, all mist from thence purge and disperse, that I might see and tell of things invisible to mortal sight'. [Milton, *Paradise Lost,* Book III.] But the price appears to be the loss of 'mortal' sight. It cannot, however, be bought by 'losing' mortal sight; to be blind, unconscious, unaware of the world visible and audible, when you are in the 'yin' state of mind, is not the solution. One must dare to be aware—consciously—of the universe that is apparent in the state of mind in which one is asleep *and* the state of mind appropriate to 'awake', Yin and Yang [Chinese concept of the negative, material, and the positive, metaphysical together constituting the Cosmos]. Therefore merely being able to concourse musically, balletically, athletically, is not enough; it must be an intercourse—a means of communication 'inter', between two states of mind. Socrates described himself as a mental midwife; perhaps the psycho-analyst is a midwife between two states of mind of the analysand; for example, Maths + Art of Fugue, Cezanne + La Montagne

Sainte-Victoire. The psycho-analytic experience consists in being able to know what it *means* when the physical quality says the age is twenty-five; what the man *means* when he says verbally that he is forty-two; and what it *means* when closer view shows lines in the skin of the face that would signify age sixty-two. Where is that conflict? Between me and myself? Or between him and his knowledge of vital statistics? Between him and his vertex of vital statistics? Or between his youth and his age? Is it his youthfulness, vigour and energy (Schopenhauer) trying to break through? Up? Out? Down? The same question with his wrinkles.

In practice (contrasted with theory, or even memory or desire) is it possible to improve one's observation, or to make a change by refining one's vocabulary—one's 'outils' for the 'atelier'? For example, if you talk English, it is imperative to know *what* English you talk and *how* you talk it. If you are a potter, you may be the kind that requires a potter's wheel. What kind? It must be the *best* kind; it will not make you into a potter, but if you are a potter it will help you to make good pottery. If you are a good cook you need a kitchen and an oven. But lying in a bath and thinking of making buns will not produce bath buns. An analyst who has an office and a technique that enables him to produce good imitations of a psycho-analytic interpretation produces artificial interpretations, *representations* of a human being, not a human being.

I was never able to be a soldier—only an artificial representation of a brave man. I could see the spire of Sequehart church 'pointing to the sky' like non-conformist banners pointing up the broad Congregational Way to Heaven—plastic and plausible, and a diversion from The Way (Tao). One cannot in a crisis fall back on Truth. Artificial representations of truth form an insecure foundation for initiation; absolute initiation—advance or retreat—has a minimum necessary condition: sincerity.

8 August 1978

[Transcription of a tape recording.]

'The faces of old ghosts look in upon the battle', Tennyson said about that last strange battle in which Arthur took part before he travelled on his journey to the Vale of Avilon. ['The Passing of Arthur', Tennyson, *Idylls of the King*.]

Once more the world has reached the same kind of place in its journey round the sun which it occupied in the battle of Amiens (8 August 1918), which was said by Ludendorff to mark a black day for the German army. The ghosts look in from the battle again; Asser, Cartwright, and Sergeant O'Toole, the poor fellow who complained that he was only an orphan, with his protuberant ears, his red flushed face, his feelings of depression and anxiety, and his confiding to me that this battle on which he was about to embark together with the rest of the tank crew (I was not one of the crew as I was now commanding the tank section and was the second-in-command of the company) would be his last. He was, of course, quite correct; very soon after the battle started, Cartwright's tank received a direct hit, and the entire crew were killed. When I came across it, the bodies were charred and blackened, and poured out of the door of the tank as if they were the entrails of some mysterious beast of a primitive kind which had simply perished then and there in the conflagration, which must have been set off by the direct hit.

This experience is similar to others I have had in the past, but the similarity refers only to the known facts, not to the unknown. In this respect there are new experiences—unlike any Eighth of August of the past—not least when Francesca and I visited the Shelley and Keats museum in Rome. We both found it an extremely profound and moving occasion, as if we were indeed participating in an experience in which Shelley was still alive. I remember noticing, and being tremendously impressed by, his description of Keats as a greater man than he, a dangerous rival who would be sure to excel him. But he said so without any of the hatred and envy that would have made it impossible for him to express the convictions to which he wished to draw the attention of his contemporaries and those who followed after him. So much generosity triumphed over hatred and rivalry and envy. These poets and artists have their methods of recording their awareness of some sort of influence, stimuli that come from without, the unknown that is so terrifying and stimulates such powerful feelings that they cannot be described in ordinary terms. They have to be considered to be perceivable only in so far as the human being has thalamic organs and thalamic experiences, and as if the human mind itself, described in physical terms, were a central nervous system that has only developed as far as the thalamus, thus leaving no real synaptic communication between the thalamus and the subsequent development of the mind, the neopallium, or whatever the appropriate term for it should be. We need to invent some form of articulate speech that could approximate to describing these realities, the phenomena that I cannot possibly describe.

Francesca showed me the letter, which I would not have noticed otherwise, written to Byron by Allegra, his daughter, from the nursery foundation run by a Catholic school—a most pathetic, touching and moving letter which apparently Byron never replied to. One could say that Byron, although appreciating the genius of Keats, could not possibly express the feelings of admiration and affection in the way that they were expressed by Shelley. Byron's *Don Juan* was no *Lament for Adonais* ['Elegy on the Death of John Keats'], which could only be written by Shelley. Similarly, one could say that *Don Juan* could only be written by Byron.

[Shelley began his preface to *Adonais* with the 'Epitaph for Bion' (c. 100 BC) by Moschus:

> A poison came, Bion, to thy lips, thou sawest the poison.
> How did it run on to thy lips and not be sweetened? And
> what mortal was so savage either to mix the poison for thee
> or to give it thee as thou didst speak? He was immune to song.

'*Nisi dominus frustra*'. [Psalm 127, i: 'Except the Lord build the house, they labour in vain that build it'.] It is a simple abbreviation, and yet it is extraordinarily significant of the way in which certain words are left out. In much the same way letters are left out of the word, 'Yaveh', because nothing else could possibly do any sort of justice to the fact that 'Yaveh' was a way of talking about a force, a power that cannot be described in articulate speech such as is appropriate when talking about omnipotence, or omniscience, or the ordinary formulations of religion—none of them adequate ways of describing the matters to which attention is to be drawn by the communication.

* * *

The people of this district [the Dordogne, France] speak of a '*crise de foie*'. It seems to me that this would be quite appropriate if it were spelt '*crise de foi*', or, '*crise deux fois*'. There is no need to suppose that the language being spoken, the appropriate language, is an articulate one rather than, say, a language that is a transition from paranoid–schizoid to depressive, from part objects to whole objects. Milton could have been talking more than one language: the articulate language, or even the poetic language, of a rational and superficial kind, as opposed to one that might be said to be much more primitive and much more like that of part objects; or objects that are not thought at all, namely the language of action before there is any discovery of an attitude that can be taken, or a technique that can be employed, between the awareness of an impulse and its translation into language. Freud described it as a state in which thought itself could be introduced as a phase leading to a pause between the impulse and the putting of that impulse into action.

One of the weaknesses of articulate speech is shown in the use of a term like 'omnipotence' to describe a situation that in fact cannot be described at all accurately with a language that is of one kind only. 'Omnipotence' must always also mean 'helplessness'; there can be no single word that describes one thing without also describing its reciprocal.

Palinurus was put to sleep by the god disguised as Somnus, and hurled into the depths of the ocean. Jesus showed that he felt betrayed when he found that God did not protect him from the murderous death that he suffered on the Cross. "Why hast thou forsaken me?" (Another possibility might be that he had a mistakenly optimistic view of the god with whom he thought he was dealing.) It is not possible to talk about 'god' unless one assumes that it also means 'devil'. The error has a very long history: in the Baghavad Gita, Arjuna is rebuked for assuming that he is able to measure the morals or the omnipotence or the mental outlook of the god by human standards; Job is reproved for having considered that he can measure Leviathan by the methods that are available for measuring ordinary human beings. Many mystics have been able to describe a situation in which it is believed that there really is a power, a force that cannot be measured or weighted or assessed by the mere human being with the mere human mind. This seems to me to be a profound assumption which has hitherto been almost completely ignored, and yet people talk about 'omnipotence' as if they knew what it meant and as if it had a simple connotation. Martin Buber came much closer to recognizing the realities of the situation when human speech is resorted to. [*I and Thou*: 'The attitude of man is twofold in accordance with the two basic words he can speak. The basic words are not single words but word pairs. One basic word is the word pair I–You. . . . This is different from the basic word I–It.'] When one talks about 'I–You', the significant thing is not the two objects related, but the *relationship*—that is, an open-ended reality in which there is no termination (in the sense that this is understood by ordinary human beings). The language of ordinary human beings is only appropriate to the rational, can only describe the rational, can only make statements in terms of rationality.

* * *

Sexual maturity is achieved very early and is frequently used as a barrier, a defence against the terrifying unknown which cannot be described in physical, sensuous terms—or if it is, it is much more likely to mislead than to illuminate. The 'thing itself' is a different problem altogether. A term like 'love' cannot describe something even as well as the term, 'the love of God'—that at least makes an attempt to introduce an element that shows that it is not a discussion about something that is so simple as physical love known to the human animal. A lioness nuzzles and shows every sign of feelings of love and affection—if interpreted in human terms—for prey it has destroyed; but it is murderous love, the love that destroys the loved object. Such visual images may be used to talk about love, even what we imagine to be mature love, but there is some other love that is mature from an absolute standard. This other love, vaguely adumbrated, vaguely foreshadowed in human speech, is of an entirely different character; it is not simply a quantitative difference in the kind of love one animal has for another or which the baby has for the breast. It is the further extension to 'absolute love', which cannot be described in the terms of sensuous reality or experience. For that there has to be a language of infra-sensuous and ultra-sensuous, something that lies outside the spectrum of sensuous experience and articulate language. It may be approximated to by methods of communication that are not purely sensuous; the artist who paints a little street in Delft can see and communicate a reality to the observer who then sees something that is quite different from any brick wall or little house that he has ever known or seen in his life. Even in science, Heisenberg's description of the Uncertainty Principle shows that already a crisis has arisen—a '*crise de foi*'.

* * *

This crisis of 'I and You', or 'We and They', can indeed be one of very great proportions, partly because there is no language with which it can be expressed. I could try to put it this way: the fundamental reality is 'infinity', the unknown, the situation for which there is no language—not even that borrowed from the artist or the religious—which gets anywhere near to describing it. Nor can it be assumed that there is a relationship between Smith and Jones, because 'Smith and Jones' is a language that is used to describe a physical reality in which there are *physical* boundaries, but not a *mental* reality; we do not know where the mental boundaries are, nor do we know where the impulses commence.

* * *

I think it may be erroneous to assume that because there is a past that seems to bear a certain resemblance to the present, the present therefore bears a resemblance to the future, which can be described in terms of the past. I can perfectly well see that there may be a crisis of development in which the human being is absolutely terrified by the fact that the future is unknown, cannot be known by himself at the present time, and may only be known to certain people, described in terms of 'genius' or 'mystic', who have a peculiar relationship with reality. It is possible that the human being is indeed doomed to extinction because he is incapable of further development; some quite different species may be required to go on from the point that has been reached so far by the human animal, in the way that the saurians were replaced by the mammalians. However feeble embryonic mammals may have been, they were nevertheless superior to the saurians.

[April 1979]

[Transcription of a tape recording.]

...under the domination of what I call the 'vogue', by which I mean something that is extremely powerful, not merely the passing fashion which happens to change from hour to hour, day to day, month to month. I mean something that persists and that is part and parcel of the permanent equipment of the human being. I think there is the same dominating force that dictates the form taken by thought itself, whether that thought be historical or musical—after all, the Lydian airs of the Greeks would not be particularly appealing to us, any more than the Art of Fugue would be appealing to the Greeks, or would even be understood by them. I think there are also vogues in religion. Freud talks about 'the future of an illusion' as if he thought that religion itself was an illusion; it may be, but I think it is a *basic* illusion [*see* p. 379 for Bion's annotation to his copy of *The Future of an Illusion*]. Any particular religion changes with the prevalent fashion, but the fundamental thing, religion itself, does not. It is a very powerful force, as can be seen by the evidence of what would appear to be a sign or symptom of the thought of a period dug up by the archaeologists who excavated the Death Pit at Ur. Apparently, when the ruling authority died, the court also died with him; they were all buried in the same pit and took the same dose of whatever drug was used before they were buried alive. That itself would seem to suggest that the religious force is a very powerful one, whether it is located in God, or the people, or the priesthood, or the court authorities. That can alter; perhaps a few thousand years hence the archaeologists may excavate signs of the state of mind that existed in Guyana in 1978 [over 900 followers of the Rev. Jim Jones, leader of the People's Temple, died on 18 November 1978 in a mass suicide ritual]. Of course, the recording now is so ephemeral—it is not in tablets of stone but on paper, and the bodies are removed from the original site. So the evidence may be less, or different. We do not know what record could exist in the future history of the world of this latest manifestation of religion—not the Jewish, or the Christian, or the Buddhist, but Religion.

* * *

Philosophical discussion in Edessa became suppressed and then disappeared, but re-emerged in a peculiar way because the Christian religion was carried to Damascus in terms of the Greek language. The Greek method of communication survived, and as a result there also survived with it the Greek way of thought; then, via Syria and Damascus, it came back to Greece. So once more the philosophy of Greece, of Plato, re-emerged when Constantinople fell; the thought that was locked up in Constantinople was then able to reassert itself with formidable consequences, which we call the Renaissance—the renaissance of culture in the western world. It is a very peculiar history—that philosophical thought should be suppressed or destroyed, go, as it were, 'underground', get lost to sight, and then re-emerge in these strange ways via the Arab culture, suppressed by the Turks, locked up in Constantinople, and then again released by the fall of the Byzantine Empire.

It is difficult to see what the trouble was when, according to Plato, Socrates—who had described himself in the Theaetetus as being a midwife (if Plato is to be relied on)—was condemned to death for having corrupted the youth. But so it was. In more recent times there seems to be a kind of dissatisfaction with the familiar philosophical views as being inadequate for the purposes for which they are needed. There were rumours during my time at Oxford about a thing called 'psycho-analysis' and somebody called Freud. I knew nothing about it, nor was much known about it at the university.

I made some enquiries but was persuaded that it wasn't really very much good—there were a lot of foreigners and Jews mixed up with it, so it was better not to get involved.

However, when I was fortunate enough to come across John Rickman, I decided to launch out onto an analysis with him.

That I found to be extremely illuminating; to my surprise, psycho-analysis seemed to have a distinct relationship to what I thought was common sense. Then, alas, came the threat of war, and I found my analytic experience terminated.

After the war, Rickman did not feel that it was possible to continue with me because we had had plenty of experience together during the war. However, I took the plunge and went to see Melanie Klein. I found that what she said, while seeming very often to be rather extraordinary stuff, had a kind of common sense about it—not altogether what I would have regarded as obvious or clear to me, but on the other hand not divorced from what I knew about myself or other people, or even about my war experience.

In due course I found myself officially qualified by the British Psycho-Analytic Society and gradually more and more involved in matters I was unfamiliar with—including those that I was not at all qualified to cope with, such as the President of the British Psycho-Analytic Society. I never felt that I had been trained to fill such a prestigious position.

I had a good deal of opportunity for hearing about my various failings and defects, and also those of psycho-analysis, from my patients. Much the same sort of thing happened when I transferred my activities—for a short space of time, I thought, perhaps five years—to the United States. It took a long time to get used once again to the fact that nobody had ever heard of me, except one or two people who seemed to feel for some reason that they wanted further assistance. At the same time there were attributed to me qualities or abilities that seemed to be very wide of the mark; if I had had the qualifications or the addiction, I could have found myself thrust into the role of a sort of messiah or deity. All this ran parallel with its being made crystal clear to me that I was a mere human being, that psycho-analysis was, after all, only a form of verbal communication, and that there were limits to what could be done by it—especially as one was dependent on having somebody who would listen to what one had to say. So, what with having to say something, and also having to have somebody there who would listen to what I said, it was clear that the position that was being thrust upon me, or that I was being invited to take, was one not at all within my compass or capacity.

Comparing my own personal experience with the history of psycho-analysis, and even the history of human thought that I have tried to sketch out roughly, it does seem to be rather ridiculous that one finds oneself in a position of being supposed to be in that line of succession, instead of just one of the units in it. It is still more ridiculous that one is expected to participate in a sort of competition for precedence as to who is top. Top of what? Where does it come in this history? Where does psycho-analysis itself come? What is the dispute about? What is this dispute in which one is supposed to be interested? I am always hearing—as I have always done—that I am a Kleinian, that I am crazy. Is it possible to be interested in that sort of dispute? I find it very difficult to see how this could possibly be relevant against the background of the struggle of the human being to emerge from barbarism and a purely animal existence, to something one could call a civilized society.

One of the reasons why I am talking like this here is because I think it might be useful if we were to remind ourselves of the scale of the thing in which we are engaged, and whereabouts a little niche could be occupied by ourselves.

[Bion's copy of *The Future of an Illusion* (1927c) is heavily annotated. The following passage is written at the end of Chapter II, p. 14 (*see opposite*).]

Reading this chapter seems to show the extent to which the advance of psycho-analysis renders its own formulation obsolete. Freud has for the foundation of his discussion, as its realization, his own conjectures on the nature of the civilization. He then has theories about the conjectures. Because the conjectures are those of a man of genius, they command attention. But there is no recognition of the status of the conjectures or of the status of theories about conjectures. In psycho-analysis it is assumed that a theory is false if it does not seem to minister to the 'good' of the majority of mankind. And it is a commonplace idea of good. The whole idea of 'cure', of therapeutic activity, remains unscrutinized. It is largely determined by the expectations of the patient though this is questioned in good analysis (as I know it). But in nuclear physics a theory is considered to be good if it aids the construction of a bomb that destroys Hiroshima. Too much of the thinking about psycho-analysis precludes the possibility of regarding as good a theory that would destroy the individual or the group. Yet there will never be a scientific scrutiny of analytic theories until it includes critical appraisal of a theory that by its very soundness could lead to a destruction of mental stability, e.g. a theory that increased memory and desire to a point where they rendered sanity impossible.

long since,[1] art offers substitutive satisfactions for the oldest and still most deeply felt cultural renunciations, and for that reason it serves as nothing else does to reconcile a man to the sacrifices he has made on behalf of civilization. On the other hand, the creations of art heighten his feelings of identification, of which every cultural unit stands in so much need, by providing an occasion for sharing highly valued emotional experiences. And when those creations picture the achievements of his particular culture and bring to his mind its ideals in an impressive manner, they also minister to his narcissistic satisfaction.

But also escape from [illegible] polemic.

No mention has yet been made of what is perhaps the most important item in the psychical inventory of a civilization. This consists in its religious ideas in the widest sense—in other words (which will be justified later) in its illusions.

[1] [Cf., for instance, 'Creative Writers and Day-Dreaming' (1908e).]

Reading this chapter seems to show the extent to which the advance of psycho-analysis renders its own formulations obsolete. Freud has for the foundation of his discussion, as its realization, his own conjectures on the nature of the civilization. He then has theories about the conjectures. Because the conjectures are those of a man of genius they command attention. But there is no recognition of the status of the conjectures or of the status of theories about conjectures. In psycho-analysis it is assumed that a theory is false if it does not seem to minister to the "good" of the majority of mankind. And it is a commonplace idea of good. The whole idea of "cure," of therapeutic activity, remains unscrutinized. It is largely determined by the expectations of the patient though this is questioned in good analysis (as I know it). But in nuclear physics a theory is considered to be good if it aids the construction of a bomb that destroys Hiroshima. Too much of the thinking about psycho-analysis precludes the possibility of regarding as good a theory that would destroy the individual or the group. Yet there will never be a scientific scrutiny of analytic theories until it includes critical appraisal of a theory that by its very soundness would lead to a destruction of mental stability, e.g. a theory that increased memory and desire to a point where they rendered sanity impossible.

Notes on memory and desire

Memory is always misleading as a record of fact since it is distorted by the influence of unconscious forces. Desires interfere, by absence of mind when observation is essential, with the operation of judgement. Desires distort judgement by selection and suppression of material to be judged.

Memory and Desire exercise and intensify those aspects of the mind that derive from sensuous experience. They thus promote capacity derived from sense impressions and designed to serve impressions of sense. They deal, respectively, with sense impressions of what is supposed to have happened and sense impressions of what has not yet happened.

Psychoanalytic 'observation' is concerned neither with what has happened nor with what is going to happen, but with what is happening. Furthermore, it is not concerned with sense impressions or objects of sense. Any psychoanalyst knows

---

First published in 1967 in *The Psychoanalytic Forum*, Vol. 2, No. 3, and reprinted here by kind permission of John A. Lindon, M.D., Editor.

depression, anxiety, fear, and other aspects of psychic reality, whether those aspects have been or can be successfully named or not. These are the psychoanalyst's real world. Of its reality he has no doubt. Yet anxiety, to take one example, has no shape, no smell, no taste; awareness of the sensuous accompaniments of emotional experience are a hindrance to the psychoanalyst's intuition of the reality with which he must be at one.

Every session attended by the psychoanalyst must have no history and no future.

What is 'known' about the patient is of no further consequence: it is either false or irrelevant. If it is 'known' by patient and analyst, it is obsolete. If it is 'known' by the one but not the other, a defence or grid category 2 element (1,2) (see Grid, p. 295) is operating. The only point of importance in any session is the unknown. Nothing must be allowed to distract from intuiting that.

In any session, evolution takes place. Out of the darkness and formlessness something evolves. That evolution can bear a superficial resemblance to memory, but once it has been experienced, it can never be confounded with memory. It shares with dreams the quality of being wholly present or unaccountably and suddenly absent. This evolution is what the psychoanalyst must be ready to interpret.

To do this, he needs to discipline his thoughts. First and foremost, as every psychoanalyst knows, he must have had as thorough an analysis as possible; nothing said here must be taken as casting doubt on that. Second, he must cultivate a watchful avoidance of memory. Notes should be confined to matters that *can* be recorded—the programme of appointments is an obvious example.

Obey the following rules:

1. *Memory:* Do not remember past sessions. The greater the impulse to remember what has been said or done, the more the need to resist it. This impulse can present itself as a wish to remember something that has happened because it appears to have precipitated an emotional crisis: *no* crisis should be allowed to breach this rule. The supposed events

must not be allowed to occupy the mind. Otherwise the evolution of the session will not be observed at the only time when it can be observed—while it is taking place.

2. *Desires:* The psychoanalyst can start by avoiding any desires for the approaching end of the session (or week, or term). Desires for results, 'cure' or even understanding must not be allowed to proliferate.

These rules must be obeyed *all* the time and not simply during the sessions. In time the psychoanalyst will become more aware of the pressure of memories and desires and more skilled at eschewing them.

If this discipline is followed, there will be an increase of anxiety in the psychoanalyst at first, but it must not interfere with preservation of the rules. The procedure should be started at once and not abandoned on any pretext whatever.

The pattern of analysis will change. Roughly speaking, the patient will not appear to develop over a period of time, but each session will be complete in itself. 'Progress' will be measured by the increased number and variety of moods, ideas, and attitudes seen in any given session. There will be less clogging of the sessions by the repetition of material that should have disappeared and, consequently, a quickened tempo within each session every session.

The psychoanalyst should aim at achieving a state of mind so that at every session he feels he has not seen the patient before. If he feels he has, he is treating the wrong patient.

This procedure is extremely penetrating. Therefore the psychoanalyst must aim at a steady exclusion of memory and desire and not be too disturbed if the results appear alarming at first. He will become used to it and he will have the consolation of building his psychoanalytic technique on a firm basis of intuiting evolution and NOT on the shifting sand of slight experience imperfectly remembered, which rapidly gives way not to experience, but to neurologically certain decay of mental faculty. The evolving session is unmistakable, and the intuiting of it does not deteriorate. If given a chance, it starts early and decays late.

The foregoing is a brief account distilled from putting the precepts advocated into practice. The theoretical implications can be worked out by each psychoanalyst for himself. His interpretations should gain in force and conviction—both for himself and his patient—because they derive from the emotional experience with a unique individual and not from generalized theories imperfectly 'remembered'.

Discussants

The discussants commenting on this paper were: Thomas French, M.D. (Chicago, Illinois, U.S.A.); John A. Lindon, M.D. (Los Angeles, California, U.S.A.); Avelino González, M.D. (Mexico D.F., Mexico); Marjorie Brierley, M.B.B.S. (Keswick, Cumberland, England); Herbert H. Herskovitz, M.D. (Bala-Cynwyd, Pennsylvania, U.S.A.).

Author's Response

The discussants of my 'Notes on Memory and Desire' help to make it clear that some of the confusion arises through the ambiguity of the terms 'memory' and 'desire'. I realize that it would be helpful if I could distinguish between two different phenomena that are both usually and indifferently called 'memory'. This I have tried to do by speaking of one as 'evolution', by which I mean the experience where some idea or pictorial impression floats into the mind unbidden and as a whole. From this I wish to distinguish ideas that present themselves in response to a deliberate and conscious attempt at recall; for this last I reserve the term 'memory'. 'Memory' I keep for experience related predominantly to sensuous impressions: 'evolution' I regard as based on experience that has no sensuous background but is expressed in terms that are derived from the language of sensuous experience. For example, I 'see' meaning I intuit through the medium of a visual impression.

'Desire' should not be distinguished from 'memory', as I prefer that the terms should represent one phenomenon that is a suffusion of both. I have tried to express this by saying 'memory' is the past tense of 'desire', 'anticipation' being its future tense.

These definitory hypotheses have a limited value, and I suggest that every psychoanalyst should make up his mind for himself by simple experimentation as to what these terms represent. For example, he should school himself to avoid thinking of the end of the session, week, or term (having made previous provision for terminating the session at the correct time as a matter of administration), and when he has done this for a sufficient period without trying to hurry himself, make up his mind about what *he* would call 'Memory' and 'Desire'. When he has done this, he can proceed to the next stage of extending his suppressions of the experience he has discovered in this way. I must warn psychoanalysts that I do not think they should extend this procedure hurriedly or without discussion with other psychoanalysts with a view to consolidating each step before taking another.

This procedure seems to me to approximate a state which Freud described in a letter to Lou Andreas-Salomé, 25 May 1916: "I know that I have artificially blinded myself at my work in order to concentrate all the light on the one dark passage." In my experience this procedure makes it possible to intuit a present 'evolution' and lay the foundations for future 'evolutions'. The more firmly this is done, the less the psychoanalyst has to bother about remembering.

I hope this makes clear some of the points to which Dr French objects, though I am doubtful whether this method should be used if he really feels that he is 'completely unable' to understand. Indeed, I would not 'desire' anyone to employ this approach unless, like Dr Lindon, he feels it has some meaning for him.

The experience that Dr Lindon describes appears to me to afford the foundation for exploring the whole question of psychoanalytic observation. I agree with his feeling that 'memory' and 'desire' are obstacles intervening between the psychoanalysts and the emotional experience of the session. When it is considered how little opportunity even five sessions a week affords the psychoanalyst, any obstacle to appreciation becomes serious.

Dr González draws attention to a defect of which I am very conscious. My own feeling is that my views have 'evolved', and although this must mean they have changed, I think the 'change' less significant than the 'evolution'.

I think the expressions he rightly quotes from *Elements of Psycho-Analysis* are wrongly framed, but wrong though the formulations now seem to me to be, they were good enough to lead me to my present formulations, which I think are better. In particular, I think the use of language based on the experience of the senses led me to fail to recognize that one does not in fact 'see' (feel, touch, smell, etc.) anxiety. I hope that my experience will be repeated by others who have tried to read these earlier formulations. If it is, I shall feel less remorseful.

I hope that my quotation from Freud will convince Dr Brierley that I am attempting to elaborate on the importance of rapport. I feel some unease if it is suggested that I am departing from psychoanalytic technique, not because I have any objection to innovation if it seems to be necessary, but because it is unlikely that the intuitions of experienced psychoanalysts can be lightly laid aside. I do hope, however, that the points I make may help psychoanalysts to think themselves into closer contact with the psychoanalytic experience.

Darwin expressed the view that judgement was inimical to observation, but, as Dr Brierley points out, the psychoanalyst has to formulate judgements while observations are being made. I hope the distinction I have tried to draw between 'evolution' and 'memory' may help to meet her objections. I believe it would go some way towards meeting Dr Herskovitz's objection to 'illogicalities'. I do in any case feel doubts about the value of a logical theory to represent the realizations of psychoanalysis. I think the 'logical' theory and the 'illogicalities' of the psychoanalytic experience should be permitted to coexist until the observed disharmony is resolved by 'evolution'.

BION'S WORKS

1940 The War of Nerves. In *The Neuroses in War,* edited by Emanuel Miller & H. Crichton-Miller (London: Macmillan).

1943 Intra-group Tensions in Therapy: Their Study as the Task of the Group. *The Lancet* (27 November).

1946 The Leaderless Group Project. *Bulletin of the Menninger Clinic, 10* (May).

1948 Psychiatry at a Time of Crisis. *British Journal of Medical Psychology, 21.*

1948–1951 *Experiences in Groups, Vols. 1–4* (Human Relations. Subsequently London: Tavistock, 1961).

1950 The Imaginary Twin. Presented to The British Psycho-Analytic Society (November) [Bion's membership paper]. *International Journal of Psycho-Analysis* (1955). Also in *Second Thoughts* [see 1967 below].

1952 Group Dynamics: A Re-view. *International Journal of Psycho-Analysis, 33.* Also in *New Directions in Psycho-Analysis,* edited by M. Klein, P. Heimann, & R. Money-Kyrle (London: Tavistock, 1955; reprinted London: Karnac Books, 1985) and in *Experiences in Groups* (London: Tavistock, 1961).

1953 Notes on the Theory of Schizophrenia. Presented at the Eighteenth International Psycho-Analytic Congress. *International Journal of Psycho-Analysis, 35* (1954). Also in *Second Thoughts* [see 1967 below].

1955 Language and the Schizophrenic. In *New Directions in Psycho-Analysis* edited by M. Klein, P. Heimann, & R. Money-Kyrle (London: Tavistock; reprinted London: Karnac Books, 1985).

1956 Development of Schizophrenic Thought. *International Journal of Psycho-Analysis, 37.* Also in *Second Thoughts* [see 1967 below].

1957 Differentiation of the Psychotic from the Non-psychotic Personalities. *International Journal of Psycho-Analysis, 38.* Also in *Second Thoughts* [see 1967 below].

1957 On Arrogance. Presented at the Twentieth International Psycho-Analytic Congress, Paris. *International Journal of*

Psycho-Analysis, 39 (1958). Also in *Second Thoughts* [see 1967 below].

1958 On Hallucination. *International Journal of Psycho-Analysis, 39.* Also in *Second Thoughts* [see 1967 below].

1959 Attacks on Linking. *International Journal of Psycho-Analysis, 40.* Also in *Second Thoughts* [see 1967 below].

1962 A Theory of Thinking. *International Journal of Psycho-Analysis, 53.* Also in *Second Thoughts* [see 1967 below].

1962 *Learning from Experience* (Heinemann Medical; reprinted London: Karnac Books, 1984). Also in *Seven Servants* [see 1977 below].

1963 *Elements of Psycho-Analysis* (Heinemann Medical; reprinted London: Karnac Books, 1984). Also in *Seven Servants* [see 1977 below].

1965 *Transformations* (Heinemann Medical; reprinted London: Karnac Books, 1984). Also in *Seven Servants* [see 1977 below].

1966 Catastrophic Change. *Bulletin No. 5,* British Psycho-Analytic Society. Also in *Attention and Interpretation* (chapter 12) [see 1970 below].

1967 *Second Thoughts* (Heinemann Medical; reprinted London: Karnac Books, 1984) [contains the papers indicated above, together with a Commentary].

1967 Notes on Memory and Desire. *The Psychoanalytic Forum, 2,* No. 3 (Los Angeles, California). Also in *Cogitations* (new extended edition) [see 1992 below].

1970 *Attention and Interpretation* (London: Tavistock Publications; reprinted London: Karnac Books, 1984). Also in *Seven Servants* [see 1977 below].

1973 *Brazilian Lectures, 1* (Rio de Janeiro, Brazil: Imago Editora). Also in *Brazilian Lectures* [see 1990 below].

1974 *Brazilian Lectures, 2* (Rio de Janeiro, Brazil: Imago Editora). Also in *Brazilian Lectures* [see 1990 below].

1975 A *Memoir of the Future, Book One: The Dream* (Rio de Janeiro, Brazil: Imago Editora). Also in A *Memoir of the Future* [see 1990 below].

1976 Emotional Turbulence. Paper given at the International Conference on Borderline Disorders, Topeka, Kansas (March). Published in the book of the conference (New York: International Universities Press, Inc., 1977). Also in *Clinical Seminars and Four Papers* [see 1987 below].

1976 On a Quotation from Freud. Paper given at the International Conference on Borderline Disorders, Topeka, Kansas (March). Published in the book of the conference (New York: International Universities Press, Inc., 1977). Also in *Clinical Seminars and Four Papers* [see 1987 below].

1976 Evidence. *Bulletin 8,* British Psycho-Analytic Society. Also in *Clinical Seminars and Four Papers* [see 1987 below].

1976 Interview with Anthony G. Banet. Published in *The International Journal for Group Facilitators: Group and Organization Studies, 2* (3).

1977 *Seven Servants* (New York: Jason Aronson, Inc.) [contains the four books indicated above].

1977 A *Memoir of the Future, Book Two: The Past Presented* (Rio de Janeiro, Brazil: Imago Editora). Also in A *Memoir of the Future* [see 1990 below].

1977 *Two Papers: The Grid and Caesura* [originally presented as talks to the Los Angeles Psycho-Analytic Society, in 1971 and 1975, respectively] (Rio de Janeiro, Brazil: Imago Editora). [New edition, London: Karnac Books, 1989.]

1978 *Four Discussions with W. R. Bion* (Strathclyde: Clunie Press). Also in *Clinical Seminars and Other Works* [see 1994 below].

1979 A *Memoir of the Future, Book Three: The Dawn of Oblivion* (Strathclyde: Clunie Press). Also in *A Memoir of the Future* [see 1990 below].

1979 Making the Best of a Bad Job. *Bulletin,* British Psycho-Analytic Society (February). Also in *Clinical Seminars and Four Papers* [see 1987 below].

1980 *Bion in New York and Sao Paulo* (Strathclyde: Clunie Press).

1981 A *Key to a Memoir of the Future* (Strathclyde: Clunie Press). Also in A *Memoir of the Future* [see 1990 below].

1982 *The Long Week-End—1897–1919* (Oxford: Fleetwood Press).

1985 *All My Sins Remembered* and *The Other Side of Genius* (Oxford: Fleetwood Press).

1986 *Seminari Italiani* (Rome: Borla) [published in Italian only].

1987 *Clinical Seminars and Four Papers* (Oxford: Fleetwood Press). Also in *Clinical Seminars and Other Works* [see 1994 below].

1990 *Brazilian Lectures* (London: Karnac Books, 1990) [a new one-volume edition of the two books listed above].

1990 *A Memoir of the Future* (London: Karnac Books) [a new one-volume edition of the four books listed above].

1992 *Cogitations* (London: Karnac Books). [New extended edition, London: Karnac Books, 1994.]

1994 *Clinical Seminars and Other Works* (London: Karnac Books) [a new one-volume edition of the two books listed above].

GENERAL BIBLIOGRAPHY

[The authors and works listed below are those referred to by Bion in this book. Publication details refer to editions in his personal library; they are not, therefore, necessarily still in print. Those I have been unable to trace are marked with an asterisk. Ed.]

Adrian, E. D., *The Physical Background of Perception* (Oxford: Clarendon Press, 1947).

Bagehot, Walter, *Physics and Politics* (London: Kegan Paul, Trench, Trubner and Co., Ltd. [undated]).

*Bell, Eric Temple, *Men of Mathematics* [out of print].

Bennett, Arnold, *The Old Wives' Tale* (London: Hodder and Stoughton, 1911).

Berkeley, G., *Selections from Berkeley* (Oxford: Clarendon Press, 1910).

Bolgar, *The Classical Heritage* (Cambridge: Cambridge University Press, 1954).

Bradley, F. H., *The Principles of Logic,* 2 vols. (London: Oxford University Press, 1922).

Braithwaite, R. B., *Scientific Explanation* (Cambridge: Cambridge University Press, 1955).

Boswell, James, *Boswell's Life of Johnson,* 6 vols. (Oxford: Clarendon Press, 1934).

Buber, Martin, *I and Thou* (New York: Charles Scribner's Sons, 1970).

Byron, George Gordon, Lord, *Poetical Works of Lord Byron* (London: Oxford University Press, 1952).

Carroll, Lewis, *Complete Works of Lewis Carroll* (London: Nonesuch Press, 1939).

Clark, Kenneth, *The Nude* (London: John Murray, 1956).

Copleston, F., *A History of Philosophy,* 7 vols. (London: Burns Oates and Washbourne, 1958–1963).

Descartes, René, *Philosophical Works of Descartes,* 2 vols. (Cambridge: Cambridge University Press, 1975).

Euclid, *Thirteen Books of Euclid's Elements,* 3 vols. (Cambridge: Cambridge University Press, 1956).

Freud, S., *The Standard Edition of the Complete Psychological Works of Sigmund Freud,* edited by James Strachey (London: Hogarth Press and the Institute of Psycho-Analysis, 1974 [details of original years and volume numbers in the text]).

[In addition to the *Standard Edition,* Bion used the following Freud sources:]

A General Selection from the Works of Sigmund Freud, edited by John Rickman (London: Hogarth Press, 1937).

Inhibition, Symptoms and Anxiety (London: Hogarth Press, 1949).

New Introductory Lectures on Psycho-Analysis (London: Hogarth Press, 1949).

An Outline of Psycho-Analysis (London: Hogarth Press, 1949).

The Origins of Psycho-Analysis: Letters to Wilhelm Fliess, Drafts and Notes: 1887–1902 (London: Imago Publishing Company Ltd., 1954).

Letters of Sigmund Freud, 1873–1939 (London: Hogarth Press, 1961).

Fenollosa, E., *The Chinese Written Character as a Medium for Poetry* (London: Stanley Nott, 1936).

Flügel, J. C., *Man, Morals and Society* (London: Duckworth, 1945).

Heisenberg, W., *Physics and Philosophy* (London: G. Allen & Unwin Ltd., 1958).

Heyting, A., *Intuitionism* (Amsterdam: North-Holland Publishing Co., 1971).

Hopkins, Gerard Manley, *The Poems of Gerard Manley Hopkins* (London: Oxford University Press, 1949 and 1970).

Hume, David, in: N. Kemp Smith, *The Philosophy of David Hume* (New York: Macmillan & Co., 1960).

Hume, David, *Hume's Enquiries* (Oxford: Clarendon Press, 1962).

Kipling, Rudyard, *Rudyard Kipling's Verse* (London: Hodder & Stoughton, 1946).

Klein, Melanie, *Developments in Psycho-Analysis* (London: Hogarth Press, 1952).

Klein, Melanie, *Envy and Gratitude* (London: Tavistock Publications Ltd., 1957).

Milton, John [the following editions are selected from numerous copies in Bion's library]

Paradise Lost, A Poem in Twelve Books (together with *Paradise Regained* and *Samson Agonistes.* Printed by Miles Flesher for Jacob Tonson, 'at the Judge's-Head in Chancery-lane near Fleetstreet', 1688. The list of over five hundred subscribers, headed 'The Names of the Nobility and Gentry that Encourag'd, by Subscription, The Printing this Edition of Milton's Paradise Lost', includes John Dryden).

Areopagitica (printed at the Doves Press, 1907, from the first edition of 1644).

The Manuscript of Milton's Paradise Lost, Book I (Oxford: Clarendon Press, 1931).

The Poetical Works of John Milton, 2 vols. (Oxford: Clarendon Press, 1952).

Moschus, *Theocritus, Bion and Moschus* (London: Macmillan & Co. Ltd., 1911).

Niebuhr, R., *The Nature and Destiny of Man,* 2 vols. (Welwyn, Hertfordshire: Nisbet & Co. Ltd., 1941).

Onians, R. B., *Origins of European Thought* (Cambridge: Cambridge University Press, 1951).

Peirce, C. S., *Collected Papers of Charles Sanders Peirce, Vol. VII, Science and Philosophy* (Cambridge, MA: Harvard University Press, 1958).

Plato, *The Republic and Other Works* (New York: Dolphin Books, 1960).

Poincaré, H., *Science and Method* (New York: Dover Publications Inc. [undated]).

Popper, Karl R., *The Logic of Scientific Discovery* (London: Hutchinson, 1959).

Powicke, F. M., *King Henry III and the Lord Edward,* 2 vols. (Oxford: Clarendon Press, 1947).

Prichard, H. A., *Knowledge and Perception* (Oxford: Clarendon Press, 1950).

Quine, W. van Orman, *Mathematical Logic* (Cambridge, MA: Harvard University Press, 1955).

Ritchie, A. D., *Studies in the History and Methods of the Sciences* (Edinburgh: Edinburgh University Press, 1958).

Russell, Bertrand, *Algebraic Projective Geometry* (Oxford: Clarendon Press, 1956).

Russell, Bertrand, *History of Western Philosophy* (London: George Allen & Unwin Ltd., 1974).

Semple & Kneebone, *Algebraic Geometry* (Oxford: Clarendon Press, 1949).

Shelley, Percy Bysshe, *The Complete Poetical Works of Percy Bysshe Shelley* (London: Oxford University Press, 1965).

Teilhard de Chardin, Pierre, *The Phenomenon of Man* (London: Collins, 1959).

Tennyson, Alfred, Lord, *The Poems of Tennyson* (London: Longmans, 1969).

Toynbee, Arnold, *A Study of History,* 6 vols. (London: Oxford University Press, 1948).

Whitehead, A. N., & Russell, B., *Principia Mathematica,* 3 vols. (Cambridge: Cambridge University Press, 1925 and 1927).

*Woodger, J. H., *Technique of Theory Construction* [out of print].

INDEX

(Entries in bold type indicate section headings in text.)